Environmental Management for Real Estate Professionals

Editorial Consultants
J. T. Abercrombie, CPM®
Beverly J. Diefenderfer, CPM®
Cher R. Zucker-Maltese, CPM®

Joseph T. Lannon
Publishing and Curriculum Development Manager

Caroline Scoulas
Senior Editor

Stephanie H. Mathurin
Project Editor

Environmental Management for Real Estate Professionals

David C. Parks

Institute of Real Estate Management
of the NATIONAL ASSOCIATION OF REALTORS ®
430 NORTH MICHIGAN AVENUE · CHICAGO, ILLINOIS 60611

This publication is designed to provide accurate and authoritative information in regard to the subject matter covered; however, due to the changing and varying nature of federal, state, and local laws, independent legal and other professional advice should be sought in the application of the information covered in this book. Forms, documents, and other exhibits in this book are samples only. This publication is sold with the understanding that the publisher is not engaged in rendering legal, accounting, or any other professional service. Because of varying state and local laws, competent advice should be secured before the use of any form, document, exhibit, or information herein.

The contents of this publication are based on the best available information at the time of its preparation. The author and publisher recognize that laws and regulations are changed from time to time and that new scientific or other evidence may intensify or diminish some environmental problems. Appropriate professional advice should be sought whenever specific environmental concerns are raised.

The opinions expressed in this text are those of the author, David C. Parks, and do not necessarily reflect the policies or positions of the Institute of Real Estate Management.

Identification of other organizations does not constitute an endorsement of any organization or of any positions they may advocate.

Library of Congress Cataloging-in-Publication Data

Parks, David C., 1960–
   Environmental management for real estate professionals / David C.
Parks
      p. cm.
   Includes index.
   ISBN 0-944298-69-9
   1. Liability for environmental damages--United States. 2. Real
property--United States. 3. Environmental law--United States.
4. Real estate development--Environmental aspects--United States.
I. Title.
KF1298.P37   1992
344.73'046--dc20
[347.30446]   91-45631
                                                  CIP

Printed in the United States of America

1 2 3 4 5 6 7 8 9 10 Printing / Year 01 00 99 98 97 96 95 94 93 92

To my wife, Debbie,
and our sons, Christopher and Jonathan,
whose assistance, support, and patience
were critical to this work,
and to my parents and grandparents
who instilled in me a love of learning and teaching.

Preface

Working as a property manager, I have been keenly aware of the impact that environmental issues have made on the real estate industry. I believe that these issues are among the key "new" concerns in our business today. Assuming the position of Director of Environmental Operations for Trammell Crow Company, North Carolina Division, I built on my knowledge of environmental topics and gained valuable experience in the environmental arena. As my knowledge grew, I recognized that I had information at my fingertips that many of my colleagues did not have access to—information that could be put to use by a wide range of industry professionals. When I was unable to identify a book that introduced basic environmental issues from the perspective of real estate professionals, I began to assemble some of the information that I thought would be helpful to property owners, managers, developers, and investors.

From this effort, I developed *Environmental Management for Real Estate Professionals*. My intention was to write a basic book that would introduce the real estate professional to the environmental terms, concepts, and issues that he or she might encounter in the field. I did not presume a great deal of prior knowledge on the part of my reader; this is not a book for environmental professionals. Quite the contrary, one of my primary objectives when writing this book was to equip real estate professionals with sufficient knowledge to know when it is necessary to hire environmental specialists.

Using this Book

As you will see, *Environmental Management for Real Estate Professionals* is divided into ten chapters, the first of which is substantially different in tone and content from the remainder of the book. In chapter 1, I have tried to present an overview of those environmental issues that have global consequences as well as those that are most likely to be encountered by real estate professionals. I wanted to create an environmental primer so that all my readers would begin *Environmental Management for Real Estate Professionals* with the same foundation of knowledge. Like chapter 1, chapter 2 is very factual; in it I have shared information about the main aspects of federal environmental legislation.

Chapter 3 introduces one of the most crucial topics of the book— liability. Today, many real estate professionals face the possibility of incurring liability for an "environmental" problem. Indeed, this is one of the primary reasons that environmental awareness is so important to people in our industry.

Environmental site assessments are explored in chapter 4. In recent years, the site assessment has become the method of choice for thoroughly investigating the environmental condition of a property. By performing the proper site assessments, the real estate professional has made a documented effort to investigate the environmental condition of the subject property. If done correctly, this effort can reduce some of the liability risk—and I have explained how. I have also explained the differences among various types of site assessments because this is a subject that is often surrounded by confusion.

Chapters 5 and 6 address specific real estate professionals. Chapter 5 examines the unique concerns of the those individuals who are purchasing or selling real estate. Chapter 6 takes a look at the environmental issues associated with real estate development.

In chapter 7, I explore issues that relate to leases and leasing. These are topics of interest for owners, lenders, investors, leasing agents, and managers alike.

Chapters 8 and 9 were written with the property manager in mind. The beginning of chapter 8 explores the management contract and environmental considerations for negotiating such an agreement. It concludes with a discussion of those management duties that are to some extent environmental by nature (e.g., conducting inspections). Chapter 9 is more hands-on in its approach and includes discussions of emergency procedures for possible environmental situations.

Chapter 10 is really a roundup of topics that have not been addressed in earlier chapters. In it, I cover four topics that truly warrant attention: working with environmental professionals, public relations and "green" marketing, ethics, and the role of the environmental manager.

Seven appendixes and a glossary complete the text. This material includes some suggestions concerning legal clauses that might prove useful in environmental contexts and a list of conditions that signal possible contamination. The last appendix, "Sources of Information," suggests resources for those who seek additional information. A glossary defines the key environmental terms that are used in this book and provides a list of acronyms for easier access to information.

The Nature of the Material

One of the biggest challenges that I encountered while planning *Environmental Management for Real Estate Professionals* was developing a book that would not become dated quickly. I have tried to explore the fundamental topics related to environmental concerns and provide knowledge that can be easily augmented. There is no denying that environmental legislation—federal, state, and local—changes with remarkable rapidity. Furthermore, laws vary from one location to another. It is absolutely crucial for the reader of this book to be aware of the current laws as well as the laws that prevail in his or her area. Developing such awareness often involves enlisting the services of an expert (e.g., an environmental attorney). Similarly, technology changes and the appropriate environmental engineer or consultant can keep the real estate professional informed.

The forms, legal clauses, and checklists in this book are offered as samples only. Contents of individual forms, checklists, and legal documents should be dictated by need, by location, and by prevailing laws. Again, it is essential to obtain the assistance of appropriate professional(s) when confronted with an environmental issue. I have tried to lay the proper groundwork so that real estate professionals will be better equipped to ask the right questions about environmental issues after they have read this book. It is my hope that I have achieved that goal.

ACKNOWLEDGMENTS

The following people and organizations provided me with resources and reference material, advice regarding technical or legal topics, assistance with organizational and administrative tasks, moral support, and suggestions for book inclusions. My thanks are extended to all of them including Bill Maddux, David Tipple, and Kenya McFadden of Trammell Crow Company in Charlotte, North Carolina; Kevin Murray of Parry, Murray, and Cannon in Salt Lake City, Utah; James Frantes of Versar Incorporated in Fair Oaks, California; K. Lyle Dokken of Versar Incorporated in Greeley, Colorado; Roy Parker of Avendt Environmental in Charlotte, North Carolina; Cindy Edwards of Oxford Management in Greenbelt, Maryland; Jim Boomgarden of Cooper Environmental in Charlotte, North Carolina; North Carolina Department of Environmental Management in Mooresville, North Carolina; Greenpeace USA in Washington, D.C.; Moore and Van Allen in Raleigh, North Carolina; Aetna Life and Casualty in Dallas, Texas; Marine Midland Bank in New York, New York; and Duke Power Company, Nations Bank, First Union National Bank, and Wachovia National Bank, all in Charlotte, North Carolina.

Special thanks to the Institute of Real Estate Management (IREM) and Joe Lannon, Caroline Scoulas, and Stephanie Mathurin whose encouragement, patience, and expertise in publishing and editing were invaluable throughout the project. I would especially like to thank the three editorial consultants who reviewed the manuscript to assure that it was accurate, easy to understand, and appropriately focused for its intended audience. This panel included J. T. Abercrombie, CPM®, Principal of Abercrombie Real Estate Services in San Diego, California; Beverly J. Diefenderfer, CPM®, Corporate Treasurer of Loeltz Property Management, Inc., in La Jolla, California; and Cher R. Zucker-Maltese, CPM®, Vice President of Prudential Realty Group in Newark, New Jersey.

David C. Parks

Contents

General Environmental Issues

April 22, 1970, might well be called the birthday of environmental activism in the United States; on that day, Americans celebrated Earth Day for the first time. Earth Day brought nationwide attention to environmental issues and initiated the "environmental movement." Now, years later, it is necessary to take stock of the progress Americans have made toward the goal of preserving the environment.

Through environmental awareness, activism, and legislation, much has been accomplished toward improving the condition of the environment in the United States. This stands in sharp contrast to the situation in some eastern European cities where air pollution is particularly bad. There, one can find special free "clinics" in which citizens spend fifteen minutes in a room containing pure oxygen to be able to return to their work outdoors. Medical experts have estimated that 10 percent of all deaths in some eastern European countries can be attributed to pollution.

While environmental issues were moving toward the forefront of public concerns in the United States, a significant amount of related legislation was enacted on the local, state, and federal level. Such legislation pulled additional individuals and industries into the environmental arena—and real estate is one such industry. Today, more and more real estate professionals are affected by environmental issues (a trend that is likely to continue in the future). It is becoming increasingly important for everyone in the industry to have a basic understanding of the range of environmental problems that might be encountered on a property, the means to respond legally and ethically to such problems, and the prevailing laws that dictate specific actions.

This book is intended as an introduction to those particular environmental issues that are most likely to affect the real estate professional. It is best, however, to begin with some general information concerning environmental problems.

GLOBAL CONCERNS

To gain a "big picture" understanding of important environmental issues and to appreciate public sentiment and outcry, it is necessary for the real estate professional to know what is truly meant by such terms as acid rain, ozone depletion, and global warming. Because such issues may have indirect effects on all types of real properties, property managers and other real estate professionals may need more than token awareness of environmental issues. Unfortunately, environmental activists and the so-called "media" are not always effective when they explain these problems to the public. Many people do not understand the nature of commonly discussed environmental problems. The next few sections of the text include descriptions of some of the significant environmental problems that have gained attention worldwide.

Acid Rain

"Acid rain" is actually acid precipitation. It is snow, sleet, hail, mist, fog, dew, and humidity that are acidic (i.e., have a low pH or hydrogen-ion concentration). The pH scale measures acidity and alkalinity; its values are 0 to 14, with 7.0 representing neutrality. Measurements above 7 represent increasing alkalinity; those below 7 represent increasing acidity (the lower the number, the greater the acidity). Acid rain is not discernably acidic by human senses, but its potential for creating problems is significant. Here is a reminder that even the most minute changes (by human standards) can have disastrous effects on the environment.

Acid rain is caused by the addition of sulfur dioxide (SO_2) and nitrogen oxides (NO_x) to the air. These gases react with water to form acids (e.g., sulfuric acid, nitric acid). Normal precipitation brings these acids back to earth. More than one-half of all sulfur dioxide is produced by the burning of coal and other fossil fuels such as heating oil, and other petroleum derivatives (gasoline, diesel fuel, etc.) to generate electricity and to operate motor vehicles of all types. More than 80 percent of nitrogen oxides are produced by the same processes; approximately one-half of nitrogen oxides in the atmosphere are produced by motor vehicles. Nitrogen oxides are also used as anesthetics and to provide pressure for aerosol products (e.g., hairspray, whipped cream).

The most noticeable negative consequences of acid rain, and those most publicized, are its effects on rivers, lakes, and woodlands. A lowering of the pH level of rivers, streams, and lakes has damaging effects on the fish and plant life. There are also negative effects when plants on land come into contact with acid rain; in some cases, forests and grasslands are being destroyed, and new growth is virtually impossible as long as acidic rain prevails.

When streams and lakes become more acidic, so do the underground water supplies that provide most of the population's drinking water. This presents human health risks of its own. Acidic water may leach toxic metals such as copper and lead into drinking water systems. Most people are aware of the effects of lead poisoning, but they may not realize that the consumption of other toxic metals has been associated with kidney failure, high blood pressure, stroke, and other serious conditions. Children are particularly susceptible to the life-threatening diseases caused by toxic metals.

Some scientists believe that acid rain may be the third greatest cause of lung cancer (behind active and passive smoking) because the elements that cause acid rain are the same elements associated with lung cancer. Recalling that the term "rain" includes fog, mist, humidity, and other vapors, it is easy to understand how acid rain could be inhaled into the lungs or even absorbed through the skin.

The most acidic rain in the United States usually falls in the East (especially the Northeast), and along the West Coast. In California, acid fog has been measured at pH levels more acidic than pure lemon juice. *Comparative Scale of pH Values, Exhibit 1.1,* shows some of the anticipated effects of lowering the pH of waterways; it also indicates some acid rain pH measurements to put this information into perspective. While acid rain may not seem to be a major concern of real estate professionals, large-scale furnaces, boilers, and other types of equipment that burn fossil fuels are subject to regulations and requirements that are imposed in an effort to reduce the acidity of precipitation. Acid rain has made—and will continue to make—an impact on the cost of electrical power and the importance of energy-efficient building design.

Ozone Depletion and the Ozone "Hole"

What is ozone? Although the words "ozone" and "ozone layer" are often used, they are not frequently defined. In chemical terms, ozone is O_3, a form of oxygen with three atoms (triatomic) that forms naturally in the upper atmosphere. Ozone is also created for commercial purposes to be used as a disinfectant or bleach.

There are two areas where ozone is found in the earth's atmosphere. One is from ground level to seven miles above the earth's surface (the troposphere) and the other is from seven miles above the earth's surface to the outer reaches of our atmosphere (the stratosphere). Within the troposphere, ozone is a major pollutant; in the stratosphere, ozone serves as a natural protective shield.

Tropospheric ozone oxidizes metals that are absorbed by humans, plants,

E X H I B I T   1.1

Comparative Scale of pH Values

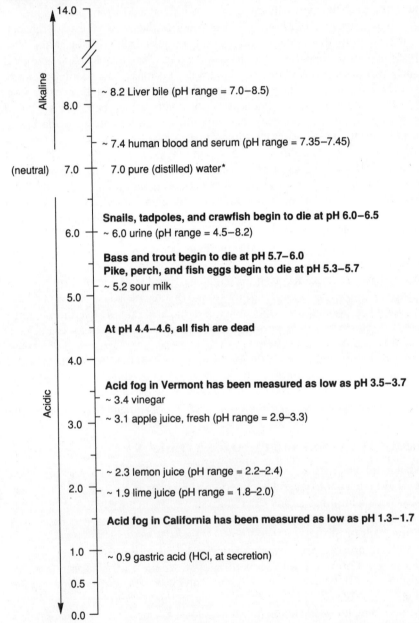

~ 8.2 Liver bile (pH range = 7.0–8.5)

~ 7.4 human blood and serum (pH range = 7.35–7.45)

7.0 pure (distilled) water*

Snails, tadpoles, and crawfish begin to die at pH 6.0–6.5
~ 6.0 urine (pH range = 4.5–8.2)

Bass and trout begin to die at pH 5.7–6.0
Pike, perch, and fish eggs begin to die at pH 5.3–5.7
~ 5.2 sour milk

At pH 4.4–4.6, all fish are dead

Acid fog in Vermont has been measured as low as pH 3.5–3.7
~ 3.4 vinegar
~ 3.1 apple juice, fresh (pH range = 2.9–3.3)

~ 2.3 lemon juice (pH range = 2.2–2.4)
~ 1.9 lime juice (pH range = 1.8–2.0)

Acid fog in California has been measured as low as pH 1.3–1.7

~ 0.9 gastric acid (HCl, at secretion)

*The pH of natural water varies with the source, with soil water being generally acidic and seawater alkaline—groundwater (soil), pH 4.5–8.5; river water, pH 6.8–8.6; spring water, pH 6.2–8.2; and seawater pH 7.8–8.6.

and water systems. It can affect the eyes and the respiratory system; scientists believe that contact with ozone through exposure or inhalation can result in such things as cataracts, blindness, strokes, heart attacks, lung tumors, and lung cancer.

This surface ozone is produced by chemical processes such as the manufacturing of bleaches for textiles and paper and the treatment of water supplies. It is also produced by a natural photochemical reaction that takes place when nitrogen oxides are exposed to sunlight. Pollution control laws are created with specific ozone production limitations in mind.

Stratospheric ozone protects the earth and all its life forms because it absorbs and reflects ultraviolet radiation from the sun, preventing the radiation from reaching the earth's surface. Increased exposure to ultraviolet radiation not only increases the risk of cataracts and skin cancer, but also causes drought and crop destruction. Hence, the protection provided by the ozone layer is essential. Some scientists speculate that the ozone layer also reflects heat from the sun; this theory identifies ozone depletion as a contributor to global warming (a general warming of the earth's atmosphere).

The ozone "hole," as it is sometimes called, is located over Antarctica at the South Pole. Estimates suggest that the "hole" is larger than the area of the continental United States; furthermore, it may already be spreading to the southern portions of Australia and South America. It is not, as the name suggests, a real hole. The ozone "hole" is actually a thinning that occurs in the ozone layer—a reduction in thickness that may be measurably equivalent to the height of Mount Everest. This thinning is most pronounced from August through November, when it is "springtime" in Antarctica.

The destruction of the ozone shield is primarily caused by three gaseous substances: nitrogen oxides, carbon dioxide, and chlorofluorocarbons (CFCs). The production of nitrogen oxides was discussed earlier.

Carbon dioxide gas (CO_2) is created by fermentation, decomposition of organic matter and, of course, the burning of petroleum products and other fossil fuels. The approximate proportions of different "contributors" of CO_2 are indicated in *Carbon Dioxide from Burning Fossil Fuels, Exhibit 1.2*. This pie chart only addresses carbon dioxide produced by *unnatural* means; CO_2 is also created when humans—and other mammals—breathe. It is therefore impossible to eliminate carbon dioxide completely; as the population grows,

---

The chart on the opposite page indicates some of the dangers of increasing acidity in the environment (items in boldface type). To provide perspective, the chart includes some common acids as well as selected human body fluids, which have pH values ranging from definitely alkaline to extremely acidic.

Note that increasing acidity affects various aquatic life forms adversely. In a slightly acid environment, snails, tadpoles, and crawfish begin to die. With increasing acidity, bass and trout begin to die and hardier forms—pike, perch, and fish eggs—have difficulty surviving. Fish cannot survive at all in a very acid environment.

EXHIBIT 1.2

**Carbon Dioxide from Burning Fossil Fuels
(Proportionate Distribution of Sources)**

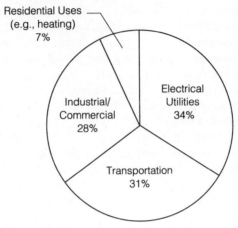

Residential Uses (e.g., heating) 7%

Industrial/Commercial 28%

Electrical Utilities 34%

Transportation 31%

Source: U.S. Environmental Protection Agency

so does the amount of CO_2 in the air. Excess carbon dioxide gives rise to problems.

Chlorofluorocarbons (CFCs) present the greatest threat to the ozone layer. These manufactured molecules have chlorine (Cl) and fluorine (F) atoms replacing hydrogen atoms in hydrocarbon structures. They are used as refrigerants and coolants in refrigeration and air-conditioning systems, and as aerosol propellants, solvents, cleaners, blowing agents (used to "foam" polystyrene and other substances), etc. Because CFCs do not occur naturally, they are not destroyed by natural processes in the lower atmosphere. They are generally used as liquids; in the gaseous form, CFCs rise into the upper atmosphere where they destroy ozone molecules (one CFC molecule can destroy up to 100,000 ozone molecules). It should be noted that a molecule of CFC has a life span of approximately 100 years.

Ozone destruction as such is not a major day-to-day consideration for the real estate professional. Nevertheless, choosing less-damaging refrigerants and opting for products that do not include CFC aerosol propellants will help in a small way to lessen the potential damage to the ozone layer.

The "Greenhouse Effect"

An issue often heard in the news is something commonly called the "greenhouse effect." Although the term "greenhouse effect" may sound pleasant, it represents a potentially serious problem and is one explanation for the phenomenon of global warming.

While the characteristics of global warming may be considered similar to the conditions in a greenhouse (increased temperature and precipitation), global warming does not have the same positive connotations as a greenhouse. There is no "glass" or "shroud" surrounding the earth and intensifying the solar effect. Instead, solar heat and radiation that ordinarily would be reflected back into space are being retained on the earth's surface (raising the earth's average temperature).

The earth's atmosphere allows solar radiation to enter with little difficulty (reduced penetration by ultraviolet radiation, caused by the shielding ozone layer, is the exception) but allows only a portion of the radiation reflected by the earth to return to space. By absorbing a portion of the reflected radiation, the earth's atmosphere keeps the planet's average temperature warmer than it would be if all reflected radiation escaped.

The gases in the atmosphere that absorb the sun's energy are carbon dioxide, methane, chlorofluorocarbons (CFCs), nitrogen oxides, ozone, and water vapors. Of these, carbon dioxide is by far the most abundant. *Gases That Contribute to Global Warming, Exhibit 1.3,* indicates proportionate levels of the so-called "greenhouse gases."

Methane gas is generated by burning wood, the decomposition of organic wastes (garbage dumps and landfill sites are generally vented to allow methane to escape), and mammalian fecal deposits. The major component of natural gas, methane is also a by-product of coal formation and is often released during oil and gas exploration, production, and refining. Because radiation from sunlight is needed as a catalyst for the breakdown of methane, the more methane produced, the more solar heat retained. Sunlight is also required as a catalyst for the breakdown of nitrogen oxides, and solar heat is retained by these compounds, too.

Oxygen is a major constituent of the air we breathe; in the process known as photosynthesis, oxygen is produced by plants as a by-product of converting CO_2 to complex hydrocarbons (carbohydrates). Burning one gallon of gasoline takes all the oxygen produced by a 100-year old tree in the span of one year. With that knowledge, the deforestation of approximately 50,000 to 75,000 square miles of rain forest each year seems all the more significant.

In addition to photosynthesis, plants convert NO_2 to carbon-nitrogen compounds through a process known as nitrogen fixation. Again, it is necessary to remember that each year, there are fewer plants available to break down nitrogen oxides through nitrogen fixing and carbon dioxide through photosynthesis.

Chlorofluorocarbons (CFCs).   CFCs are significant contributors to environmental problems (both in terms of ozone depletion and global warming). In 1986 alone, about 2.6 billion pounds of CFCs were used.

CFCs are simple hydrocarbon molecules (like methane or ethane gas) in which *all* the hydrogen atoms have been replaced by halogens (specifically

EXHIBIT   1.3

Gases That Contribute to Global Warming

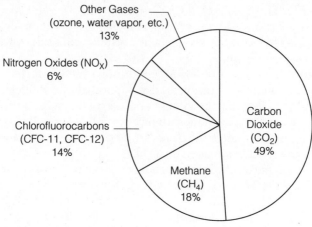

Source: U.S. Environmental Protection Agency

chlorine and fluorine). Developed for commercial use in 1928, CFCs made certain "comfort" products possible, including air conditioners, refrigerators, freezers, and aerosol sprays. CFCs are used in liquid form, but they are readily vaporized to gaseous form in the atmosphere.

Today, the refrigeration, food-processing, and automotive industries account for approximately 70 percent of CFC usage in the United States; aerosols account for only 4 percent. *Global and U.S. Usage of CFCs (1986), Exhibit 1.4,* provides an informative breakdown of CFC use.

In September 1987, forty-nine nations, including the United States, signed an agreement regulating CFCs; this agreement is known as the Montreal Protocol. Later, federal and state legislation ratified the major provisions of the agreement, establishing a $1 to $5 tax for each pound of CFCs produced and regulating CFC containment, recovery, recycling, disposal, and loss prevention. Basically, the agreement banned the use of CFCs in nonessential areas (e.g., hairsprays and other convenience aerosols). The Montreal Protocol was amended in June 1990 to provide for the complete phase-out of CFCs (provisions were made to cut the use of CFCs in half by 1995 and eliminate their use by January 1, 2000). The 1990 Clean Air Act passed by the United States Congress incorporated the CFC phase-out of the Montreal Protocol.

The Act goes even further by establishing an additional phase-out schedule for halogenated hydrocarbons (HCFCs), currently used as the best alternative to CFCs. HCFCs are created through the addition of hydrogen to CFCs. HCFCs decompose faster than CFCs, reducing their ability to react with other

EXHIBIT 1.4

Global and U.S. Usage of CFCs (1986)

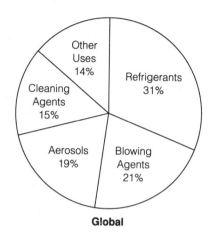

Global

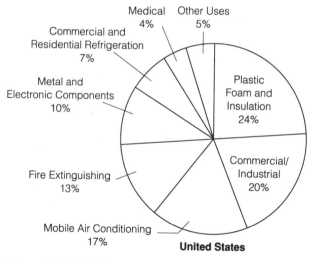

United States

Source: U.S. Environmental Protection Agency

compounds. While this is good news for the environment, it does not eliminate all problems. The phase-out schedule of the Clean Air Act should result
in a total CFC and HCFC production ban by the year 2030.

Common CFCs and HCFCs, Exhibit 1.5, compares the two most common
CFCs used in 1991 (CFC-11 and CFC-12) with the two most popular HCFC
alternatives (HCFC-123 and HCFC-22). The American Society of Heating,
Refrigerating, and Air-Conditioning Engineers (ASHRAE) uses CFC-11 (R-11)

EXHIBIT   1.5

Common CFCs and HCFCs

	Life Span (years)	ODP	GWP
CFC-11	70	1.0	1.0
CFC-12	144	1.0	3.05
HCFC-123	1.9	0.016	0.019
HCFC-22	19	0.05	0.037

In this table, ozone depletion potential (ODP) and greenhouse warming potential (GWP) are both measured relative to CFC-11, which serves as a baseline (hence, its ODP and GWP are 1.0). Based on these comparisons, HCFCs would appear to have much lower ODP and GWP values and are therefore preferable to CFCs for comparable uses.

as the "baseline" compound to determine two things: (1) the Ozone Depletion Potential (ODP), which is the effect a chemical has on the protective ozone layer and (2) the greenhouse warming potential (GWP), which is the amount of global warming gases produced. In many instances, the alternatives are more efficient than CFC-11 or CFC-12. These materials are refrigerants that are currently available and may be used with existing heating, ventilating, and air conditioning (HVAC) and other mechanical systems.

The use of alternative compounds is not the only option. Technology does exist that reduces waste CFC products; special equipment can be attached to older HVAC systems to effectively "recycle" the existing coolants. This process provides substantial savings in some instances and substantial waste prevention and environmental damage control in all instances. With such equipment, it is prudent to utilize leak detectors and air-monitoring alarms to detect escaping waste CFC products (and therefore wasted energy and refrigerants). As is the case in all environmental issues, knowledge makes the difference. More information about alternative refrigerants and available technology can be obtained by contacting a chapter of the American Society of Heating, Refrigerating, and Air-Conditioning Engineers (ASHRAE). HVAC engineering and manufacturing companies are other sources.

Hydrofluorocarbons (HFCs). Newer alternative refrigerants, HFCs, were developed to replace CFCs and HCFCs per the Montreal Protocol and the Clean Air Act. Hydrofluorocarbons are used for the same purposes as CFCs and HCFCs; unlike those compounds, HFCs are not chlorinated, and they have no damaging effects on stratospheric ozone.

Like HCFCs, HFCs are halogenated hydrocarbons (again, the difference being that the former are chlorinated while the latter are not). One such compound, HFC-134a, is sold under the brand names SuvaCold and Klea. Its chemical formula is CH_2FCF_3 and it is nonflammable. This substance can be used in modern mechanical rooms without changing fire or air-quality monitors. It is not listed as a carcinogen under federal regulations, and it is noncorrosive.

Several methods are available for modifying current mechanical equipment so that it can use HFC-134a. Gear changes can be made to the chiller, or other mechanical adjustments can be considered. These alterations may be done quickly—even while the chiller is down for repairs. Modification costs will vary with the age and type of the equipment. Again, information about such modifications and the associated costs can be obtained through the American Society of Heating, Refrigerating, and Air Conditioning Engineers (ASHRAE).

Actual conversions have already been made, providing information on the effects. Per manufacturers' specifications, HFC-134a should decrease capacity by 1 to 10 percent and keep energy efficiency at the same level (plus or minus 1 percent). Actual results have indicated increases in energy efficiency that stretch to 10 percent, and a loss of about 10 percent of capacity.

HFCs are the wave of the future. They work, and conversions of existing equipment are effective. As an alternative to CFCs and HCFCs, HFCs are the best substitute available for dealing with existing machinery.

REAL ESTATE-RELATED ENVIRONMENTAL ISSUES

Everyone is affected by acid rain, ozone depletion, and global warming—certainly the real estate professional is no exception. Not only are these environmental issues of general human concern, they may also prompt legislation that has a direct impact on such expense items as waste disposal and energy use.

There are also those environmental matters—asbestos, radon, and recycling, to name a few—that have already had a direct effect on the real estate community. These problems affect the real estate professional profoundly and must be part of his or her base of knowledge.

Asbestos

The discovery of asbestos in a building can be an owner's nightmare (although it does not have to be). In the worst cases, asbestos can cause severe financial difficulties, make marketing a challenge, and create problems with insurance—and that is only the beginning. One of the most publicized environmental problems, it is also one of the most likely to elicit overreaction.

Asbestos is a naturally occurring mineral. In the past, it was used in the construction industry as a component of floor tiles, concrete, roofing felt and shingles, insulation material, ceiling tiles, etc. Literally tons of asbestos were used in construction from the 1930s to the 1970s. While the presence of asbestos in and of itself may not be dangerous, so-called "friable" asbestos has the potential to create an unsafe level of asbestos in the air, and airborne asbestos fibers *are* a health hazard. (Asbestos that is breaking up into a powder is termed "friable.") Ingestion and inhalation of asbestos have been linked to asbestosis (a scarring of the lungs) and various forms of cancer.

The health hazards posed by asbestos were officially recognized in 1973 when the United States Environmental Protection Agency (EPA) banned the use of sprayed asbestos insulation. (Note: All allusions to the EPA will refer to the United States EPA—unless otherwise stated.) Since that first action in 1973, the EPA and the Occupational Safety and Health Administration (OSHA) have established tolerable limits of exposure to asbestos. OSHA has also created regulations that govern employee exposure to asbestos. The Asbestos Hazard Emergency Response Act (AHERA) of 1986 regulates the presence of asbestos in school buildings.

There are many responses to the presence of asbestos. It can be left alone, contained, or removed. Clearly, there are significant differences between living with the problem and abating it. Decisions should be made on a case-by-case basis. A recent study on asbestos, performed by Harvard University, indicates that asbestos should not necessarily be removed if it is undamaged and not friable. The study indicates that the exposure risk from removing "safe" asbestos is actually greater than if it is left in place. The EPA and the scientific community are both beginning to concur with this opinion.

The presence of asbestos can complicate the sale or purchase of real property. However, its discovery is just as likely to create problems related to current management and operations. To minimize the impact of the discovery of asbestos, the property manager should prepare a special response plan to deal with notifying the owner, tenants, staff, authorities, etc. Such plans should always be done, just as emergency procedures are detailed for fire, explosion, earthquake, or any other natural disaster (this topic is addressed in greater detail in chapter 9).

Because asbestos is naturally occurring, it is regularly found in air and in water supplies. The latter results when water comes into contact with natural formations containing asbestos. A simple filter attachment will help remove asbestos from a water supply.

If asbestos is discovered, a detailed study should be made, and insured asbestos experts should determine if removal is required or even necessary. If removal is judged to be necessary, it should be performed by a qualified removal contractor and all contracts and correspondence—including certificates of insurance—should be reviewed by an environmental attorney.

The EPA offers a helpful publication concerning asbestos. *Managing As-*

bestos in Place: A Building Owner's Guide to Operations and Maintenance Programs for Asbestos-Containing Materials can be obtained by contacting the EPA in Washington, D.C.

Radon

Property managers should understand the concerns associated with radon. The technical designation for radon is Rn-222; it is the only naturally occurring radioactive gas known. Its atomic number is 86, and it is a by-product of the decomposition of Radium-226 in soil or rocks. There are several other isotopes (atoms with the same number of protons) with the atomic number 86 and, therefore, more than one form of radon. The other isotopes, however, are solids that may cling to soil or dust particles and be inhaled. Only Rn-222 is a true gas.

Radon enters buildings in many ways—through the soil, via underground water, and in natural gas. It seeps through all but the most airtight substances and infiltrates a structure along water lines, gas lines, and walls. As energy efficiency improves and dwellings become more airtight, radon that enters homes is less and less likely to escape. The states with the highest radon levels are Pennsylvania (the highest), followed by Utah, Colorado, and New Jersey, with Kentucky, Virginia, and Wyoming sharing fifth place. The states with the lowest radon levels are Arkansas (the lowest), followed by Louisiana, Indiana, Delaware, and California.

Radon is not usually considered a problem in commercial properties because, compared to residences, commercial buildings have a smaller percentage of underground or foundational area per square foot of occupied space. Also, airflow requirements tend to be more stringent for commercial buildings than for residential ones. While it should be noted that radon is seldom a hazard in commercial buildings, one should never rule out the possibility of the presence of radon in any structure.

Lung cancer is the health risk most frequently associated with the inhalation of radon. Even though the life span of radon is only about three days, it can damage someone's lungs in a short period of time. Given the fact that radon testing is very inexpensive, it is easy to understand why testing for radon is just plain good business practice.

The most important factors regarding radon accumulation relate to the ratio of invasion versus the rate of ventilation (i.e., if more comes in than goes out, there is a problem). Therefore, time of day, weather, and the seasons have a great deal of effect on whether radon accumulates to dangerous levels.

Wind helps interior radon levels to abate, much as it helps water to evaporate. The more wind, the greater the imbalance between inside and outside pressures, and the better the odds that radon will escape. In fact, radon levels are often at their lowest in the evening when there tends to be more wind.

Weather conditions have an impact on radon levels. Radon levels tend to be lower during the spring and fall of the year when many households or commercial buildings utilize ventilation from windows, dampers, or attic fans. When summer heat and winter cold arrive, people begin to utilize cooling and heating systems and buildings are closed. As one might expect, radon levels increase during summer and winter. Winter is the season most likely to produce the highest radon concentrations. When snow, rain, ice, or fallen leaves block radon diffusion through the soil outside, radon tends to move through the path of least resistance, which is usually a home basement or foundation slab. In those areas of the United States where coal, coal oil, and natural gas are used as heating agents, the impact of radon may be even greater. Radon is known to be carried with natural gas and, as the temperatures decrease, natural gas usage increases. Radon is also commonly found in coal deposits and coal mines (especially in Pennsylvania where a great portion of coal used in heating is produced).

There are a number of ways to check for the presence of radon. Test "kits" may be purchased in hardware stores for less than $40. However, commercial properties should be tested by a professional ambient air quality engineer; radon concentration (and by association, the level of concern) will vary with the size and nature of the building. Professional testing will cost more than a do-it-yourself kit, but radon testing is still not as expensive as other air quality tests.

The radon test is fairly simple. A sampler device containing a charcoal filter is left in the same area for several days. A qualified engineer can coordinate weather patterns, seasons, and building ventilation systems to determine if there are areas of a structure to be concerned about and, if so, where they are located. The engineer will install and pick up the sampler devices and have them tested at a local laboratory; results are often back within a few weeks. Another, more expensive, option is the use of a highly sensitive device similar to a temperature change or electrical usage monitor that checks actual radon levels and charts them on a circular pad. Such a device may remain in place for long periods (perhaps as long as a year to detect seasonal patterns), and it must be observed by a qualified engineer. Although testing of this nature is expensive, the results are extremely accurate.

There are two effective methods for combating radon. One approach is to seal foundations, basement floors, walls, and other areas of the structure that come into direct contact with the ground. Alternatively, ventilation can be added to a building (e.g., fans, piping, etc.) to help diffuse and dissipate radon. Most people address radon problems through a combination of these methods.

One ventilation method that has met with some success is the installation of a series of underground pipes beneath the foundation and/or around the basement walls; these pipes vent above ground. This method actually provides an alternative route for radon, preventing it from entering the building in the first place. Sometimes piping and fans are placed in critical areas. An attic fan is another effective tool for removing radon—and one that many people already have.

Polychlorinated Biphenyls (PCBs)

Like asbestos, PCBs have been known to incite overreaction. The mere fact that PCBs have been discovered does not necessarily make the situation life-threatening.

PCBs, short for polychlorinated biphenyls, are biphenyls in which many hydrogen atoms have been replaced by chlorine atoms. They are manufactured rather than naturally occurring. Biphenyls are complex liquids used as heat transfer agents (i.e., to remove heat from the source generating it); they are also used as antifungal coatings on the interior of citrus fruit crates. Non-chlorinated biphenyls have a low toxicity rating and are not generally a major concern or problem in industrial situations. However, once biphenyls are chlorinated, the resultant PCBs are toxic and have a long life span. Many PCBs share characteristics with dichloro-diphenyl-trichloroethane (DDT), an insecticide that has been banned because it is associated with dioxin (pesticides and dioxin are discussed later in the chapter). The EPA has classified PCBs as human carcinogens, hazardous materials, and priority toxic pollutants. When introduced into the environment, PCBs contaminate soil, water, plants, and animals and can eventually contaminate the entire food chain. Contamination from PCBs affects the eyes, throat, liver, and skin; children are especially sensitive to exposure. PCBs that may have adhered to soil or dust particles may also be inhaled. Physical side effects in humans include skin cancer, liver cancer, cirrhosis of the liver, anorexia, and permanent eye damage. Exposure may halt fetal development and result in miscarriages or severe birth defects. For this reason, PCBs are classified as "embryotoxic."

There are more than 200 compounds which, when chlorinated, become PCBs. At the industrial level, a generic PCB solution may contain fifty or more different polychlorinated biphenyls. Each unique PCB is a very stable, non-flammable compound. Liquid PCBs may be mixed with other compounds to form nonflammable solids. Mixing PCBs with other compounds provides greater alternatives for their use. PCBs are most commonly used as insulation for electrical products such as cables, wiring, and transformers. They may also be found in the high-pressure, high-heat liquids used in train braking and other hydraulic systems. The Toxic Substances Control Act of 1976 (TSCA) banned the use of PCBs in new electrical transformers.

The presence of PCBs may complicate a real estate sale or purchase, but it is more likely to be of concern to the property manager. A property manager who has to contend with the presence of PCBs is most likely to find them in electrical transformers. PCB-containing transformers have been around for many years; some of them are still in use and have presented no threat to the environment. However, when PCBs are discovered on a property, it is crucial to take the time to determine the best, safest, and most cost-effective plan of action regarding them.

"Wet" transformers, as PCB-containing transformers are called, are not a danger to the environment unless they leak, burn, or explode. It is impossible to tell whether a transformer is wet just by looking at it. Utility companies have recycled older ones and converted them to "dry" (non-PCB-containing) transformers; hence, the age of a transformer is not always an indicator of its contents. (Although testing is often considered something to be avoided because of the inconvenience to tenants, the time involved, and its significant costs, testing and sampling are absolutely necessary to verify the presence— or absence—of PCBs.)

Replacing wet transformers with dry ones can be tremendously expensive and, in some instances, cost prohibitive. The law prohibits PCBs in new transformers, so any new transformer installed by the utility company (and any existing ones that were installed after 1976) will be dry. By waiting for the utility to replace old or defective transformers at its own expense, the owner will save the cost of conversion or replacement (assuming, of course, that the transformers are not privately owned).

Routine inspections of on-site transformers will determine whether or not a transformer is a potential problem. A leaking transformer is always a potential problem, especially if its PCB status is unknown. The discovery of a leaking transformer should be followed immediately by notification of the local utility. This advice applies regardless of ownership (i.e., whether the transformer is owned privately or by the utility). As a rule, the local utility offers the most expertise in the matter of PCBs. Utilities are also sensitive about their public image and highly motivated to help people in the community (consider the amount of publicity generated by utility rate increases and the widespread negative responses that often follow). Granted, utilities are not likely to perform cost-free testing of privately-owned transformers, but any environmental engineer would charge a fee for the same work. If the local utility will do the testing, it is best to have them do the job.

In addition to evidence of leakage, other indications of problems include unexpectedly high electrical bills, burned or blackened areas on the transformer itself, or arcing or electrical sparking at the panels or transformer. Any one of these conditions calls for immediate action—repairs should be made with appropriate haste. Assuming the transformers are not privately owned, the first step is notification of the utility. Necessary repairs are likely to be made at the utility's expense.

Even if testing a transformer results in the discovery of the presence of very low levels of PCBs, this should not be cause for panic. The PCBs may be merely residual. While many old transformers have been recycled using non-PCB-containing materials, it is almost impossible to remove 100 percent of the PCBs from the interior of a transformer. A low level of PCBs may lead to detection, but it is not likely to pose a threat to the environment or to humans. Again, when in doubt, contact the utility company.

It is worthwhile to note that two of the world's most fire-resistant substances, asbestos and PCBs, also pose significant health risks. When evaluating fire-retardant substances or applications, it is important to obtain all the appropriate material safety data sheets (MSDSs) and federal substance hazard index listings to determine the chemical components of the substance under consideration. *Example Format for a Material Safety Data Sheet, Exhibit 1.6,* indicates the type of information that is likely to be imparted by an MSDS. To obtain an MSDS on a given substance, one can contact the manufacturer (who is responsible for preparing the MSDS).

Pesticides

It can be said that the most common sources of toxic chemicals and toxic fumes are among the most commonly used substances in property management. Pesticides are poisons. In some cases, exposure through skin contact or inhalation may be serious enough to cause illness, pain, debilitating injuries, and even death.

The term "pesticide" is generic and is used to refer to any chemical used to kill pests. A pesticide can be a herbicide (used to kill plants such as weeds), an insecticide (used to kill or control insects), a rodenticide (used to kill rodents such as rats and mice), or a fungicide (used to control mold, mildew, etc.). Pesticides are formulated as liquid emulsions or solutions, granulated solids, and dusts, and are used in diluted form in agriculture, household pest control, landscaping treatments, etc. Most of the information available on these substances focuses on insecticides rather than herbicides. Insecticides are used on everything from the food we eat to the cabinets in which we store our eating utensils. Hence, the EPA and most environmental groups have given priority to an examination of the risks associated with various insecticides on the market. Herbicides are primarily used outdoors where diffusion into the air is greater; as a result, they have been studied less than insecticides. Herbicides are used in the growing of food as well as on lawns, shrubs, and indoor plants. Because of this, they should not be discounted as health risks. Some property managers may actually use more herbicides than insecticides in the course of normal operations.

Sensitivity to pesticides can manifest itself in many ways. Symptoms may parallel other illnesses such as flu, stomach viruses, and even unusual or exotic cancers. As always, children are most susceptible to the toxic effects. Typical side effects of exposure to some pesticides include kidney, thyroid, and neurological disorders.

It is also important to note that chemical fertilizers may pose problems; fertilizers are not studied as intensely as pesticides. Overuse of chemical fertilizers can actually damage the soil—killing necessary organisms and making

E X H I B I T　1.6

Example Format for a Material Safety Data Sheet

MATERIAL SAFETY DATA SHEET

CHEMICAL NAME:	
SYNONYMS:	CHEMICAL FAMILY:
FORMULA:	MOLECULAR WEIGHT:
TRADE NAME AND SYNONYMS:	

I. PHYSICAL DATA

BOILING POINT, 760 mm.Hg		FREEZING POINT	
SPECIFIC GRAVITY ($H_2O=1$)		VAPOR PRESSURE at 20^0 C.	
VAPOR DENSITY (air = 1)		SOLUBILITY IN WATER, % by wt. at 20^0 C.	
PER CENT VOLATILES BY VOLUME		EVAPORATION RATE (Butyl Acetate = 1)	
APPEARANCE AND ODOR			

II. HAZARDOUS INGREDIENTS

MATERIAL	%	TLV (Units)

III. FIRE AND EXPLOSION HAZARD DATA

FLASH POINT (test method)		AUTOIGNITION TEMPERATURE			
FLAMMABLE LIMITS IN AIR, % by volume		LOWER		UPPER	
EXTINGUISHING MEDIA					
UNUSUAL FIRE AND EXPLOSION HAZARDS					
SPECIAL FIRE FIGHTING PROCEDURES					

landscaping more difficult and expensive to maintain. In addition, fertilizers often contain a high concentration of nitrates, which have been associated with birth defects, heart disease, childhood brain tumors, and other illnesses. For this reason, any use of chemical fertilizers (as opposed to organic or natural fertilizers) should be monitored by the property manager or environmental manager.

IV. HEALTH HAZARD DATA

ACUTE ORAL TOXICITY LD$_{50}$	
DERMAL IRRITATION	
EYE IRRITATION	
THRESHOLD LIMIT VALUE	
EFFECTS OF OVEREXPOSURE	
EMERGENCY AND FIRST AID PROCEDURES	

V. REACTIVITY DATA

STABILITY			
UNSTABLE	STABLE	CONDITIONS TO AVOID	
INCOMPATIBILTY (materials to avoid)			
HAZARDOUS POLYMERIZATION			
May Occur	Will not Occur	CONDITIONS TO AVOID	
HAZARDOUS DECOMPOSITION PRODUCTS			

VI. SPILL OR LEAK PROCEDURES

STEPS TO BE TAKEN IF MATERIAL IS RELEASED OR SPILLED	
WASTE DISPOSAL METHOD	

VII. SPECIAL PROTECTION INFORMATION

RESPIRATORY PROTECTION (specify type)			
VENTILATION	LOCAL EXHAUST	SPECIAL	
	MECHANICAL (general)	OTHER	
PROTECTIVE GLOVES		EYE PROTECTION	
OTHER PROTECTIVE EQUIPMENT			

VIII. SPECIAL PRECAUTIONS

PRECAUTIONARY LABELING	
OTHER HANDLING AND STORAGE CONDITIONS	

EMERGENCY PHONE NUMBERS

All pesticides must be registered by the EPA. However, registration of a pesticide is not a guarantee that it is safe for use. Laws regulating pesticides and the EPA evaluation procedures contain loopholes through which "unsafe" pesticides can slip.

Under the Federal Insecticide, Fungicide, and Rodenticide Act (FIFRA), only the "active" ingredients or the components that cause the desired effect are required to be identified specifically on the product labels. These labels must include warnings regarding specific hazards, but only those of the identified components need to be given. Dioxins and organophosphates (byproducts of the production of some pesticidal chemicals) are rarely, if ever, "active" ingredients in pesticide formulations. For that reason, they are not registered with the EPA or listed on product labels. Ironically, organophosphates are derivative chemicals similar in composition and effect to some chemical weapons, which the United States has been trying to outlaw internationally for years. In addition, the EPA conducts its reviews of pesticides based on industry-supplied data and test results rather than on independent studies or its own tests. In fact, the EPA does not perform tests on these products at all; it requires manufacturers to supply all the product information, use data, and test results on which the registration of a pesticide is based.

Property managers are likely to deal directly with problems related to controlling termites; exterminating household pests such as mice, cockroaches, and silverfish; and reducing weeds in lawns and landscaped areas. Because the application of pesticides is frequently required in the operation of all types of properties, it is important for the property manager to be cognizant of the laws regarding pesticides and their use. For example, some pesticides can no longer be used. Federal, state, and local laws may also govern who can apply these substances; license requirements exist for the application of some pesticides. Before any property manager can make an assessment of the safety and health risks posed by a given pesticide, he or she must know what substances can and cannot be used.

While certain pesticides may be common or popular, there are numerous alternatives available on the market. Many of these are much safer and equally economical and effective as the popular brands. There are also so-called "organic" or natural methods of pest control and landscape maintenance (in actuality, most manufactured pesticides contain carbon and are therefore also "organic"). An effective combination of the two can be implemented; some of these options may even save money.

The property manager should always know what hazardous chemicals are being used and how best to minimize exposure to them. In many cases, it may take no more than a scheduling change to allow for sufficient ventilation or irrigation time. In any event, the fewer tenants, residents, employees, and visitors exposed, the safer the owner and management company are from liability.

The landscape maintenance contractor or pest control contractor should be able to provide an MSDS for each chemical used on a property (see exhibit 1.6). These sheets detail both the specific hazards of and the most effective protection from exposure. Maintaining these sheets is an OSHA requirement. One should be wary of any contractor who is reluctant to provide copies of MSDSs when requested to do so.

Many national, state, and local organizations can provide information on specific pesticidal chemicals, as well as alternative chemicals or procedures that may be just as effective. The National Coalition Against the Misuse of Pesticides (NCAMP) in Washington, D.C., is one such source, and they can also provide information on how to contact the National Coalition for Alternatives to Pesticides (NCAP).

Dioxin. Dioxin is a catch-all name for a group of approximately seventy-five similar compounds, the most common of which is 2,3,7,8-tetrachlorodi-benzo-*p*-dioxin or TCDD. Dioxin is a by-product of paper bleaching, as well as the manufacture of pesticides, refined oil products, and chlorophenols. It is also produced during the incineration of municipal, industrial, and medical wastes. Dioxin is rarely listed on warning labels because labeling laws require only "active" or useful ingredients to be listed. As a by-product of the chemical process, dioxin becomes a part of the chemical that is being manufactured. Dioxin is considered a carcinogen, a hazardous waste, and a priority toxic pollutant by the EPA.

Given that dioxin is an inherent component of pesticidal chemicals, it follows that insects and plants containing the substance are consumed and brought into the food chain. Dioxin collects in the fatty tissue of animal bodies and thus becomes more concentrated as it moves up the food chain. Nursing infants are considered higher on the food chain than adults because their food is manufactured by the mother's body, so they are at an even greater risk.

The more than 15,000 studies to date on dioxin and its effects on human health and the environment have led to an overall consensus that there are no "safe" levels of exposure. Because dioxin may be present in chemicals used on a property or can result from the degradation of such chemicals in place, it is the property manager who is most likely to encounter this potential problem. While elimination of dioxin will be difficult (if not impossible), the property manager can make certain decisions in contracting for landscaping and pest control to prevent some dioxin contamination. The first step is to obtain MSDSs from landscape contractors and pest control contractors. No chemical applications should be allowed unless the manager has an MSDS for each chemical to be used. Although the contractor will be liable to a certain extent for any problems resulting from the chemicals or their applications, it is always the owner of the property who will be held absolutely liable.

Electromagnetic Fields (EMFs)

Among environmental issues, electromagnetic fields (EMFs) might be considered one of the most controversial. An electromagnetic field is defined as a field of force associated with electric charge in motion having both electric and magnetic components and containing a definite amount of energy. In general, EMFs are divided into two types—an EMF has an energy level above

300 hertz (Hz), while low-level EMFs actually exist wherever electricity flows (i.e., in one's home, office, or car).

While some scientific data suggest a link between EMFs and certain diseases (e.g., potential risks have been associated with living beneath high-tension power lines), none of the evidence is conclusive. Also, their impact on the environment is not clear. The effects of EMFs on electrical equipment are undisputed, however. An EMF overload in a limited area of a building may cause such problems as utility brown-outs, breaker overloads, and functional problems with equipment. Electromagnetic overload has been known to render entire floors of high-rise office buildings useless for high-tech operations.

Indoor Air Quality (IAQ)

Indoor air quality (IAQ) is truly a "hot" environmental topic in real estate, especially in office buildings. In truth, most properties have acceptable air quality and few property managers will ever have to handle IAQ problems. Nevertheless, it is necessary to be aware that certain human symptoms have been related to poor-quality indoor air. When a number of people in a building exhibit symptoms related to poor IAQ, the building may be "sick"—*sick building syndrome (SBS)* is a label used for buildings with poor IAQ. Such symptoms include watery eyes, shortness of breath, nasal irritations, rashes, headaches, fatigue, dizziness, nausea, flu-like symptoms, and more.

IAQ is affected by a building's structure as well as its internal systems, and by outdoor conditions, tenant usage, and location. It is important for the property manager to understand the four major contributors to IAQ (as defined by the EPA): (1) outside sources, (2) HVAC systems, (3) building occupants, and (4) construction materials.

Outside Sources.   The 1990 Clean Air Act (CAA) and some earlier local ordinances instituted requirements concerning "ambient" air (i.e., "fresh" air from the outside surroundings). These regulations stipulate that a certain percentage of the air in a building has to be ambient air. Such regulations are worthwhile in most areas of the country, but there are central business districts (CBDs) where the pollution from traffic and general operations may render outside air more polluted than the air recycled throughout buildings. Radon can also enter buildings from outside, and circulating air from outside can cause problems for people inside who suffer from allergies during certain times of year. Some of the problems caused by outside sources can be addressed by filtration, but this process is not necessarily effective.

Heating, Ventilation, and Air-Conditioning (HVAC) Systems. HVAC systems not only control temperature (which affects the growth of a variety of organisms—including microscopic ones), they also regulate air supply (inflow and return). Too much inflow or return in certain areas of the building can lead to buildup of dust and other residues, cause drafts that may increase human exposure to certain substances, or create "cold-spots" and "hot-spots" in the building. Ventilation equipment must be properly maintained. When maintenance is inadequate, contributors to poor IAQ may include accumulation of dust in HVAC ducts as well as growth of microbes and other organisms in ducts and drip pans.

Building age is likely to affect the types of IAQ problems encountered. While older buildings are not as airtight as newer ones, their HVAC systems may not be equipped to serve occupants as effectively. No amount of maintenance can "heal" an inadequate ventilation system. When air distribution and "fresh" air supply is not sufficient, problems can arise from other sources. Fumes from cleaning products used by janitorial crews may be circulated through the HVAC system and contribute to poor IAQ. (For this reason, it is advisable to do heavy-duty jobs at night using ventilation from other sources than the building HVAC systems.) Emissions from office equipment during the day (e.g., ammonia from blue print machines, chemicals from printing and photo developing processes, etc.) may create problems. Even simple "desk chemicals" (e.g., glue, ink, "white-out," etc.) can contribute to poor IAQ.

Building Occupants.   Given that IAQ is affected by temperature, humidity, air flow, and substances present in the air, it is clear that the day-to-day activities of building occupants have an impact. From the perspective of IAQ, the most detrimental human activity is smoking. While most smokers inhale 70 to 90 percent of their cigarette smoke, the remainder is released into the atmosphere for others to breathe (so-called "secondhand smoke"). This residual smoke gets into the air return system and leaves a residue in ducts and other HVAC system components.

People also bring odors and germs into a building, engage in activities that involve the use of chemicals, and generate trash that may have unpleasant odors. All these activities have an effect on IAQ—even breathing increases the concentration of carbon dioxide in the air.

Construction Materials.   Every building is made up of a different combination of materials, each of which has a unique impact on IAQ. For example, formaldehyde gas may be emitted by building materials and other products that contain formaldehyde (e.g., some types of foam insulation, particle board, plywood, glues, adhesives, solvents, fumigants, and carpeting). Asbestos used as insulation can be damaged, yielding fibers that may become airborne and create IAQ problems. Some caulks and sealants release volatile organic compounds (VOCs) that have an adverse effect on IAQ. VOCs have been linked to certain human symptoms that are associated with sick building syndrome (e.g., watery eyes, headaches, fatigue, and dizziness). Literally hundreds of VOCs are in the air; the vast array of sources includes tobacco smoke, paints, refrigerants, disinfectants, cleaning products, and much more (see chapter 9 for additional discussion of VOCs and IAQ).

Indeed, the possible contributors to poor IAQ comprise a very long list.

Although real estate professionals do not need highly technical knowledge regarding IAQ, it is wise for them to have a basic understanding of typical IAQ problems, their origins, and possible solutions. The issue of IAQ becomes more and more important every day as public awareness of sick building syndrome increases.

Municipal Waste and Recycling

As this book was being written, Americans were generating 160 million tons of municipal waste per year. The three most common methods of waste disposal are landfill, incineration (including waste-to-energy conversion), and recycling. All three methods are expensive: Refuse costs approximately $40 to $60 per ton to dispose as landfill, $70 to $120 per ton to incinerate, and $20 to $30 per ton to recycle (costs vary regionally). *Municipal Waste Composition and Disposal (1989), Exhibit 1.7,* indicates the percentages of different kinds of wastes generated and the proportionate use of the three most popular waste disposal methods in the United States in 1989.

There are approximately 6,000 active landfill sites now operating in the United States. Federal, state, and local regulations, plus public awareness and opinion, have resulted in restrictions regarding the creation of new landfill sites. The U.S. EPA estimates that by 1992, capacity for landfill disposal in the United States will be reduced by thirty-six million tons per year. That is thirty-six million tons of waste that must be eliminated in some other way.

The use of waste incinerators, while more expensive, is an alternative that is becoming more popular. New technology has decreased smokestack pollution and increased the ability to generate electricity from the process of incineration. Nevertheless, incinerator ash by-products are a concern. Through burning, the volume of waste is reduced to approximately 10 percent of its original volume, but the ash contains high percentages of heavy metals and dioxin. Incinerator ash is deposited as landfill, but there is little information available regarding what happens to the ash once it is deposited.

The least expensive waste disposal alternative is also the most environmentally friendly. *Recycling* reduces the volume of waste to be disposed and makes fewer demands on the world's nonrenewable resources. As a consequence, less energy is consumed in obtaining these resources. For example, recycling one ton of aluminum eliminates the need for approximately four tons of bauxite, one ton of coke, and one ton of pitch, which are consumed as virgin (previously unmined and nonrenewable) materials in the production of metallic aluminum.

Recycling is likely to become mandatory throughout the United States. In the first six months of 1990, sixty-five recycling laws were passed in twenty-seven states. While transition to a recycling system may not be implemented by an owner or manager prior to statutory requirements, studies of anticipated needs can save a lot of time when recycling becomes mandatory. Sources for information on recycling alternatives include local government

E X H I B I T   1.7

Municipal Waste Composition and Disposal (1989)

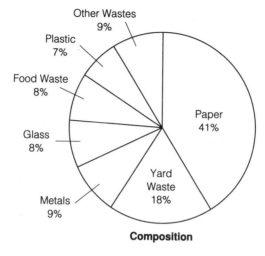

Composition

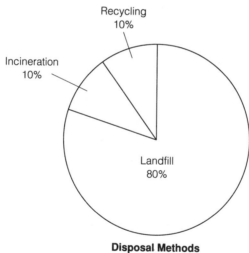

Disposal Methods

Source: U.S. Environmental Protection Agency

---

offices and private waste disposal firms (look under "recycling" in the yellow pages telephone directory).

Recycling is one of the environmental issues that is most likely to influence the property manager directly. Not only should he or she be aware of any applicable recycling requirements, the property manager should also be aware of the means to establish recycling programs. Finally, he or she should understand that there is another reason to establish a recycling program besides following legal requirements and being environmentally conscientious—recycling programs can save money.

Of all the municipal waste produced in the United States, more than 40 percent is paper. The recycling of a ton of wastepaper saves approximately 17 trees and 7,000 gallons of water in the production of new paper. Of the waste generated in the United States in 1989, only 1 percent of all plastics, 12 percent of glass, 23 percent of white paper, 35 percent of newspaper, and 55 percent of aluminum cans were recycled. It can be said conclusively that local recycling regulations and legislation at the federal, state, and local level will become more prevalent.

In a very broad sense, the real estate industry will be one of the largest sources of recyclable materials in the country. The volume of scrap materials from development and then subsequent reconstruction of tenant spaces is substantial. During initial construction phases, separation of various types of recyclable waste is relatively simple, but the costs for removal of the separated materials will be increased because additional receptacles are required and a variety of disposal facilities will have to be used.

Existing and newly completed projects will also generate hundreds of thousands of tons of waste through the operation of businesses and the day-to-day living activities of tenants and residents. In retail and industrial projects, tenants are usually responsible for their own waste disposal contracts. Recycling clauses can be added to lease documents so that the costs of placing additional dumpsters in a central location and removing them under separate disposal contracts may be added to the common area maintenance (CAM) charges (each tenant pays a pro rata share). In this way, the only inconvenience to the tenants would be separating the waste as it is generated. While the most efficient method is separation at the source, this becomes more difficult in the case of an office building where each individual is a source. In addition to educating employees about recycling, central receptacles should be available in each office to provide employees with a separate place to discard recyclable materials. This will permit the janitorial crew to separate and remove more waste more efficiently.

In large residential developments, centralized containers are the most efficient means of waste storage and removal. Individual residents should be required to separate their wastes. Depending on the size and acreage of the property, tenants would be required either to take their separated wastes to the appropriate receptacles or to set out the separated wastes for property maintenance personnel to collect. A residential property's requirements for additional dumpsters in more locations will depend on the number of units and the area to be served.

Hazardous Waste.   Commercial enterprises are most likely to be generators of hazardous wastes, some of them incidental to their specific operations (e.g., the solvents used by dry cleaners). Collection, transportation, and disposal of hazardous wastes are all closely regulated. State permits are required for the generator, the transporter, and the disposer (often a landfill site). Specific labeling of hazardous waste is mandatory. These particular regulations and requirements have been and are evolving, but they were not always in place. A real estate transaction involving a property contaminated by a hazardous waste is one that it may be preferable to avoid.

THE BOTTOM LINE: STAYING INFORMED

Any general discussion of environmental issues should include a reference to the legislative picture. While the subject of environmental legislation is a topic that will be addressed at length in chapter 2, this introduction to the environmental concerns of real estate professionals should close with a few thoughts regarding the law and knowledge of it.

Environmental legislation changes constantly—and ignorance of the law is not an acceptable defense. Any one property is likely to fall under the jurisdiction of local, state, and federal agencies. To understand the prevailing legislation, it is often necessary to sift through layers of overlapping laws that are imposed at more than one level—local, state, and federal. It is absolutely essential for the property manager to understand which regulations prevail or at least know when it is necessary to secure assistance from a professional.

One example of a confusing issue involves the Environmental Protection Agency (EPA). As stated earlier in the chapter, all reference to the EPA in this text will mean the United States Environmental Protection Agency (unless otherwise stated). It is important to remember that states have their own agencies whose role it is to protect the environment. Some state agencies may actually go by the name EPA, although the names of these agencies vary greatly from state to state (as do the roles they play and the regulations they impose).

It is clear that staying informed is the key to dealing with any type of environmental problem effectively. This chapter presents an overview of some of the issues that real estate professionals should understand. It is rarely necessary for the real estate professional to have highly technical knowledge of these topics. Some of the most worthwhile environmental information involves knowing when it is time to solicit the help of environmental specialists and who should be involved—few lessons are more important. The following material will build on the foundation of knowledge established by this chapter and include some hands-on advice for dealing with specific problems. For those who seek additional details regarding any environmental issues, there are many sources (e.g., experts, libraries, institutions of higher learning); some of these are listed in Appendix G, Sources of Information.

Environmental Legislation

Environmental legislation can be confusing and contradictory. Although the first truly comprehensive environmental legislation was passed many years ago, attorneys, the court systems, the United States Congress, the EPA, and others are still trying to define its purpose, power, and limitations. The effects of environmental legislation, however, have been widespread and significant.

The legislative issue of greatest concern to the real estate industry is the doctrine of "absolute liability" and the ways it relates to the property owner. Absolute liability involves assessing liability for an act or situation that causes harm, without consideration of the person or persons at fault. Current environmental laws apply absolute liability to property owners, making an owner liable for any sort of environmental contamination on his or her property, regardless of how or when the contamination occurred or who was responsible. In other words, someone could buy a property today and become absolutely liable for contamination that has existed on that property for many, many years. This does not mean that previous owners are protected from liability, however. Although current owners are most likely to be liable for costs associated with environmental problems, they can include any previous owner in a liability lawsuit.

Absolute liability is designed with the intention of being *equally unfair to everyone* and, therefore, fair after all. Considering such issues as absolute liability, it is easy to recognize the importance of understanding major environmental laws and the ways these laws affect real estate owners and managers.

Exceptions to the "rule" of absolute liability involve the violation of laws concerning information disclosure. The owner of a property has a legal obligation to inform prospective purchasers of any environmental problem of which he or she is aware. Should it be revealed that the seller of a property failed to make the buyer aware of a known problem prior to the purchase, the new owner is not liable for costs related to the problem. The previous owner is not only liable for those costs but also subject to penalties.

HISTORY

Laws, and changes in them, have made environmental issues a critical factor in many real estate transactions. A list of significant legislation would include the Clean Air Act of 1970 (amended significantly in 1990), the Federal Water Pollution Control Act of 1972, the Resource Conservation and Recovery Act (RCRA) of 1976 (amended in 1984), and the Comprehensive Environmental Response, Compensation, and Liability Act (CERCLA or SUPERFUND) of 1980 (amended in 1986).

For the real estate owner, purchaser, or professional, concern about incurring liability is of the utmost importance. Unfortunately, the specter of liability is present during even the most basic real estate deals. Another sobering detail is the fact that EPA litigators can—and do—prosecute criminal charges against individuals. Ownership and management present some serious risks; these risks have created new service businesses (e.g., environmental law, consulting, and testing firms) and a need for in-house specialists who analyze and interpret information from these environmental professionals.

At the end of fiscal 1990, the EPA announced that it had referred approximately 375 civil cases and 65 criminal cases to Justice Department prosecutors. In addition, more than 50 people were convicted and sentenced for environmental crimes. (It should be noted that environmental law does not provide for protection of the individual through a corporate entity, a topic that will be addressed in chapter 3.) In the same year, the courts sentenced individuals to more than 700 months of prison time and collected millions of dollars in fines. The largest single fine in 1990 was approximately $15 million for a violation of the Clean Water Act.

Clean Air Act (CAA) 1970/1990

The Clean Air Act (CAA) of 1970 was originally intended to decrease the amount of air pollution created by heavy industry and automobiles. Its immediate effect on commercial and residential real estate was minimal. Developers of industrial real estate, however, faced design and construction regulations. The Clear Air Act had the greatest effect on the so-called "smokestack" industries.

In the real estate industry, CAA had the most profound effect on the incineration of waste and the generation of electrical power. When adjustments were made to comply with the new regulations, waste disposal and electricity costs increased significantly. Increased expenses in these areas were a major contributor to the now commonplace use of net, net-net, and triple-net leases throughout the industry, passing property operating expenses through to the tenant.

Scientific research over the past twenty years has increased our understanding of issues such as global warming, acid rain, and ozone depletion. In response to this new information, Congress passed a new Clean Air Act in 1990. At the time of writing this book, it is impossible to explain the total impact of the 1990 Act. Nevertheless, the Act includes issues of concern to the real estate industry that should be highlighted.

The 1990 regulations tighten the requirements on "smokestack" industries and automobiles. Like earlier regulations, the new ones will have a sizable impact on the costs of waste disposal and electrical power. Although the use of triple-net leases will protect property owners and investors from major operating cost increases, increased tenant costs are often passed down to the consumer. (Sometimes owners may have to change their expectations for base rent, however. When tenants' costs increase substantially, they may be motivated to reduce their leased space or move to a less-expensive location.)

Obvious changes brought about by the Act will be heightened awareness of electricity usage and efficiency, increased regulation of HVAC system emissions, and intensified pursuit of alternative energy sources. Congress designed the Act with the intention of promoting technological advances in these and many other areas.

Due to the problems associated with electrical power generation, the new law has increased restrictions on the waste products produced by these processes. The costs associated with electrical power are expected to rise dramatically as the new restrictions are put in place, providing an impetus to generate electricity more efficiently.

Trends toward energy-saving bulbs, light fixtures, insulation, construction, and design will continue, and new technology is expected. Simple cost-cutting measures that should become commonplace include decreasing the number of lights burning twenty-four hours a day in offices and retail establishments, adding motion and noise sensor switches to restrooms and storage areas to decrease electricity consumption when facilities are empty, and relying on mechanical sensor alarms rather than lighting retail spaces at night. Replacing photocells with light timers in parking lots can substantially reduce the amount of time that lights burn. Adding a security patrol to parking garages and requiring drivers to turn on their headlights can reduce the required lighting by as much as 50 percent (without compromising security).

Energy-efficient windows, insulation, and ceiling tiles can be installed in new buildings or when tenants change; these items increase energy efficiency by reducing heating and cooling losses. Energy-efficient bulbs, ballasts, and reflector panels are all currently available, and alterations of light fixtures to accommodate them may halve the number of bulbs required.

The 1990 Clean Air Act will dramatically affect the HVAC industry. Regulation of CFCs and HCFCs will force the development of better-designed, more-efficient systems. Technologists will have to create the means to contain and recycle these emissions—or eliminate them altogether. All this will affect the initial design and construction of new projects as well as the alteration of existing properties.

Incentives for developing alternative energy sources have been boosted immensely by the new Act. Solar and wind power technologies already in use will contribute efficient and "clean" power that can be utilized in a variety of ways. In addition to reducing the demand for commercially generated electricity, these types of technology can help decrease the annual operating costs of many buildings.

To assure compliance with new federal emissions and pollution standards, the use of gasoline containing ethanol will become more common. Incentives to change vehicles over to natural gas or butane operation should increase the numbers of fleets using these fuels. Some governmental agencies, municipalities, and hospitals have already begun using emergency generators and fleets of vehicles that run on natural gas.

The 1990 Clean Air Act will have a major impact on American industry as a whole. Perhaps the most far-reaching environmental legislation in history, it may be years before its ramifications will be completely understood.

Clean Water Act (CWA) 1972

Formerly known as the Federal Water Pollution Control Act, the Clean Water Act (CWA) has been amended several times over the past two decades. Originally designed to restrict industrial polluters, its regulations affect real estate in several ways.

Most of its effects are experienced at the development stage. National Pollutant Discharge Elimination System (NPDES) regulations affect sewer and storm water drainage and wastewater treatment as well as grading, storm run-off, and run-off from fill dirt brought to or removed from construction sites.

"Wetlands" is a term most people have heard, yet few know exactly what it means. Simply defined, wetlands are areas where water is a major determinant of plant life, animal life, and the environment as a whole. While this is not a formal definition (formal definitions are not common in environmental law), it is a useful one. Wetlands regulations are very complex and involve more than one governmental agency. These regulations affect site selection, type of construction, and construction costs in a very complex and potentially disastrous way for the uninitiated developer.

The determination of whether an area is classified as wetlands is generally the responsibility of the U.S. Army Corps of Engineers (as specified by Section 404 of the Clean Water Act). The Corps of Engineers draws its definition of "wetlands" from the Code of Federal Regulations, which reads as follows: "Those areas that are inundated or saturated by surface or groundwater at a frequency and duration sufficient to support, and that under normal circumstances do support, a prevalence of vegetation typically adapted for life in saturated soil conditions. Wetlands generally include swamps, marshes, bogs, and similar areas." (From "Recognizing Wetlands," a pamphlet published and distributed by the Army Corps of Engineers.)

The Clean Water Act also allows other federal agencies to get involved in the process of determining wetlands; these agencies are given the power to veto the Corps' interpretation when it is deemed necessary. Some of these other agencies include the Fish and Wildlife Service, the Soil Conservation Service, the Department of Agriculture and, of course, the EPA.

In order to build on a wetlands area, developers must obtain a permit under Section 404. When someone proposes to alter the wetlands classification of a given piece of land, he or she must establish an equivalent amount of wetlands elsewhere. Hence, developers, farmers, etc., are significantly affected by legislation that is designed to preserve wetlands. Given these CWA requirements, the costs of some proposed developments may be prohibitive.

The process of obtaining a permit for development on wetlands areas is technical, involved, and lengthy. In order to issue a permit under Section 404, the Corps may be required to comply, not only with the Clean Water Act, but also with the National Environmental Policy Act, the Fish and Wildlife Act, the Endangered Species Act, and countless others. The developer may also be required to obtain permits from state and local governments. These state and local permits are generally a prerequisite for filing section 404 permit applications. Even after a section 404 permit is authorized, the deal is not "done"— the EPA has the right to void it.

Before anyone purchases land with the intention of developing it, he or she should either verify that the land is not categorized as wetlands or determine that permits of a similar nature have been granted previously in the area. The developer should also be sure that any prior permits were issued quite recently; sometimes development is prohibited in areas where it was once allowed. For example, some property owners on the South Carolina coast were surprised to discover that they could not rebuild their beachfront homes that had been destroyed by hurricane Hugo because such "development" was no longer allowed in that area. (See chapter 6 for additional discussion concerning development on wetlands.)

The National Pollutant Discharge Elimination System (NPDES) permitting process is designed to control private wastewater discharges. These regulations generally apply when developing a project that does not have access to a public waterway or sewer system or when planning a project that will discharge wastes other than regular consumer waste products into a public system. These permits are also required for "pretreatment plants" or wastewater discharges that are pretreated on site before being passed into a public waterway or sewer system.

In both a legal and an engineering sense, the NPDES permitting process is highly technical. The best way to ensure that everything is done correctly is to use an attorney and an engineer, both of whom specialize in NPDES permitting. There are no shortcuts to the procedure; the inexperienced may never get through the system on their own. It is well worth the time and effort to do things right from the beginning—substantial federal fines may be assessed for each day that a project is not in compliance.

When private wastewater treatment or pretreatment plants are installed, it is advisable to have a qualified engineering firm conduct compliance inspections twice a year. If a property is a multitenant or multibuilding site served by one treatment plant, compliance inspections should be performed after every new addition. A wastewater system problem is easily overloaded, and substantial fines can be imposed at both federal and state levels.

The technical nature of the Clean Water Act (especially in regard to wetlands and NPDES permitting procedures) often results in a need for the services of one or more specialists. The real estate owner, manager, and developer should know when to call in professionals and the right people to call.

Resource Conservation and Recovery Act (RCRA) 1976

Amended in 1984 by the Hazardous and Solid Waste Amendments (HSWA), RCRA has two primary purposes and objectives. First, it provides for the licensing and regulation of all solid waste treatment, storage, and disposal (as landfill) as well as the creation and transportation of hazardous wastes. It requires each state to maintain an up-to-date listing of all hazardous waste sites and generators—regardless of size. Second, it provides for "cradle-to-grave" monitoring of hazardous wastes generated; this helps to prevent dumping and other contamination. It also allows for the monitoring and advancement of waste minimization technologies in business and industry. Essentially, RCRA is in place to control errant hazardous waste generation and disposal.

To understand how RCRA affects owners, managers, and developers of real estate, it is necessary to examine its contents. First of all, the Act defines a "hazardous" waste as a waste product that has either or both of the following qualities.

1. It can cause or significantly contribute to an increase in mortality or irreversible illness.
2. It can cause a potential hazard to human health or the environment when improperly stored, treated, or disposed.

Even if a waste is not hazardous according to these guidelines, RCRA still applies. The Act also regulates wastes that have the following characteristics either individually or combined.

1. *Ignitability,* or the capability of causing or feeding a fire.
2. *Corrosivity,* or the ability to corrode metal and/or harm human tissue or aquatic life.
3. *Toxicity,* or the potential to leach chemicals (primarily inorganic) into soil or ground water.
4. *Reactivity,* or the capability of explosion or production of toxic clouds and gases when mixed.

Given these guidelines, the impact of RCRA on the real estate owner is significant. The following is a list of only a few of the types of waste that fall under RCRA regulation.

- Waste oils and automotive fluids
- Cleaning chemicals
- Used batteries (flashlight, automotive, etc.)
- Liquid and powdered chlorine and bleach
- Dry cleaning and laundry cleaning fluids
- Machinery lubricants
- Roofing materials
- Concrete and masonry cleansers and sealants
- Water treatment chemicals
- Freons and HVAC charging chemicals
- Copier toner and inks
- Fertilizers
- Dyes, paints, and thinners
- Pesticides
- Asbestos
- Preservatives
- Used cooking oils
- Medical wastes

RCRA recognizes two types of hazardous waste generators. A Large Quantity Generator (LQG) produces more than 1,000 kilograms (2,205 pounds) of hazardous waste per month. A Small Quantity Generator (SQG) produces less than 1,000 (but more than 100) kilograms per month. Most office and retail developments will only be associated with SQGs. Some industrial and warehouse projects may encounter LQGs. A few examples of SQGs follow.

- Fast food restaurants
- "Quick change" oil and lube operations

- Copying centers
- Tire storage and distribution centers
- Auto "detailing" shops
- Automatic car washes
- Car rental operations
- Grocery operations
- Drug stores
- Dry cleaners
- Hardware stores
- Janitorial supply operations
- Medical offices

Improper storage, disposal, transportation, etc., of RCRA-regulated wastes directly affect the property owner because he or she is absolutely liable for any problems on the property. Regardless of the identity of the individual or individuals creating the problem, the law will require the owner to rectify it. For this reason, tenants' leases should include clauses written to protect the owner, and property inspections should be conducted regularly. These actions reduce an owner's liability exposure.

Each state carries out its own monitoring and enforcement programs (authorized by RCRA). While state programs may establish requirements that are more strict than federal standards, they can never establish less strict ones. Federal fines for violations are assessed for every day that an unacceptable situation remains uncorrected; these fines can be sizable. State fines may be assessed in lieu of or in addition to fines assessed on the federal level. These fines may be in any amount designated by the state, either more or less than the federal limits.

It is important to beware of the term "solid waste," which is often used in association with RCRA. Section 1004 (27) of the Act defines "solid waste" as "solid, liquid, semi-solid or contained gaseous materials." Essentially, the only wastes not covered in this definition are those wastes regulated by the Federal Water Pollution Control Act and the Clean Air Act.

Comprehensive Environmental Response, Compensation, and Liability Act (CERCLA or Superfund) 1980

The original act promulgated in 1980 (CERCLA) was amended in 1986 by the Superfund Amendments and Reauthorization Act (SARA). In this book, the word "Superfund" will refer to both CERCLA and SARA legislation. Superfund has four primary objectives. First, it provides for monitoring and regulation of "inactive" disposal facilities, dump sites, landfills, and spill sites. ("Inactive" in this instance means that there are no disposal or spill activities taking place at the site.) The Act provides for the identification, classification, and priority rating of these sites through the National Priority List (NPL). Sites called "Superfund Sites" are generally listed on the NPL.

Second, Superfund provides regulations and requirements for the *remediation* or *cleanup* of these sites and any associated contamination. State and federal regulations both apply. Superfund defines and regulates fund collection and cost allocations for state and federal programs. *Remediation* has become a commonly used term that refers to the act or process of remedying a problem. *Cleanup* refers to a more involved program that completely cleans up or removes the problem. (A more detailed discussion of these two terms appears in chapter 4.)

Next, the SARA amendments of 1986 increase the reporting and response requirements for spills and releases. In the case of emergencies, SARA Title III establishes clear direction regarding public notification as well as notification of local, state, and federal agencies. Failure to comply with the reporting requirements of Superfund can translate into millions of dollars in fines—and even jail terms for individuals involved.

Finally, Superfund is the basis for what has become the most critical environmental issue facing the real estate industry today—the issue of absolute liability. This is the assignment of liability for remediation or cleanup costs of contaminated sites, regardless of fault.

One of the aims of Superfund was to unite the different corrective actions required by all environmental laws and create a single set of guidelines. This goal was achieved in the areas of monitoring, remediation (or cleanup), regulation, cost recovery, and enforcement. Superfund guidelines cover every possible aspect of the environment from air to water to land. It is the only law of its kind in this respect—it is unique in the history of American law.

The basis for the liability issue is Superfund's identification of the "owner or operator" as the primary person or persons who are liable. The current owner or operator of the property becomes absolutely liable for all costs associated with remediation or cleanup of a problem. Unfortunately, many people have difficulty accepting that *neither the courts nor the government will bend on the issue of absolute liability, regardless of the consequences.* This fact cannot be overly emphasized.

As specified by the Act, "owner or operator" includes any and all possible owners and/or operators of a piece of property. Literally any person or entity associated with the chain of title may be considered an "owner or operator." This group includes lenders and majority stockholders. In the words of the Act: "The term 'owner or operator' means (i) in the case of a vessel, any person owning, operating or chartering by demise, such vessel, (ii) in the case of an *on shore facility* (emphasis added) or an off shore facility, any person owning or operating such facility." [42 U.S.C. §9601; 101 (20)(A)] Although current owners are those most likely to be liable for costs related to environmental problems, previous owners can be included through lawsuits. There is no absolute protection for anyone who has been associated with the chain of title for a property.

The Act also defines the term "person" as, "an individual, firm, corporation, association, partnership, consortium, joint venture, commercial entity, United States Government, State Government or State municipality, commission, political subdivision of a State, or any interstate body." [42 U.S.C. §9601; 101 (21)]

While these words may seem to be little more than "legalese," the Act effectively establishes who and what constitutes an "owner or operator" under the law. Similarly all-inclusive is the definition of a "facility" as specified by the Act. To the surprise of many, even someone's home qualifies as a "facility." The definition is as follows: "The term "facility" means (A) any building, structure, installation, equipment, pipe or pipeline (including any pipe into a sewer or publicly owned treatment works), well, pit, pond, lagoon, impoundment, ditch, landfill, storage container, motor vehicle, rolling stock, or aircraft, or (B) any site or area where a hazardous substance has been deposited, stored, disposed of, or placed, or otherwise come to be located." [42 U.S.C. §9601; 101 (9)]

Tenants (lessees) are not forgotten. While the actual assignment of liability is addressed in section 107 (b3) of the Act, section 101 (35) defines potentially liable parties as those with "contractual relationships" that involve the transfer of "title *or* possession" to the property or premises. Clearly, these words have made an impact on the once uncomplicated transfers associated with property, land, and building leases. What is more, they create potential liability for the fee manager who is acting as an agent of the owner.

In short, it doesn't matter whether a current property owner had the intent to pollute, was negligent, contributed to a problem, or was even alive when the contamination occurred. The fact of ownership dictates where the liability lies. A lack of knowledge about the existence of contamination is a defense only when, in the words of the law, *"all appropriate inquiry"* was made to detect possible contamination prior to purchase. Unfortunately, the Act does not explain what constitutes "all appropriate inquiry," and Congress has failed in its attempts to clarify the meaning of these words.

This very clause has resulted in the development of a series of procedures that are intended to be performed prior to purchase and provide proof that the purchaser has made all appropriate investigation regarding possible contamination. These procedures, developed by the environmental attorneys and consultants in the industry, are commonly referred to as Preliminary Site Assessments, Phase I and Phase II Site Assessments, and Phase III Remediation (to be discussed in detail in chapter 4). While there is no single set of procedures that is uniformly used, the general approach taken by most people is quite consistent throughout the real estate industry.

Due to the lack of a legislative definition of "all appropriate inquiry," there is never a guarantee of protection from liability under Superfund. For this reason, many solid real estate deals fall through because of the purchaser's anxiety concerning the possibility of facing liability. The courts have generally ruled that the discovery of a "hazardous" substance or a condition not in accordance with EPA regulations is "per se" (intrinsically or automatically) indicative of a violation under CERCLA and constitutes a "substantial endangerment." The existence of substantial endangerment opens the door to the possibility of felony prosecution—and this surely adds to the anxiety of a potential purchaser.

THE ECONOMIC EFFECTS OF ENVIRONMENTAL LEGISLATION

The economic effects of environmental legislation are pervasive and substantial. People who have become "desensitized" to environmental issues over the course of the last three decades, however, are less likely to recognize the relationship between economic impacts and environmental issues. The complexity of everyday living has created a world where cause may not be as obvious as effect.

Environmental regulations have affected motor fuel composition; automobile designs; housing design and insulation; air-conditioning and heating system design and operation; chemical treatment (and contents) of household water supplies; formulations of paints and concrete; components of cleaning fluids, etc. What is more, everyone is affected by changes in electrical power generation, chemical manufacturing processes, and waste disposal procedures. There are regulations governing landfill sites, recycling, trash incineration, pesticide components and applications, fertilizer composition, and many other commonplace items and activities, and these regulations are frequently changed. All these changes incur costs that are passed on to the owner, tenant, or consumer, increasing the cost of living. Vehicle fuel, utilities, and waste disposal in particular have become more expensive. It is estimated that new federal environmental laws will cost consumers billions of dollars over the next decade.

The effect on business is expected to increase dramatically. Loans to cover the cost of pollution control and waste reduction are already being financed through municipal industrial revenue bonds and the U.S. Small Business Administration (SBA).

The success or failure of small businesses and real estate investments have a profound effect on the economy. A headline taken from the *Wall Street Journal* on October 4, 1990, reads "Environmental Worries Slow Loans to Small Businesses." The article quotes House Small Business Committee Chairman John LaFalce (Democrat, New York) as follows: "Thousands of creditworthy small businesses can't obtain the financing they need to survive." In Congressman LaFalce's words, this is happening because lenders are fearful that "a $50,000 loan could turn into a $5 million nightmare." In truth, many businesspeople worry that new environmental rules will increase their costs beyond what they can afford.

The economic impact of environmental regulations on the financial community is characterized by a general tightening of the money supply. Financial institutions are less willing to make real estate loans. They have lowered acceptable loan-to-value ratios; raised debt coverage ratio requirements; raised loan closing and loan origination costs; and increased insurance requirements. Because of environmental concerns, the financial community is having to pay higher insurance costs, meet larger loan-loss reserve requirements, and accept lower appraisals on existing loan portfolios. In an attempt to avoid liability for environmental problems as an owner and/or operator, many lending institutions will write off loans entirely rather than foreclose on a property that shows evidence of problems.

The result is a slowdown in capital investment nationwide, which directly affects economic growth. As always, these costs are passed on to the consumer and inflation swells. Sadly, much of this impact is caused by fear of the unknown; many problems are potential rather than actual problems. However, as more real estate professionals become experienced in the environmental arena, some of the uncertainty will be eliminated.

Environmental Liability

Admittedly, the question of liability has already been emphasized. The truth is, no real estate professional can afford to underestimate the significance of liability and environmental issues. The fear of civil and criminal prosecution, fines, and the costs of cleanup make environmental liability *the* issue to be resolved in most real estate transactions.

As discussed in chapter 2, Superfund is the driving force behind the liability question. While the law specifies that the "owner or operator" is liable for environmental problems, it does not allow for protection of the individual through the corporate structure. On the contrary, *the EPA is authorized to find and prosecute the highest level individual that it can make a case against.* In at least one instance, a majority stockholder was successfully prosecuted.

The cost and time required to clean up a problem provide significant incentives to avoid liability for remediation or cleanup (some such projects take as long as thirty years). For example, in 1989, the average cost of a cleanup operation not involving groundwater contamination was $157,000. When groundwater was contaminated, the average cost was $2.5 million. In some instances, remediation costs have far exceeded the actual value of the property. Appealing EPA decisions, litigating against previous owners, and pursuing other alternatives to remediation are activities that generally take place during remediation rather than before it is begun. Many problems call for immediate responses because fines may be incurred every day that the owner fails to address the existing situation. Clearly, when the owner does not have the time to investigate other plans of action, remediation or cleanup is more expensive.

This chapter will deal with liabilities associated with different types of involvement in real estate transactions. Property owners, lenders, parent companies, parent company corporate officers, and tenants frequently face liability in environmental actions.

Of all the rapidly changing areas of environmental law, the issue of liability has been the most volatile. Lobbyists, industries, and financial institutions are fighting this aspect of existing laws. Whenever a liability question arises, it is time to consult a qualified, specialized environmental attorney.

LIABILITY OF THE OWNER AND/OR OPERATOR

The fear of liability, especially on the part of an owner and/or operator, is certainly justified (a detailed discussion of the concept of "operator" appears in chapter 8). The important thing to remember, however, is that environmental law provides for (and the courts recognize) several defenses against liability. If liability were inevitable, the purchase and sale of real estate in the United States would be virtually impossible.

It is also important to recognize that an owner and/or operator does have some means of recourse even after liability has been assigned. While a property's title will transfer with the sale of the property, the courts have generally ruled that current owners may collect damages from previous owners and from other parties responsible for environmental problems. Only a very specific waiver by the buyer can protect a seller from future recourse, and this waiver must be written into the purchase contract or closing document. This prevents unknowing assumption of someone else's problem by the purchaser and plugs a legal loophole that would allow polluters to escape liability.

Superfund is very clear regarding the obligation of the owner and/or operator to either repay the EPA's remediation or cleanup costs or to fund and manage an independent EPA-approved remediation or cleanup. This is commonly known as "remedial liability" and is the liability most feared by property owners.

The Act provides for environmental liens and superliens to guarantee that the EPA can obtain reimbursement of funds expended on a site. When the environmental impact of contamination is ongoing and substantial (e.g., Love Canal), the EPA may remediate the site immediately and send the owner the bill. In order to enforce collection, environmental liens may be placed on the property, much as a tax lien is assessed. To sell the property, the lien must be paid off and released.

So called "superliens" are liens imposed by the federal government. Superliens take precedence over any other lien on the property, including a first mortgage. This means that the government may file its lien at any time, even after the first mortgage and any other liens have been placed, and payment of the federal government's lien takes first priority. While the net dollar amount of the lien does not change with the classification to superlien, its effect on lenders can be quite dramatic.

Property valuation is also affected by environmental liability. Properties with known environmental problems lose value. Such a property would be approached cautiously by purchasers, tenants, and others who might assume it has a higher potential for future environmental problems and possible liabilities. It makes little difference whether a reduction in value is justified. Real estate is a commodity, and commodity prices are determined by the market and its perceptions—not necessarily by factual data.

LIABILITY OF THE LENDER

After an initial examination of the language of Superfund, most lenders believed that it did not affect them. After all, the law specifically exempted the person or entity who received title while trying to protect a security interest in the property. Most lenders assumed "ownership" of a property only through foreclosure (in foreclosure, the lender receives title in order to protect the security interest). So, exemption from liability was certainly a valid assumption for lenders. Unfortunately for the lender, environmental law is not this straightforward.

Two landmark court decisions changed the perspective of every lender. The decisions handed down in *United States v. Mirabile* (1985) and *United States v. Maryland Bank & Trust* (1986) brought lender liability to the forefront of issues concerning the financial community. These decisions were essentially confirmed in the Superfund amendments of 1986. The decisions in *United States v. Nicolet* (1988) and *United States v. Fleet Factors* (1990) merely added to lenders' liability concerns. As lender concerns grew, so did new areas of concern for the entire real estate industry.

Before discussing the individual court cases previously named, it is worthwhile to repeat that the primary means of assigning liability lies in the interpretation of the definition of "owner or operator" and the acts that classify one as an "owner or operator." The Superfund definition is intentionally vague to assure that someone (preferably someone other than the American taxpayer) will be able to assume financial responsibility for the cleanup. While this notion of assuring cleanup payment is not specifically referenced in Superfund, the courts have tended to collect from anyone associated with a property. Hence, the entities with the deepest pockets (i.e., the lenders) are not excluded from the classification of owner and/or operator.

In *United States v. Mirabile,* American Bank and Trust and Girard Bank were involved as primary and secondary lenders. American Bank had been the primary mortgagee of a property; Girard made additional loans to the property's mortgagor. Subsequently, American Bank foreclosed on the property in question and sold it to Mirabile. Later, when environmental problems were discovered, Mirabile was sued for reimbursement of remediation expenses and responded by countersuing the two lenders.

American Bank and Trust was released from the suit; the court found that in foreclosing, American was merely protecting its security interest. The court determined that American Bank and Trust was never actually an "owner or operator" under Superfund because it sold the property as soon as a suitable buyer was found. Girard, however, was not as fortunate.

In order to assure collection of as much of its debt as possible, Girard assigned a bank officer to the site as a "work-out" trustee for the initial property owner. This officer made regular site visits and participated in most operational decisions, having authority to change, approve, and veto certain activities. The court ruled that this made Girard an "operator" under Superfund. Girard could therefore be held liable for remediation costs.

In *United States v. Maryland Bank,* Maryland Bank had foreclosed on a property. At the foreclosure sale, Maryland Bank itself purchased the property, apparently because of a lack of adequate bids. The bank maintained ownership for a substantial period of time thereafter. Hence, the court ruled that Maryland Bank was an "owner" under Superfund and was liable for cleanup costs.

Superfund amendments in 1986 affirm the basis for both the Mirabile and the Maryland Bank decisions; this has caused widespread confusion in foreclosure proceedings. Many banks and other lenders delay foreclosure proceedings for long periods of time to avoid becoming "owners." With the impact of recession on real estate markets and overbuilding in many areas of the country, lenders who foreclose are more likely to face prolonged ownership. Additionally, it is much more risky (in terms of incurring liability) for banks to get involved with their borrowers' businesses when trying to assure payment of sums due. This broader definition of lenders' liability has resulted in tighter money and more in-depth, time-consuming *due diligence* when deciding whether to issue loans.

In legal terms, "due diligence" is often used to refer to the duty of the underwriting or selling group to ensure that the offering statement or prospectus does not misstate or omit material information. In the environmental idiom, "due diligence" is used as a general term to refer to the appropriate or sufficient level of care and attention that should be given during the examination of a property. Doing "due diligence" or making a "due diligence" effort involves undertaking a diligent examination of the subject property.

In extreme cases, when the EPA is attempting to collect costs associated with a cleanup, the old common-law definition of a mortgage has been used to attach liability to a lender. This definition assumes that true title of the property vests in the mortgagee (the lender), subject to a right of redemption of title upon payment granted to the mortgagor (the borrower). It is the origin of the expression, "the bank still owns my house," and similar phrases.

Lenders being forced to pay for remediation or cleanup is a prime example of the courts attaching liability to the parties with the "deepest pockets."

In *United States v. Nicolet,* the EPA successfully argued this interpretation. The court ruled that under common law and therefore under Superfund, the mortgagee was the "owner" of the property and liable for cleanup costs. This has been argued successfully in other cases as well (although it is not common practice). Additionally, a deed in lieu of foreclosure (the act of giving a property back to a lender without foreclosure) technically vests title in the lender who is thus susceptible to "owner" liability under Superfund.

It is important to note that just because the EPA uses common-law definitions to its advantage, it cannot be assumed that common-law defenses are valid or effective in environmental cases. In such cases, the courts have frequently ruled in ways that negate the validity of historical, normal defenses. The lesson learned is simple: *One should never assume the legitimacy of historical defenses in environmental cases.*

In *United States v. Fleet Factors,* the court ruled that the lender assumed liability for cleanup costs by making a loan while illegal activity was being conducted at the site. The judgment was justified by the fact that a loan provision granted the lender the right to influence proceedings at the site; hence, the lender was in a position to control site activities. Because the lender had the right and ability to influence compliance with environmental law, it became liable as an "operator." It made no difference that the lender had not exercised its rights as an operator, nor had it attempted to verify compliance with the law.

In light of these decisions, lenders have changed their loan document requirements. One such adjustment is the common requirement for property owners to perform regular compliance inspections and provide the lenders with copies of inspection reports as verification. Such a practice is intended to shield the lender from "operator" status, while assuring compliance with the law. In the case of leased property, the owner and/or manager should strive to monitor compliance without putting himself or herself in the classification of "operator" (a delicate situation that is examined in chapter 8). Admittedly, an owner always faces liability risk, but avoiding "operator" status reduces his or her exposure.

Lenders have also increased their level of participation in projects. Some lenders restrict certain types of tenants, pre-approve leases prior to execution, and hire independent consultants to conduct compliance inspections. While this would most likely categorize the lender as an "operator," it gives the lender more direct control and the ability to participate in its own protection.

The entire real estate industry feels the impact of lenders' liability concerns. Understanding the liability issue is the first step toward successfully pursuing project financing. To protect themselves, lenders have developed a set of guidelines for judging loan applications. Each lender will have its own environmental guidelines or checklists that must be completed before closing. These guidelines should be continually reviewed and updated to reflect changing laws and new interpretations of the law based on court decisions. Given the fact that rules and regulations vary by location, each lender's checklist will be different. A national or multinational company must maintain separate checklists for each area of the country where it does business. Some common lender requirements follow.

- A title check of property ownership extending back fifty to sixty years; this tends to indicate the various uses of the property.
- A review of aerial photos as far back as available (another indication of past and present uses of the property).
- Verification of past owners' and operators' status as waste generators.
- A check on all other properties within a radius of one-half to one mile and their owners' status as waste generators. Also, any noncompliance certificates these owners may have received.
- A waiver of the lenders' liability (part of the closing documents).
- Appropriate environmental clauses in all lease documents (used to protect the owner from liability).
- Certification that no hazardous materials are present on the property or acknowledgment and identification of any hazardous substances that are present.

In truth, the kinds of information and activities that are required by lenders parallel those things that every prospective buyer should know and do prior to a purchase of real property. Lenders rarely make unreasonable requests. For example, an assessment of the average "clean" property is relatively inexpensive, takes four to six weeks to complete, and results in an informative report that is ten to twelve pages long. To ensure the accuracy of such reports, lenders and owners use their own staff environmental specialists or hire outsiders who can monitor and control the reporting and management functions.

The significance of lender liability makes it an issue that is likely to undergo future changes. As this book was being written, some specific Superfund alterations were under consideration; the proposed changes affected lender liability. This serves as yet another reminder that environmental legislation is in a state of continual flux. Regardless of changes in the law, however, it is unlikely that lenders will ever be *completely* protected from liability and therefore disinterested in properties' potential environmental problems.

LIABILITY OF CORPORATE OFFICERS

The courts and the EPA have clearly established that an individual within a corporation can be "personally" liable for environmental contamination. Essentially, if an act of noncompliance occurs while an individual is part of a corporation, that person can be viewed as having committed a personal act of endangerment. Unfortunately, the assignment of personal liability does not relieve the corporation of liability.

By 1990, the EPA had set some legal precedents that are summarized as follows.

1. If an individual has control or authority over an operation or facility where an environmental violation occurs, he or she may be held personally liable for any act or omission causing the violation, regardless of his or her involvement in the act of noncompliance or the policy effecting it.
2. In addition, the supervisor of an individual who is responsible for a violation may also be held personally liable because the supervisor had the authority to prevent the violation.

This potential liability may (and has) extended to presidents, chief executive officers, and even the major shareholders of corporations (even when the individuals are unaware of the violations in question). In general, when an individual has the ability or authority to control or prevent a situation, that person may incur liability regardless of his or her level of direct involvement. Individuals may be liable for remediation or cleanup costs, fines, and criminal penalties. Indeed, the EPA has promoted a doctrine that would, in effect, "pierce the corporate veil" (i.e., liability could be assessed to those who have heretofore been protected by the limited liability of the corporate structure). It should be stated, however, that actual piercing of the corporate veil has, as of the writing of this book, occurred only rarely.

While the federal government allows criminal prosecution of individuals facing environmental liabilities, historically, the EPA has not pressed criminal charges against individuals in corporations unless there is proof that the individual was personally responsible for flagrant noncompliance. Nevertheless, the EPA has been directed (by Congress) to increase criminal prosecution. *Ignorance of the law is not a defense.* Therefore, noncompliance itself is a crime. The federal government has provided for and increased the incidence of mandatory jail terms for certain environmental crimes; individual states have followed suit. What is the reason for the prosecution of individuals? It forces companies to take environmental issues seriously.

LIABILITY OF TENANTS (LESSEES)

Tenants (lessees) face almost as much liability risk as owners. Once again, the basis for liability lies in the definition of "owner or operator." The tenant inhabiting a building or facility on contaminated ground can be defined as an "operator," and be liable for the facility. It makes no difference whether the tenant intends to contaminate, is negligent, or even contributes to the contamination—he or she can be held absolutely liable for remediation or cleanup.

Superfund also identifies any entity that has a contractual relationship with a contaminated property as potentially liable. These relationships are defined as "(including) land contracts, deeds, or other instruments transferring title or possession." Hence, tenants become liable by law because leases generally transfer possession. The law has made the tenant liable per se, though only when the tenant cannot defend himself or herself through proof of having exercised appropriate due diligence to detect contamination. Corporations are forced to execute appropriate due diligence before even entering into a lease agreement. Such responsibilities are best assumed by an in-house environmental specialist whose contribution may well prevent the need for expensive consultants at a later date. When no such individuals are on staff, it is necessary to enlist the part-time service of an outside expert.

THE BUSINESS COMMUNITY RESPONSE TO LIABILITY

Environmental issues and concerns are beginning to have a significant effect on the business community. Real estate developers, investors, owners, lenders, managers, and tenants were the first to become sensitive to such issues. Those "Fortune 500" and "Fortune 100" companies not actively involved in the business of real estate have been the last to make adjustments, even though their exposure to liability may be as great as or greater than that of the developer. While lenders perform or require an environmental study prior to making real estate loans, the lender's due diligence is specifically designed to protect the lender; there may be no true protection provided for the purchaser or the tenant.

The benefits of hiring an environmental operations specialist (EOS) are becoming obvious to those in the corporate world. A skilled EOS takes a great deal of disparate information and turns it into an informative, comprehensive report that will help management make informed, intelligent decisions. Some of the information that must be synthesized includes the interpretations of the regulations by environmental attorneys, technical data from environmental consultants, due diligence criteria from the lenders, and the reporting and/ or remediation requirements called for by local, state, and national regulatory agencies. It has become apparent that specially trained environmental professionals help corporations—and individuals—reduce their exposure to the risk of incurring environmental liability.

The issue of environmental liability has become a primary concern of the business community. Because incurring environmental liability can mean facing a significant financial crisis, liability assignment is part of the law that is receiving a great deal of attention (by popular demand). For example, as this book was being written, certain Superfund changes had been proposed to alter lender liability laws (something that was mentioned earlier in the chapter).

The future could bring other changes in the assignment of environmental liability. There are those people who have suggested regulations regarding due diligence practices prior to making a real estate purchase or executing a lease. Such due diligence requirements would be established to provide some legal protection from environmental liability (i.e., those who followed the legal guidelines would be assured of liability protection as specified by the law). Still other modifications of liability laws have been discussed.

It is essential to note that the material in this chapter reflects the status of environmental laws as this book was being written—it does not provide a crystal ball for the future. Legislation changes continually, and environmental legislation is likely to vary from month to month, state to state, and city to city. Every real estate professional should understand this.

Regardless of any future changes in the law, the information in this chapter is valuable because it focuses on a particularly "hot" real estate-related environmental issue and explores its complexities. Here is a topic that deserves the attention of all real estate professionals; it is unlikely that the business community will ever be able to ignore potential environmental liability.

Environmental Site Assessments

The terms associated with environmental issues can be confusing and complex—and the language of environmental site assessments is a prime example. As in all matters associated with questions of legality, it is especially important to understand definitions used for environmental issues. A misunderstanding concerning environmental terminology could create a false sense of security or result in the loss of legal protection. The impact of such errors can be sizable—and irrevocable.

It is crucial to understand the different types of environmental site assessments—although it is not always easy. Chapter 3 explained why assessments are vital; they provide defense against environmental liability. The real estate professional should understand each kind of site assessment and its function as a legal defense.

THE ASSESSMENT AS A LEGAL DEFENSE

Superfund does provide for certain defenses against the liability associated with property ownership. Anyone who has been involved with the purchase or sale of commercial real estate will already be aware of lenders' and purchasers' requirements to conduct an environmental assessment prior to closing. The fulfillment of these requirements is intended to protect lenders and owners under what is called the *Innocent Landowner's Defense*. By performing the proper assessments and judging the property to be "clean," an owner provides himself or herself with some protection from liability for those environmental problems that existed prior to the purchase.

Sections 101 (35)(A) and (35)(B) of CERCLA summarize the defenses available to "the defendant" ("defendant," for purposes of this discussion, will refer to the property owner). According to Section 101 (35), a defense is possible if: "(A) . . . the real property on which the facility concerned is located was acquired by the defendant after the disposal or placement of the hazardous substance on, in, or at the facility, and . . . (i) At the time the defendant acquired the facility the defendant did not know and had no reason to know that any hazardous substance . . . was disposed on, in, or at the facility. (ii) The defendant . . . acquired the facility by escheat, or through any other involuntary transfer or acquisition . . . (iii) The defendant acquired the facility by inheritance or bequest."

The portion of clause *(ii)* just quoted deals specifically with government entities and is not applicable in this discussion. Clause *(i)* is the text most owners use when developing a viable defense. It is qualified by an explanation of the ways to demonstrate a lack of prior knowledge of the problem to the satisfaction of the courts and federal and/or state agencies: "(B) To establish that the defendant had no reason to know, as provided in clause (i) of subparagraph (A) . . . the defendant must have undertaken, at the time of acquisition, *all appropriate inquiry* [emphasis added] into the previous ownership and uses of the property consistent with good commercial or customary practice in an effort to minimize liability . . . the court shall take into account any specialized knowledge or experience on the part of the defendant, the relationship of the purchase price to the value of the property if uncontaminated, commonly known or *reasonably ascertainable* [emphasis added] information about the property, the obviousness of the presence or likely presence of contamination at the property, and the ability to detect such contamination by appropriate inspection."

This excerpt dictates the extent and contents of environmental site assessments prior to property purchase; it has also shaped the common format of assessment reports used in the environmental arena. Unfortunately, its terminology is vague in some crucial areas; this is a constant concern for people in the real estate industry.

One highly significant section of the Act has influenced sales activity in commercial real estate. The following words are found in Section 101 35(B): "Notwithstanding this paragraph, if the defendant obtained actual knowledge of . . . a hazardous substance at such facility when the defendant owned the real property and then subsequently transferred ownership of the property to another person without disclosing such knowledge, such defendant shall be treated as liable . . . and no defense . . . shall be available to such defendant." Failure to disclose knowledge of the presence of a hazardous substance prior to sale is a violation of the law per se and, as such, is indefensible. These words effectively eliminate the notion of "caveat emptor" (i.e., "let the buyer beware"—the idea that the buyer assumes all risk). The language in this section of the law is undeniably direct and the ideas put forth are enthusiastically enforced by the courts. *An owner who has substantiated, factual data regarding an environmental problem on the property must disclose that information to potential purchasers.*

Disputes in assigning liability occur when assessments have been done and problems go undetected only to be revealed at a later date. Two issues come into question—deciding what constitutes "all appropriate inquiry" and "reasonably ascertainable" and determining how one proves "by a preponderance of the evidence" that the current owner truly qualifies as an innocent or unknowing landowner. While there have been several bills proposed to clarify the language of the law, none had been passed at the time of the writing of this book. Court interpretations have been inconsistent.

Owners will not always be aware of environmental problems on their properties and purchasers should recognize that complete protection from liability does not exist. This explains why prepurchase environmental assessments are required by buyers and lenders. Although less savvy buyers may not require an assessment on their own, it is almost certain that their lenders will require one.

At this juncture, it is worthwhile to address the confusion caused by terminology associated with site assessments. Difficulties with terminology are easy to explain. As everyone knows, words have different meanings in different areas of the country. In the Southeast, for example, property owners pay to have their properties "trashed" (cleaned), while in the Southwest people go to jail for having "trashed" (vandalized) a property. Consulting and engineering firms in the same city may use the same terminology to represent similar but different activities. For example, the terms Preliminary Site Assessment (PSA) and Phase I Site Assessment (Phase I) often create confusion because some professionals choose to use the terms interchangeably. Although the terms are used to represent similar things, their actual meanings are slightly different.

In this text, a Preliminary Site Assessment (PSA) and a Phase I Site Assessment (Phase I) will have distinct definitions. A PSA and a Phase I tend to provide different information. Understanding the differences between the two is crucial to choosing an assessment procedure and identifying the information that should be provided, the costs associated with it, and the liability protection afforded by it. *A Phase I will include all aspects of a PSA plus some additional interior and exterior testing.* A PSA does not involve any on-site testing procedures.

THE PRELIMINARY SITE ASSESSMENT (PSA)

The primary reason for conducting a PSA is to provide "reasonably ascertainable information about the property, the obviousness of the presence or likely presence of contamination at the property, and the ability to detect such contamination by appropriate inspection." It is executed in an effort to make "all appropriate inquiry" prior to purchasing a property. It is important to note that regardless of assessment type, the court decides whether these conditions have been met. If a problem is uncovered later, the fact that a PSA was done *might* allow the purchaser to seek protection as an innocent landowner.

If the owner is paying for the assessment, the resulting report is not likely to provide any opinions regarding legal or technical issues—*an owner's report typically recounts the findings only.* In this case, interpretation and opinion should remain off the record (the consultant preparing the report must be previously advised of the information that the owner wishes to obtain). If the owner would like additional advice, he or she should receive it verbally or, if in writing, in a form other than the PSA report. The opposite is true when a purchaser is paying for the assessment. Reports that are prepared for a purchaser should absolutely include speculation, recommendations for additional testing, and interpretations of report results. The environmental consultant must be made aware that the report will be reviewed with the intent of purchasing a property. A purchaser will need extra information to be able to address appropriate issues when dealing with the seller.

Some might suggest that there is a bit of duplicity in the typical seller's approach because he or she is not making every effort to discover existing contamination. It makes it absolutely necessary for each party to contract an independent study. While it is in the seller's best interest to provide results without interpretation, the buyer relies on an interpretation of the results to determine liability risk. Consequently, sellers most often conduct PSAs while buyers will usually opt for a more detailed Phase I. Lenders will generally accept either because they have their own people to interpret results and because the lenders' protection under the law is usually approached independently of the other parties.

After a PSA is performed, a report is compiled to summarize the findings. Such a report is divided into sections, the most important of which is the executive summary. Located at the beginning of the report, its purpose is to provide a condensed version of the more detailed sections that follow.

The sections following the executive summary should provide a detailed account of the entire assessment and should act as documentation of the results. In addition, they would include a property description, site evaluation, state and local agency review, tenant compliance inspection, etc. Separate discussions of the most important sections follow.

Statement of Purpose

This is a very brief section, one or two paragraphs at most. It should identify the property, its location, and the circumstances that created a need for the assessment (e.g., a loan application, possible sale of the property, requirement of state or federal agencies, etc.). It should identify the client for whom the assessment is being made and the company performing the assessment. It should name the personnel performing the actual on-site work.

Site Description

The site description is a narrative portrait of the property. It is generally supplemented by location maps (referenced as figures) and as-built drawings or pictures (depending on the nature of the project). Some reports may include illustrations indicating tenant locations in multitenanted buildings. This is often the case when trying to determine tenant-specific problems. The narrative should include a description of the property's appearance; its location relative to major thoroughfares, airports, and industrial sites; and its location relative to natural or geographic features such as lakes, streams, creeks, and national parks.

The narrative should specify the acreage of the property, applicable zoning, the most common use in the area (e.g., residential, industrial, retail), and whether the project's current use complies with zoning. If the property does not conform to present zoning, any zoning variances or concessions should be noted. Other information to be specified includes whether there were previous buildings or uses at the site and what they were.

Common additions are such things as a brief summary regarding topography of the area, soil type, and United States Geological Survey (USGS) classifications for water tables and wetlands. Generally, statements of this type are not long, nor are they highly technical. They do, however, indicate that the consultant has done his or her "homework." Such additions are not necessary for the report to be well-prepared and complete.

Site Inspection Summary

This portion of the report should summarize what was actually observed on site. Interior and exterior inspections should be performed. Before any inspection(s) take place, the property manager must make the tenants aware of the anticipated inspection date(s). The tenants should be notified of the type of inspection being performed; conveying this message in a positive way helps to reduce tenant anxiety concerning environmental assessments. Property managers are well advised to accompany anyone conducting an environmental assessment, especially during interior inspections of tenant spaces. This not only reassures the tenants, but also results in faster inspections (not to mention a better informed property manager).

The site inspection summary should itemize interior features worth noting. The presence of potential problems should be indicated (e.g., sloppy chemical racks, oily stains on the floor or near drains, special electrical transformers, cooking equipment, etc.). Certain tenants (e.g., medical, dental, and architectural) typically use special chemicals in their work; such tenant uses should be noted and any on-site storage facilities should be inspected. All hazardous or regulated substances located on the property should be listed along with the name of the tenant associated with each one. Methods of disposal for hazardous substances should be inquired about and documented.

The site inspection should include a list of available utilities and the suppliers of those utilities (especially water and sewer service). Also of note are any easements that might exist on the property (e.g., power line easements), railroad track systems, and any other on-site features or operations over which the property manager has limited control. It is important to inspect adjoining properties at the property lines as well. It is not unusual for a problem originating on an adjacent property to leak or spread across property lines (this is referred to as off-site contamination).

The exterior inspection should include a complete tour of the building's perimeter and an assessment of the appearance of the structure and surrounding grounds. Any variations in vegetation or staining of the soil should be acknowledged, as should the presence of standing liquids or unusual odors. Again, a property manager should accompany the inspector; the manager may be able to identify things that would otherwise be presented negatively in the report. Assume that a property has recently been sprayed with a herbicide for weed control and there are resultant patches of dead vegetation. By informing the environmental consultant about the recent pesticide use, the property manager prevents speculation concerning the reason for the dead plants. Even from the purchaser's perspective, it is worthwhile to have the property manager's input to clarify an otherwise questionable issue.

Exterior structures and machinery should be described in this section of the report. Gasoline pumps, emergency generators, and special fire control systems signal the presence of underground tanks. References to any repair, paint, and metalworking facilities belong here as well. The importance of this information is twofold. For the current property owner, it pinpoints the potential problems and provides documented evidence of a due diligence effort to uncover problems prior to sale. This may limit the liability if contamination is discovered in the future and the current owner is able to prove that he or she could not have contributed to it. For the prospective buyer, this information identifies areas of potential liability to be addressed prior to any transfer of title. Courts will allow the seller to indemnify the buyer against environmental problems if the indemnification has been stated in the closing documents.

Area Survey

The primary goal of the area survey is to establish the relationship of the subject property to its environment and to evaluate the potential existence of contamination that has spread from an off-site source. To do this accurately, it is necessary to conduct a detailed survey of the area within a one-half mile radius. First, a detailed list of every tenant, development, use, construction project, and other operation within a one-half mile radius is prepared. This list will include all tenants of the subject property and is presented in its entirety. Although this is a sizable task, it is far from "busy-work" or padding done simply to increase the size of the finished report. Such information provides a more accurate view of the most common use of the area and identifies those tenants and industries in the area that have a historical record of environmental problems.

During the course of listing the area's businesses, notes are made regarding facilities where underground storage tanks (USTs) may be located (e.g., the presence of gas pumps is an indicator). Notes are also made regarding above-ground storage tanks (which may have replaced USTs) and storage yards for 55-gallon drums or other containers. While evidence of these things does not necessarily signal a spill, their presence increases the probability for the existence of an undiscovered problem. The list of regional businesses in the area survey also provides something against which regulatory agency files are inspected.

The survey will also include an assessment of the subject property's relationship to other properties in terms of topography. Topography—the actual lay of the land—is important because groundwater and drainage follow similar paths (both have a tendency to run downhill). As the list of area businesses is compiled, it is important for the report to define those businesses located uphill or up-gradient from the site as well as those that are downhill or down-gradient.

There is some cause for concern if a problem is located uphill from the site. In such a case, contamination from the uphill site would logically tend to run toward the subject property. As everyone knows, however, things are not always as they seem—while a property may appear to be uphill, geologists may nevertheless determine that actual groundwater flow is in the opposite direction. Hence, a topographical survey should include a trip to the local USGS office to inspect the government's topographical maps.

Another investigation that takes place at the USGS office is the study of aerial photographs of the area (going back as far as possible). Some aerial photographs are surprisingly old. Even though airplanes are a 20th century invention, hot air balloons were used to obtain aerial photographs in earlier times.

These photographs will reveal any previous development that may present a concern of its own. The photos are generally available in 15- to 25-year increments and, as such, will indicate any long-term changes. Aerial photographs can also show visible changes in topography due to development. As mentioned earlier, visible topography is sometimes deceiving when compared to expected ground water flow. The knowledge that visible topography may not be "natural" is likely to be helpful.

Aerial photos can also show natural changes over time such as the redirection of streams or natural drainage swales. Natural disasters such as forest fires, floods, tornados, or earthquakes can cause changes in the topography and general nature of a piece of property. A forest fire can turn an area that was once lush and green into an arid meadow or grassland. The current vegetation of any area may be completely different·from its vegetation fifty years ago.

An examination of regional businesses, an investigation of local topography, and a study of aerial photography can provide a good forecast regarding the possibility of off-site contamination. While such surveys may take several days to complete, no PSA—or Phase I for that matter—would be complete without an area survey.

Chain of Title

The chain of title is critical to the report. It satisfies the Superfund requirement to make "all appropriate inquiry into the previous ownership and uses of the property." Industry standards dictate that this should be a title report that essentially lists the names of all the owners of the property for the past forty to sixty years.

Such a title report may be ordered from a title company and given to the consultant performing the assessment, or the consultant can perform the search in the appropriate county courthouse. All title information is public knowledge; choosing how to find it is a matter of determining cost effectiveness.

Essentially, the purpose of the chain of title is to ascertain whether prior ownership of the property was involved in environmentally unsound uses. While the character of some businesses is not always revealed by their names, identification of large chemical companies, well-known "smokestack" companies (i.e., heavy industries), or the United States Department of Defense as prior owners serves as a warning.

Regulatory Review

The regulatory review is the most important and the most technical portion of the PSA. It is performed at the local, state, and federal level, and requires the assistance of all the regulatory agencies involved.

Inquiries should be made at the local environmental management office or health department to determine whether anyone has expressed concerns or reported problems in the area near the subject property. As a general rule, it is up to the discretion of each agency to determine the seriousness of a report received and to initiate action. For this reason, a report made to a local agency may or may not be forwarded to the state or federal level. Any reports in the area of the subject property should be listed in the assessment and studied to determine potential problems for the subject property. Under the

Freedom of Information Act, any report filed with a governmental agency is public record and may be viewed on request.

Each state is required by RCRA to maintain its own list of all large and small quantity hazardous waste generators (LQGs and SQGs). This list is available for public inspection; in most states a copy may be obtained for a nominal charge. The list of state LQGs and SQGs may be compared to the list of businesses in and around the subject property to determine who, if anyone, is classified as a hazardous waste generator and where they are located in relation to the subject property.

Some states also maintain a list of known or suspected hazardous waste sites. Generally known as the State Superfund lists, they, too, are available for inspection. It is easy to verify the locations of sites with potential problems because properties are listed by both owner and address. In those states that do not maintain a Superfund list, the federal list may be checked.

The agency review should also include an examination of areas classified as wetlands. Wetlands classification has been known to eliminate any chance for property development. Perhaps the entire property is classified as wetlands, or the cost of creating similar new wetlands in a different location makes the project no longer feasible. Wetlands classification maps for an area may usually be found at the office of the state environmental department, or state or local branch of the USGS, Army Corps of Engineers, or the U.S. Soil Conservation Department.

Federal records are similar to state records with regard to Superfund and problem sites. Occasionally, however, the federal list may include references to sites that the states are not yet aware of, or vice versa. Under the Superfund Act, the Comprehensive Environmental Response, Compensation, and Liability Information System (CERCLIS) and the National Priority List (NPL) were created to provide a data base on contaminated properties nationwide. These lists may also be purchased (at little cost); many environmental firms keep updated copies on hand for these assessments. Obviously, these records are reviewed during the PSA to determine if any problems exist in the area of the subject property.

The fact that contaminated sites are located in the area of the property according to any such listing does not necessarily indicate a problem. The file for each of these nearby sites should be reviewed, and the nature of the problem and its potential impact on the subject property should be assessed. Properties located close to problem sites are not necessarily threatened.

Executive Summary

The first section of the report must be created last. Only then does it include a comprehensive summary of the findings. The question of point of view is crucial to the development of an executive summary. It should be written with the real estate professional—not the environmental specialist—in mind (i.e., it should be easy to read and understand and free of highly technical or complex legal language). Because the executive reading the report must understand its context, it is imperative that he or she ask questions, as necessary.

As stated earlier, the executive summary must be written in awareness of the client's position. If the client is a potential purchaser, the report should include opinions regarding any potential contamination indicated by the surveys. The summary should also include recommendations for additional testing. When the client is a seller or an owner attempting to obtain financing, however, an executive summary should be based entirely on fact—conjecture is unnecessary and inappropriate.

Under no circumstances should the report downplay the results. Any seller must learn about potential problems or questions, be able to provide assessment results to purchasers and lenders if requested, and determine the viability of various property use alternatives. Nevertheless, the information provided to others should be statements of fact; the reader can arrive at his or her own interpretation. Remember, the law specifically assigns liability to those who know about environmental problems and fail to inform other parties who are subsequently involved with the property.

When a current owner contracts a study that may eventually be given to others, a draft copy of the report must be reviewed by both the owner's environmental attorney and the owner before the consultant issues anything in final form. The owner's attorney would take the first look at a report of this nature and would then forward it to the owner. Should the owner wish to make any changes, those changes would be returned to the attorney for his or her review. This allows the owner to verify that the report has been done correctly (for his or her purposes) and assures that any editing will be reviewed by legal personnel. Taking such steps also classifies all the information contained in the report as privileged information between attorney and client.

The summary should start with a concise statement of the original goals and parameters of the study. It should include a brief description of the property and its operational type. The word "brief" is key. Anyone contracting a study of this sort will be somewhat familiar with the property (besides, more details are included in other sections of the report).

A short summary of the site inspection and the methodology should follow. For the most part, this section should include only those items that might be questionable or indicate potential problems. When there are no indications of on-site problems, the report should state this clearly and without further discussion. Unless the chain of title specifically indicates a cause for concern, it is usually not mentioned in the executive summary.

Off-site concerns should be listed, regardless of their impact on the property. Their files will have been reviewed during the regulatory review, and thus, the summary section should provide file references for *all* off-site problems (whether or not they present problems for the subject property). A problem site that is located more than one-half mile from the property is rarely mentioned. A summary statement regarding an off-site problem of limited concern might read: "ABC company reported a naphthalene spill on X-date; however, environmental testing has concluded the spill was contained on site at ABC's facility and thus has no impact on the subject property."

Finally, a summary of key findings may be included. At this point in the report, consultants generally explain their interpretations, give their opinions regarding property status, and recommend other testing if necessary. These summaries are generally included for a potential purchaser. They should be limited or omitted from the report if it is being done for an owner.

In many instances, a consultant will recommend additional testing or cite opinions. *Few consultants will promise a clean property—there is too much room for error.* Naturally, those who read summaries are likely to focus on the negative aspects. Even when the general tenor of a report is positive and the consultant indicates that the subject property is very likely to be satisfactory, a single recommendation for additional testing is likely to disturb lenders and purchasers (regardless of the severity of the potential problem).

The Preliminary Site Assessment is a very effective tool when used correctly. It is usually sufficient for most properties. Although it is less expensive than Phase I and other types of assessments, it will provide for mitigation of liability under the innocent landowner defense in most situations. There are times, however, when a question or concern may be serious enough to warrant further testing. For this reason, many owners will not perform PSAs unless specifically asked to do so. Should a potential problem come to light, one generally has to proceed with testing that can lead to the discovery of problems that, by law, must be reported. Hence, a several thousand dollar assessment can become a remediation project costing tens of thousands of dollars. It is no surprise that many owners prefer ignorance to the chance of having to make expenditures.

THE PHASE I SITE ASSESSMENT

The Phase I Site Assessment (Phase I) essentially produces the same report as the Preliminary Site Assessment (PSA) with one exception—it includes results from testing performed during the on-site inspection of both the interior and exterior of the site. The results of this testing are usually included as a separate section of the report. The Phase I is the assessment most used by potential purchasers and also by lenders when the lender specifies the type of assessment to be done.

When performing the site inspection for a Phase I report, the consultant will carry a sampling kit as he or she performs the interior and exterior inspections. The kit will contain various types of containers and sampling instruments as well as labels and a notebook for recording samples taken. The process is relatively simple and should not take much more time than the inspection for a PSA. However, when a consultant is taking samples inside a tenant's space, it is a good idea to have the property manager along to reassure any tenants who might become uneasy.

The performance of any kind of environmental inspection calls for good tenant communications. Tenants should be alerted to all upcoming environmental inspections—and the manner in which this information is shared can make a significant difference in tenants' attitudes. An announcement concerning environmental inspection must convey a sense of the positive nature of such an event. It is important to communicate that the sole purpose of any environmental inspection is to assure that the premises are free of problems.

Any speculation regarding possible inspection results should not be shared with tenants (e.g., " We are conducting an inspection because we believe that there is an asbestos problem"). Such statements may create panic among tenants before problems are even uncovered. Similarly, one should not put tenants on the defensive prior to an environmental inspection (e.g., "We are checking to make sure that your waste disposal techniques are legal"). After hearing statements that could be construed as accusatory, tenants are less inclined to cooperate.

Interior Samples

Interior sampling is done for several reasons. Sampling for asbestos, for example, is done in each and every space. This means taking unobtrusive samples of ceiling tiles, floor tiles, and insulation without damaging walls, roof shingles, pipe insulation, carpet padding, etc. All samples are carefully labelled, taken to a laboratory, and examined to determine asbestos content. *Potential Asbestos-Containing Materials (ACM), Exhibit 4.1,* provides a glimpse of the wide range of materials that may contain asbestos.

Water samples will generally be taken from all taps and water fountains located in the tenant spaces. Among other things, the water will be tested to determine lead content. Lead has long been known to be hazardous to human health; the EPA emphasizes the concern regarding lead in water supplies. Water testing is also done to determine the presence of other heavy metals such as chromium.

Many property owners may assume that a municipal water system is a sufficient guarantee that water will be safe (i.e., it complies with EPA standards). Until recently, however, most joints and solder on water pipes were made of lead-containing materials. While the use of polyvinyl chloride (PVC) piping has done away with much of the use of metal plumbing fixtures, the lines that supply water to any property may well have been installed before the widespread use of PVC.

Owners are likely to be very concerned when elevated levels of lead are found in the water systems of a commercial property or a multifamily residence. Obviously, the cost to repipe an entire building can be prohibitive.

E X H I B I T   4.1

Potential Asbestos-Containing Materials (ACM)

Acoustical plaster	Fire doors
Adhesives	Fireproofing materials
Asphalt floor tile	Flooring backing
Base flashing	Heating and electrical ducts
Blown-in insulation	High-temperature gaskets
Boiler insulation	HVAC duct insulation
Breeching insulation	Joint compounds
Caulking and putties	Laboratory gloves
Ceiling tiles	Laboratory hoods/table tops
Cement pipes	Mastics (floor tile, ceiling tile, etc.)
Cement siding	Packing materials
Cement wallboard	Pipe insulation
Chalkboards	Roofing felt
Cooling towers	Roofing shingles
Decorative plaster	Spackling compounds
Ductwork connections	Spray-applied insulation
Electrical cloth	Textured paints and coatings
Electrical panel partitions	Thermal paper products
Electric wiring insulation	Thermal taping compounds
Elevator brake shoes	Vinyl floor tile
Elevator equipment panels	Vinyl sheet flooring
Fire blankets	Vinyl wall coverings
Fire curtains	Wallboard

Compiled from U.S. EPA documents.

This list of ACM products is not comprehensive; it is intended to suggest the range and types of materials that contain asbestos.

Fortunately, an elevated level of lead in a building's water supply is a problem that is relatively easy and inexpensive to rectify. Much of the problem can be eliminated by placing filters on the taps of kitchen, restroom, and other water supply sources. The simple filter systems found in hardware stores and advertised on TV are usually sufficient. These filters can usually be installed by maintenance personnel. Furthermore, running a faucet for thirty seconds first thing in the morning reduces lead content by about 60 percent because water that sat in the pipes overnight is replenished with fresh water. This is a worthwhile "tip" to share with tenants.

In some instances, air-quality studies may also be performed. These studies are not a standard part of a Phase I; they are generally part of a Phase II. Nevertheless, the particular nature, age, type, or use of a property may signal the need for air-quality testing. Properties that suggest a need for air-quality testing are mid- and high-rise office buildings, single-family homes, and industrial manufacturing facilities. Any structure with enclosed or indoor mechanical rooms, basements, underground parking, or underground loading docks may require testing.

Air-quality surveys require monitoring equipment to be left in certain areas over a period of time (the length of time varies depending on the type of test and the equipment). Common tests check for asbestos fibers and radon in the air. Other tests will check for the presence of such substances as carbon monoxide, ozone, solvents, preservatives, etc. These substances may be present in levels that may cause tenant, resident, or employee discomfort and minor physical side effects. In rare instances, the concentration of a substance may cause extreme illness.

It is as important to check new buildings as it is to check older ones. While new buildings have more advanced heating, ventilation, and air-conditioning (HVAC) systems, they also tend to be more airtight. Adhesives and cleaners used on carpeting, wallpaper, and woodwork can be a problem if they are not used properly and according to the manufacturer's specifications. Cleaning agents used by janitorial and maintenance crews can reach dangerous concentrations in poorly ventilated areas. Improperly adjusted or maintained HVAC and mechanical rooms may become infused with high levels of hazardous substances, which may in turn be distributed throughout the areas served by the HVAC system. While a good preventive maintenance program can eliminate most such problems, environmental consultants will occasionally decide to include air-quality studies in their Phase I Site Assessment when they have reason to believe that such studies are necessary.

Exterior Testing

Exterior testing for Phase I studies is generally limited to areas of specific interest. An environmental consultant will look for certain "signs" that indicate the necessity to do soil testing (e.g., visible soil staining, areas without any vegetation, railroad track easements with staining on and around the tracks, cleared areas around electrical transformers).

Polychlorinated biphenyls (PCBs) are of particular concern; they were widely used in hydraulic fluids and oils on trains and as insulating liquids in transformers. Also of interest are petroleum hydrocarbons (which result from various oils, gasolines, hydraulic and other fluids that have been spilled or dumped on the ground), and the various "enes" and "anes" associated with cleaning solvents and coating materials. Some "enes" are toluene and trichloroethylene, while examples of "anes" are hexachloroethane and trichloroethane. Typically "enes" present much more serious problems than "anes." As a general rule, an "ene" is at a dangerous level when its concentration in parts per million reaches double digits (10 ppm, etc.).

Underground storage tanks (USTs) are a major cause for concern on any property. Evidence of a UST in the form of gas pumps, filling facilities, and clean-out valves will almost certainly be noted and tested. Testing should be done to determine whether an underground storage tank (UST) has become a leaking underground storage tank (LUST).

Three types of tests are performed on UST sites (to evaluate the soil, the tank, and the groundwater). Taking soil samples three to five feet down is standard procedure. These samples are tested for petroleum products and their derivatives to determine if there has been any spillage (from filling or dispensing) or any leakage. In conjunction with the soil sample, a "tightness" test is usually performed on tanks using an instrument positioned inside the tank. This is used to determine the presence of an LUST.

A monitoring well to test groundwater underneath the tank is always recommended in these situations. Although such tests can be very expensive and time consuming, most experts agree that any tank more than five years old has a 95 percent chance of leakage. From the property purchaser's perspective, a test of groundwater should always be performed.

When "active" tanks have annual tightness test records that go back five to seven years and reveal no leakage, soil tests are unnecessary. These records should be easy to obtain through the owner of the tank (the property owner or tenant); tank owners are required by law to make such tests and keep records of them. The tank-owning tenant should be required to provide the management company with a copy of each of these tests when completed. A manager taking over management of a property that has underground tanks and no test results on file should request tests immediately upon commencement of the management contract.

The results of Phase I tests should be included in the detailed section of the report along with copies of laboratory analyses (specific data) and testing diagrams and parameters. This support documentation is sometimes provided as appendixes to the report because of the numbers of tests involved. The executive summary should contain a synopsis of the test results.

THE PHASE II SITE ASSESSMENT

The Phase II Site Assessment (Phase II) is an extension of the PSA and Phase I. Its primary objective is to quantify the contamination discovered in a previous study. Phase II Site Assessments are based on the information determined by the PSA or Phase I and should be tailored to the problems that have been identified.

A Phase II usually has two distinct sections or stages of investigation. For purposes of clarity, these sections will be referred to as "Phase II stage one" and "Phase II stage two"—although this terminology does not reflect widespread usage. In general, one is only likely to encounter references to "Phase II Assessments" (i.e., the assessment as a single unit). It is important to recognize, however, that some Phase II Assessments are less involved than others. If testing done during the first stage of Phase II indicates that there is no reason to proceed, it is not likely that there will be a second stage.

Stage one of the Phase II involves extensive testing and a thorough investigation of the problems indicated. Such things as air-quality studies, ground-water monitoring, extensive soil sample analysis, and a battery of tests on USTs are all performed during this stage of Phase II. In terms of laboratory analysis, Phase II (stage one) is by far the most technical assessment, although it generates a relatively short executive summary. Stage two is the evaluation of a specific course of action that has been chosen from the recommendations developed in stage one.

The Phase II Report (Stage One)

The Phase II report (stage one) should consist of three sections and an appendix. While different consultants use different formats for reporting, there are three main areas to cover. These sections could be described as (1) testing goals and methods, (2) test results, and (3) the executive summary. The appendix should contain copies of all test results obtained through laboratory analysis.

The explanation of testing goals and methods should be detailed and clear. Each suspected problem should be specified, along with a detailed description of the tests done and what they were designed to determine. This section should detail all the technical basis for the testing and relate it to the PSA or Phase I results previously obtained.

The test results section should summarize the overall test results and their anticipated impact on the property. Specific results should be explained, as should the reasoning behind the assessment of property impact. This section will also contain diagrams of the property showing the location of test sites and indicating any pertinent data regarding those sites. The actual hard-copy results of each test should be included in the appendix along with a copy of the original study (the PSA or Phase I report).

The executive summary should be short and concise. It should summarize the test results in a nontechnical manner, identify areas that require specific attention, and identify the property's status within the law. A list of alternative actions should be provided by the consultant. Other plans, if feasible, should also be discussed. The following list represents the most typical decisions made by owners after recommendations have been suggested by consultants.

1. *Further Action Unnecessary.* A Phase II (stage one) study may determine that the results from the Phase I were flawed and the potential problem revealed is not a matter of concern. Phase II stage two will not be performed in such situations.

2. *Further Action Inadvisable or Impossible.* This is a common response to Phase II results when it has been demonstrated that there is a problem that is off site and migrating to the subject property. A recommendation for no further action may be a consideration when it is not

possible to control the problem from the subject property (e.g., contamination of an underground water stream). Again, when no specific remediation plans are considered, the Phase II Assessment will not include a second stage.

3. *The Second Stage of the Phase II Assessment Should be Performed.* At this time, the owner may also decide to perform a risk endangerment study to obtain a more accurate measurement of the environmental impact of identified problem(s) as well as their anticipated effects on the human population on and around the site. The results of such a study would aid the decision concerning an appropriate remediation or cleanup plan.

Before proceeding to stage two, a plan of action must be chosen. In the stage one executive summary, the environmental consultant is likely to present a number of alternatives from which to choose. The selection process should include the owner, his or her environmental attorney, and the environmental consultant or engineer.

When choosing a course of action, it is important to remember that the plan must be sufficiently well-defined to be able to assess its viability during stage two of the Phase II Assessment. It is necessary to decide on a specific course of action (or inaction) that is intended to lead to a predetermined level of remediation; anticipated results should be quantified. *Obviously, any plan must comply with local, state, and federal guidelines.* Maintaining the existing conditions (i.e., status quo) is always an alternative as long as that particular plan meets with local, state, and/or federal agency approval.

Exercising any one of these options calls for careful planning, proper documentation, and the use of legal counsel. Technical advice should be provided by an environmental consultant or engineer.

It is important to understand that performing a Phase II (stage one) does not mean that contamination is a foregone conclusion. Preliminary assessments may be incorrect—hazardous substances may exist naturally, and mechanical and handling errors do occur. In the event of suspected off-site contamination, a Phase II (stage one) can actually prove that a property is not being affected. Nevertheless, as soon as a problem has been identified and a plan of action selected, it is time to conduct the second stage of the Phase II.

The Phase II Report (Stage Two)

Stage two of a Phase II Site Assessment is done to demonstrate that a certain course of action is the one most beneficial to the environment, agreeable to regulatory agencies, and acceptable to the owner. Stage two may involve additional testing to accurately define the extent of the problem. It may also include testing that is designed to determine the effects of approaching the problem as planned (e.g., environmental, safety, and other impacts). Some proposed plans may be ruled out after doing a cost-benefit analysis, considering economic feasibility, investigating technological capabilities, and researching remediation mechanics.

The stage two report should include a summary of the proposed action and the anticipated results, as well as the projected time frame and the estimated costs for executing the plan. Goals should be stated in quantitative, measurable terms.

The completed Phase II (stage one *and* two), with previous reports included in the appendixes, must be presented to the appropriate agencies for their approval. *Agency approval is required before a Phase III plan can be initiated.* Federal and state agencies require a written report that includes a recommended plan of action (if it is unnecessary to perform a second stage of the Phase II Site Assessment, this submission occurs after stage one is completed). At this time, the appropriate agencies may either confirm the recommendation or require that alternative plans be put in place.

The final course of action is most often referred to as Phase III. It is the implementation of a chosen program that has received agency approval (e.g., remediation, cleanup, maintenance and monitoring of the status quo).

THE PHASE III PROGRAM

Unlike the PSA, Phase I, and Phase II site assessments, Phase III programs are designed to address existing problems. A Phase III program might deal with such things as PCB contamination, wastewater discharge, air pollution, water pollution, indoor air-quality problems, lead contamination, noise pollution, and more. There are as many Phase III plans as there are environmental problems and real properties. Consequently, Phase III plans are difficult to define because each is tailored specifically for the situation identified in the Phase II study.

In general, Phase III is defined as the remediation or cleanup of an environmental contamination problem. Remediation, however, may refer to a range of activities that includes everything from maintaining and monitoring the current problem to a complete eradication of the problem—and all options in between. The development of Phase III procedures is dictated by such things as the location of the property, the extent of the contamination, and the age and identity of the contaminating substance. Other influencing factors include available technology, local geological and atmospheric conditions, and local, state, and federal laws.

During any explanation of Phase III remediation, it is worthwhile to begin with a short discussion regarding terminology. Two words that are frequently used in the context of environmental issues are "remediate" and "remediation." As indicated earlier, the word "remediation" refers to the act of remedying an existing problem. *It is important to understand that "remediate" is not necessarily a synonym for "clean."*

The EPA determines the maximum contaminant levels (MCLs) for certain substances. Each maximum contaminant level is established using certain assumptions: (1) that a one-in-a-million chance of becoming seriously ill because of chemical exposure (including development of cancer) is an acceptable risk, (2) that the substance specified by the MCL is the only substance of concern (interaction with other substances creates too many variables to allow for setting acceptable levels), and (3) that the elaborate calculations involved in determining "acceptable" exposure cover all known exposure pathways, systemic effects of the substance, and all other variables that could affect the aforementioned one-in-a-million chance.

Once the MCL has been set for any one of the hazardous substances regulated by the EPA, it becomes the guideline for comparing test results. Thus, if the MCL for trichloroethylene (TCE) in water is five parts per million and a groundwater sample contains TCE at 10 parts per million, the groundwater sample is contaminated because it has TCE levels above the EPA mandated MCL. In other words, the level of TCE in the groundwater has become a liability problem.

Now for the issue of terminology. Any plan designed to lower the groundwater contamination to 5 parts per million or below is a *remediation* plan. Such a plan would remediate the problem and achieve a level of TCE in the groundwater that is acceptable to the EPA. A plan designed to *clean* the groundwater would involve the removal of virtually all the TCE (reducing its presence to zero parts per million). In this case, the difference between remediation and cleaning could amount to years of work and millions of dollars.

It should be noted that the terms "remediation" and "cleanup" are sometimes used interchangeably. Just as the differences between a Preliminary Site Assessment and a Phase I Site Assessment have been blurred, so have the differences between remediation and cleanup. Nevertheless, there is a distinction to be drawn: All cleanup programs are forms of remediation, but all remedial actions are *not* cleanup programs.

Sometimes remediating a site is the same as cleaning it. A remediation plan that calls for the removal of all asbestos in a building represents a complete "cleaning." On occasion, less radical action may be judged to be the best and safest. For example, an asbestos remediation plan may be classified as an operation and maintenance (O & M) plan (i.e., the asbestos remains where it is and is carefully monitored). Operating and maintaining undamaged asbestos that exists in a building may be the safest and most economical way to protect people from exposure to asbestos fibers. Undamaged asbestos may be sealed, and building maintenance engineers can be trained to monitor and maintain the integrity of the asbestos-containing material (ACM). The average cost of an asbestos O & M program is much less than the average cost of removal. A plan to manage asbestos in place should involve regular professional inspections to provide ongoing monitoring of the effectiveness of the program.

Like the asbestos O & M plan described, some Phase III programs involve monitoring the situation to ensure that it does not get worse. Typical reasons to assume such an approach include a lack of available technology, insignificant demonstration of environmental impact, and the likelihood that taking action will only worsen the situation. The most common reason for Phase III "inaction" is the discovery that contamination is generated off site. Off-site contaminants may pollute groundwater, air, or waterways. Clearly, there is no way to remediate a problem until the source is located, and once it is located, the "contaminator" can only be compelled to comply with prevailing laws.

In summary, any owner seeking recommendations for Phase III procedures, must understand the difference between the proposed remediation plan and actual cleaning of the site (if indeed there is a difference). He or she should quantify any differences by doing a cost-benefit analysis and evaluating the effectiveness of the options proposed. Each Phase III program should be customized to address the particular site and the existing problem(s). The Phase III procedures should be designed by insured, experienced specialists including an environmental engineer who has experience with the specific problem that must be addressed and an environmental attorney.

CLARIFYING TERMINOLOGY

Having drawn clear distinctions among the PSA, the Phase I, Phase II, and Phase III, it is prudent to define some related terminology that is frequently used in the industry. For example, references to environmental site assessments (ESAs) describe activities that parallel the assessments discussed in this chapter. Hence, the term "Phase I ESA" is synonymous with "Phase I" as used in this text (a similar correspondence exists between Phase II ESA and Phase II, Phase III ESA and Phase III).

The phrase "environmental audit" refers to the entire scope of environmental studies performed on a property. Assume that a Phase I assessment of a property is completed and does not reveal problems. Because there are no indications of need for a Phase II, no Phase II is done. In this case, the Phase I Assessment would constitute the environmental audit. At the same time, the environmental audit for a property with problems would include any Phase II and Phase III activities that were necessarily performed.

Another kind of study, the Environmental Impact Analysis, is highly detailed and *not* to be confused with any kind of site assessment. From the results of an environmental impact analysis, a document known as an environmental impact statement (EIS) or an environmental impact report (EIR) is created as a presentation of results and conclusions. The purpose of the EIS is to document the *total* environmental impact of a proposed action. An environmental impact analysis is appropriate when any kind of new construction or activity is planned, but because of the high level of scrutiny involved, it is not likely that someone would voluntarily perform such a study. Sometimes, however, an EIS is required (e.g., when federal funding or federal agencies are involved, when a court order has specified the requirement). It is essential for the real estate professional to recognize the difference between the highly specialized EIS and a report that presents the findings of a site assessment.

SITE ASSESSMENTS—A RECAPITULATION

The PSA is a useful tool. It is generally a sufficient environmental assessment for most properties and is less expensive and faster to conclude than a Phase I. For a seller or an owner who is refinancing, the PSA is the preferred study. The Phase I Site Assessment is more technical, costly, and time consuming. It is also more comprehensive and, for that reason, is preferred by purchasers and lenders.

Regardless of the procedure used, there is always the risk of discovering problems. Perhaps the assessment reveals an example of noncompliance with existing environmental law; perhaps it uncovers information that will make it difficult to sell the property or obtain financing. A necessary caveat: Because environmental laws have a tendency to be retroactive, a seemingly insignificant problem today can become a major liability tomorrow. For this reason, many owners will not perform reassessments on existing property unless it is unavoidable.

Phase II Assessments and Phase III remediations are merely extensions of the Phase I or PSA. In some instances, a PSA may reveal problems that suggest the need to do a Phase II; in such situations, the Phase I may be skipped altogether. Although Phase II Assessments are generally performed when potential problems have been identified, it is important to note that a great many of the Phase II analyses performed will not indicate a need for Phase III remediation. In fact, Phase II analysis may erase all concerns. A property transfer deal should never be terminated merely because a Phase II Site Assessment has begun.

The Phase II Assessment that reveals a genuine problem will involve the testing of a proposed plan. Assuming that tests confirm the viability of the chosen course of action, Phase III remediation will occur as soon as agency approval is secured. During Phase III, existing problems are addressed. The broad range of types of Phase III plans includes everything from full scale contamination cleanups to the implementation of operations and maintenance (O & M) programs.

Purchasing and Selling Land and Existing Facilities

As the 1990s began, several significant economic problems could be attributed (directly or indirectly) to real estate related issues (e.g., the collapse of the savings and loan industry, the weakness in the banking and financial industries, and the cash and equity problems in the insurance industry). With increased conservatism in the financial world, changes in common approaches to financial due diligence have become substantial; every potential purchase is evaluated for environmental risk. Today, it is fair to say that the purchase of either land or existing facilities is rarely seriously considered until the property has been carefully inspected. Due diligence periods have lengthened and more time is necessary for property closings—a trend that is likely to continue in the future.

From an owner's or potential owner's perspective, environmental liability transfers with the title to the property. While the previous owner is not relieved of liability (unless this has been done contractually), the most probable target for environmental litigation is the current property owner and/or operator. For this reason, environmental due diligence and inspection is as important a process as financial due diligence; an error in either can become a disaster. Therefore, from the purchaser's or lender's perspective, it is important to control any and all environmental assessments performed on the property, rather than relying on the seller to do so. Although this may increase costs, any related spending is usually justified.

While it is important to perform an environmental audit, it is just as crucial to be aware of what the audit does and does not do. Some potential purchasers are misinformed regarding this issue. *Regardless of the level of scrutiny, an environmental audit will not prove that a property is completely free of environmental problems.* Its purpose is to provide incontrovertible evidence that the purchaser made "all appropriate inquiry" to determine if problems or contamination exists. Environmental audits are done with the intention of protecting the property owner from environmental liability. Audits are performed with the knowledge that there is probably no property on earth that is entirely "clean."

Rarely do sellers agree to pay for environmental audits and, when they do, they usually demand the right to contract and review the studies themselves. While this might be acceptable in certain instances, it is necessary to understand that sellers will usually choose the fastest and least expensive method of assessment and may edit the final report. This forces the purchaser to hire a consultant to review the report and issue an opinion—something few consultants are willing to do when they have no familiarity with the property or the audit procedures. Consultants who will issue opinions on third-party reports generally charge a substantial fee for doing so and they will rarely, if ever, give substantive guarantees of their interpretations.

For this reason, it is usually safer, faster, and wiser for the purchaser to conduct and pay for his or her own audit. In this way, the purchaser receives a report uninfluenced by the owner.

The selection of an environmental consultant should be made using certain qualifications; to some extent these will vary by client. Desirable qualifications include good references from past assessment contracts similar to the one that is to be performed, sufficient insurance coverage (including errors and omissions coverage of one to two million dollars), and experience in the geographic area where the property is located. Some people request a financial statement from the consultant's company and information concerning support staff. The consultant's company should also be classified as "approved" (i.e., certified, licensed, or accredited) in state or local agency listings of environmental service companies. This may be determined by phoning the appropriate agency for verification.

Once the consultant is chosen, he or she should make a brief, on-site visit along with the purchaser's representative, the consultant's project coordinator, and the owner's representative. At this time, the consultant can recommend either a Preliminary Site Assessment (PSA) or a Phase I Site Assessment (Phase I) and should be able to point out the reasons for choosing one over the other. This allows the client to better understand the projected scope of work as well as the report that is issued stating the findings and test results from the assessment. (The range of assessment possibilities was addressed in chapter 4.)

PURCHASING UNDEVELOPED LAND

As used here, the term "undeveloped land" will refer to land being purchased for a use other than its current one. This means the land may be vacant or have existing structures that will be removed or destroyed. "Undeveloped land" will not refer to land purchased for redevelopment or rehabilitation.

Generally speaking, a Preliminary Site Assessment is sufficient environmental investigation prior to the purchase of undeveloped land. One exception to this rule occurs when "undeveloped land" includes structures that the purchaser intends to move or destroy (in which case the purchaser should perform a Phase I Assessment—and perhaps others—to determine the environmental ramifications of removing or destroying the existing structures). The majority of undeveloped land in the United States consists of farmlands, prairie, and woodlands. While many corporations and the federal government own undeveloped land, much of it is investment land that is not commercially active.

When purchasing woodland or prairie sites, a Phase I is usually a waste of time and money. This is not always the case, however. When investigating farmlands, there are numerous reasons for performing a complete Phase I.

The American farm and ranch system is among the most efficient in the world, producing a significant proportion of the global food supply. American farmers and ranchers are some of the most independent businesspeople the world has ever seen. As a result, they have a reputation for self-sufficiency—even in the areas of fulfilling energy, fuel, and maintenance requirements.

Self-sufficiency of the owner is not necessarily a good thing as far as a potential buyer is concerned. Environmental problems associated with farms and ranches are often associated with the machinery required for day-to-day activities. (It should be noted here that farming tends to be more mechanically oriented than ranching.)

Barns and maintenance sheds on these properties usually remain in the same location for the life of the business; many such structures have been standing for years and years. This is where farm machinery, vehicles, and other equipment are maintained and serviced. Oil, lubricants, fuels, and solvents are not only used and stored in these facilities, but also generally disposed in and around them.

As awareness of environmental problems increased, some farmers and ranchers began to dispose of these wastes properly. To the industry's credit, the independent American farmer and rancher have generally been quick to take action to remedy environmental or ecological problems.

Another situation, not specific to farms, but typical of undeveloped land in the United States, is the accumulation of abandoned autos. Trucks, cars, and motorized vehicles of all types are disposed in many different locations around the country. Sometimes older vehicles are left in the same area by a supplier of parts for other vehicles. Whether a vehicle is abandoned or being saved for parts, it will leak, rust, and deteriorate where it sits. This will eventually create environmental problems that may extend beyond the topsoil.

Trash disposal in rural areas is rarely monitored and seldom controlled by the small towns nearby. In many instances, each household will have a mini-landfill for dumping wastes. The waste in such facilities is routinely burned to decrease the volume, and what remains after incineration may contain toxic substances. Over time, these substances gradually leach into the ground and/or the groundwater.

Very few rural areas have municipal water and sewerage facilities. Most homes outside of incorporated cities and towns use wells for water and cesspools or septic tanks for sewage. Over time, these facilities may not receive the type of care and maintenance they require. Many people do not realize that well water from a well located in close proximity to a cesspool or septic tank may be unsafe for human consumption.

Another very common situation is the presence of either underground or aboveground fuel storage tanks. Most American farms and ranches, especially in the Southwest and Western United States, will have their own fueling equipment. This allows them to buy in bulk for discounts, avoiding long trips to service stations and increasing their overall efficiency. Unfortunately, these tanks also tend to leak, and the use of spillage protection technology varies widely.

In states with oil fields, land that was developed for oil and gas production may, in some instances, no longer be used in that capacity. Such land may be offered for sale to real estate developers as populations expand. It is crucial for the developer to be aware of the land's previous use. The development of oil and gas wells involves heavy machinery, raw and refined petroleum products, and "sludge pits" or areas where sludge and water from drilling are pumped during the well development stage ("sludge pits" are rarely free of hazardous materials).

Indeed, there is a broad range of problem indicators. In situations that suggest potential problems, a Phase I is advisable. Alternatively, the consultant might be advised to begin doing a PSA, with the instructions to expand to a Phase I assessment if anything suspicious is discovered.

It is essential to understand exactly what Preliminary Site Assessments and Phase I Site Assessments will *not* do. They do not give concrete evidence of contamination or other environmental problems. They will not pinpoint the location of a problem or define its extent and seriousness. In many instances, such assessments will not even precisely identify the problem.

Site assessments are specifically designed to protect a property owner from liability when problems are discovered after the purchase (because he or she can demonstrate that "all appropriate inquiry" was made prior to purchase). Even the more extensive Phase I Site Assessment is only designed to demonstrate whether the possibility of a problem exists and to indicate issues of concern. While laboratory testing is generally very accurate, the limited number of samples taken during a Phase I Assessment rarely provides positive proof of anything. When the possibility of problems exists, it is time to do additional testing in the form of a Phase II Site Assessment.

PURCHASING EXISTING FACILITIES

The purchase of existing facilities should be preceded by all the care prescribed for the purchase of undeveloped land—and more. The PSA that is likely to be performed on undeveloped land represents the most basic type of assessment in the industry. Such an assessment should be the minimum acceptable standard when considering the purchase of existing facilities, regardless of the anticipated future use of the facilities.

Even if the facilities are newly constructed, the buyer should insist on a Phase I Site Assessment. Construction codes, tenant use, regulatory guidelines, etc., might have been changed since the subject property was built—it happens all the time. If violations and problems are not discovered prior to purchase, the new owner could be "on the hook" for remediation or cleanup costs later through liability as the owner and/or operator.

The aerial photographs, title checks, and area surveys of a PSA will not show potential problems on the interior of the structure. Granted, a Phase I of existing buildings, especially office space, is more expensive and time consuming than a PSA. The Phase I includes more on-site sampling, additional laboratory analyses of the samples, and a longer, more detailed report. A Phase I pays for itself, however, if it prevents the assumption of liability for costly environmental remediation.

Phase I Assessments of existing buildings should include several different types of tests. The final written report should separate these tests into categories such as: (1) building construction, (2) building operational and mechanical systems, and (3) building occupancy services. While consultants may name the sections differently, each item as discussed below should be addressed at some point in the report.

Building Construction

The older the building, the more important it is to test construction material. Because building standards are changed continually, materials that were approved in the past may not be acceptable today. When existing tenants leave, federal regulations and/or building codes may require some construction that would have been unnecessary had the previous tenant stayed in the building (grandfather clauses may allow newly-restricted building materials to remain in place until the existing tenant leaves). A buyer should be aware of such possible costs.

Ceiling tiles, carpeting, carpet padding, floor tiles, and any special insulation should be sampled and analyzed. The presence of asbestos is an obvious concern, but it is far from the only one. Such things as dyes in carpeting and adhesives used in installing tiles also affect air quality. It is essential to understand that all construction items are of concern—everything from the original structure to all subsequent improvements.

Building Operational and Mechanical Systems

Certain maintenance operations and mechanical equipment will be common to every structure, from a high-rise office building to an industrial distribution facility. In some buildings, specialized operations are performed and unique equipment is necessary. *All equipment should be examined.*

It is especially important to inspect any on-site equipment that utilizes a petroleum-based product such as oil, hydraulic fluid, diesel fuel, gasoline, etc. These substances are regulated by environmental law and the EPA; the improper disposal of them may be a significant violation of environmental law. The owner may be liable for remediation or cleanup expenses.

A good consultant would recommend that one obtain a list and copies of all notices of violation (NOVs), and a comprehensive purchase contract would call for the same. It is also prudent to require copies of tightness tests for underground storate tanks and paid registration fees for any back-up generators. If any NOVs are on record, records of all corrective action taken should be copied as well as subsequent releases of NOVs by environmental authorities.

HVAC systems and their maintenance records should be examined. It is important to investigate water-treatment processes and the types and amounts of chemicals used as well as all contracts for disposal of used chemicals, refrigerants, oils, cleaners, etc. When contractors used for disposal are small businesses or relatively unknown, their standings with the appropriate governmental agencies should be verified and any past violations should be researched. A good consultant should determine whether current water treatment, waste disposal, and cooling processes will be affected by anticipated changes of environmental laws (e.g., the presence of CFC coolants is a condition that would have to be addressed in the future).

Electrical systems and any on-site transformers should be investigated for PCBs and other environmentally regulated chemicals. While some transformers may be insulated with mineral oil at the present time, they may have contained PCBs in the past, and it is likely that a residue will remain. The local electrical utility can supply information regarding this issue

Building Occupancy Services

Building occupancy services refer to those basic items and services that must be provided for the tenants occupying the property. This includes such things as acceptable indoor air quality and a safe water supply as well as janitorial services.

Water samples should be taken from faucets and drinking fountains to determine the presence of lead and other heavy metals. These samples are usually taken during the early morning hours to collect water that has been static in the system for a while. A second sample is often taken after running the water continuously for thirty seconds or more; this will determine water contents during active use periods.

Air quality studies are done to determine the presence of substances in the air that may affect human health. Buildings are screened for asbestos, radon, lead, preservatives, adhesives, solvents, and other chemicals or fibers that may be hazardous. Once identified, most indoor air quality problems are easily resolved through increased ventilation, preventive maintenance programs, repairs, and filters.

Janitorial and other cleaning services are usually investigated to identify the cleaning chemicals used and how these chemicals are disposed. Janitorial companies are usually characterized as small quantity generators (SQGs), and must be examined according to normal site assessment procedures.

A detailed Phase I Site Assessment of facilities will include all these items (and more, if the nature of the property dictates). As building size and system complexity increase, so too should the detail and intensity of the study being done.

SELLING LAND AND FACILITIES

As stated previously, the objectives of an owner performing a site assessment will be diametrically opposed to the objectives of a purchaser performing a site assessment of the same property. While the purchaser is trying very hard to discover any environmental problems, the current owner is trying very hard *not* to discover environmental problems. This is why the seller is likely to perform a PSA on existing facilities.

At issue is the fact that a Phase I includes physical testing and provides quantitative data. The availability of quantitative results decreases one's ability to "interpret" report results. State and federal laws designate certain acceptable limits for the presence of specific substances. Referred to earlier, these limits are known as maximum contaminant levels (MCLs). As soon as a test indicates that a substance exists in excess of the range of acceptability, additional testing and reporting is required.

Choosing a PSA is effective for owners who wish to determine potential questions or areas of concern prior to listing a property for sale. Nevertheless, it is illegal for the property owner who is aware of a problem to use a PSA to influence a third party and conceal the existence of the problem from the purchaser. Such duplicity makes the current owner automatically liable under federal law for any costs associated with the existing problems.

Simply being aware that past ownership or uses of a property might have created an environmental problem does *not* obligate the owner to determine whether this is the case. A notable exception to this is the knowledge that the land was formerly a landfill site. However, as soon as the owner receives a test result indicating the presence of a hazardous substance at or above the MCL, he or she may be obligated to do additional testing—or even clean up or remediate the problem.

AFTER PROBLEMS HAVE BEEN DISCOVERED

More and more real estate deals fall through because of the discovery of environmental problems. The assignment of liability and the costs associated with cleanup and remediation are driving purchasers and lenders away from potentially profitable deals. While financial analysis has always been essential to real estate deals, environmental analysis is becoming increasingly important. Unfortunately, environmental analysis is a process that is filled with speculation rather than quantification. Many deals are terminated as soon as the need for a Phase II Site Assessment is indicated (more out of fear of what may be discovered than from an unwillingness to tackle a clearly defined problem).

The real estate industry, regulatory agencies, and the courts have begun to recognize and enforce certain contractual agreements that facilitate the completion of real estate transactions in the face of existing environmental problems. While any agreement can be subjected to a court review, those agreements that are written clearly and carefully are generally upheld. When any such agreement is made, however, an environmental attorney for each party should be involved.

These agreements may be part of the sales contract or the closing documents; they may also be separate documents that are intended to stand on their own. As such agreements gain popularity and are supported more in the court systems, the industry should experience fewer unnecessary deal terminations. The following types of agreements are the most popular and the least risky for the parties involved. All are being seen more often in real estate transactions.

Owner Indemnification

The most popular request from purchasers and lenders dealing with problem properties is an indemnification against liability from the current owner. Such an agreement will survive the closing and prevent the lender or the new owner from incurring liability for problems discovered during environmental due diligence. The new owner will be secured against responsibility for costs of additional testing, remediation, and the use of environmental professionals (as long as these expenses are required and associated with the specified areas of concern).

The EPA, state regulatory agencies, and the courts have generally ruled in favor of the validity of indemnifications; this makes indemnification a viable defense from liability for a new owner or lender. The courts have set certain precedents, however; they require very detailed identification of the specific problems and liabilities that the new owner is indemnified against, the length of the term of indemnification, and the limits involved (e.g., financial limits, the extent to which a purchaser is or will be protected from problems that were beyond the previous owner's control).

In most instances, the scope of an indemnification is very narrow. A seller may agree to be responsible for any problems associated with those things that were uncovered during the environmental due diligence (clearly defined problems as well as the potential for problems). Only those things specifically identified will be included in the indemnification. *It is unreasonable to expect blanket indemnification from an owner.* Any problems caused by existing tenants are generally considered beyond the control of the owner and are not typically included in the indemnification.

There is usually a dollar limit; when expenses exceed the limit, the new owner is responsible. Acceptable expense items include consulting and legal fees, testing and remediation costs, and other things such as fines. The person or entity granting the indemnification will usually retain the right to sue previous property owners for damages without being required to pay the purchaser any proceeds from judgments won.

This option provides a means to continue real estate deals after possible problems have been discovered and Phase II and Phase III programs are underway. The protection it affords a purchaser is substantial; it removes one significant variable from a financial analysis—environmental liability. A seller should never offer indemnification unless a specific problem is addressed; purchasers should usually expect the seller to remove indemnification clauses in sales contracts and closing documents.

Assumption of Assessment or Remediation Continuation

While not an indemnification, this type of agreement protects a purchaser or lender from the costs associated with ongoing problems and remediation activities. Simply stated, a seller agrees to continue current remediation or cleanup activities until they are completed and to pay all associated costs. In some instances, an escrow account may be established from which payments are made at periodic intervals to cover the remediation costs. The seller should be careful to assure that the agreement requires that the property is to be "remediated" rather than "cleaned."

The courts appear to interpret these agreements as if they imply indemnification of the purchaser from liability associated with the problem(s) being addressed. Because the agreements usually require the seller to perform periodic monitoring for a prescribed period of time, the purchaser is relieved of concern regarding the question of making "all appropriate inquiry" regarding the specified problem(s).

Again, these agreements usually limit the period of the seller's liability as well as the amount of money the seller must spend to cover the scope of the remediation. An escrow may be set up for payment of associated costs, and the seller will most likely maintain the right to file suit against previous owners and other potentially responsible parties (PRPs).

Agency Waivers

From the purchaser's perspective, a highly desirable deal involving a property with environmental problems would involve an agreement with governmental agencies not to hold current or future owners liable for a known problem or potential problem. Such a waiver may be issued by the local, state, or federal agency handling the situation and is the greatest protection available. It is also the most difficult to obtain and is only given under special circumstances.

Off-site Sources. If the source of an identified problem cannot be identified or controlled by the owner, an application for an agency waiver should be considered. Ultimately the primary concern of the governing agency is to stop the contamination and prevent additional problems. If an owner has no control over the source of the contamination, it is highly unlikely that the problem can be remediated until that source is eliminated. Groundwater contamination sometimes presents such a situation.

Economic Feasibility. The economic feasibility of remediation may have an impact on the kind of deal that is made. Some agencies will waive liability for remediation if current remediation technology is either insufficient to properly address the problem or tremendously expensive (provided the problem is not currently making an environmental impact, spreading, or increasing in intensity). Such a waiver will usually be conditional and require regular monitoring.

Other Alternatives. While an agreement releasing current and future owners from liability and assigning liability to a previous owner is most unusual, it may be obtained in certain instances. Such agreements have been granted when the previous owner was a state or federal governmental agency.

The federal government has been known to create some environmental problems. Activities of the U.S. Department of State and Department of Defense have resulted in billions of dollars of remediation expense over the years. State and federal departments of transportation are also involved in environmentally sensitive activities. For this reason, the EPA and state environmental agencies tend to be more willing to release property owners from liability when problems are directly attributable to governmental agencies. Because the law requires these agencies to pay for cleanup and remediation, environmental agencies are generally assured the problem will be addressed.

Requests for such waivers require the combined efforts of an environmental engineer or consultant and an attorney who must spend time gathering evidence and preparing a case. Such waivers are generally made after a study reveals the presence of contamination, current or previous government ownership of the property, and the current or previous presence of governmental operations that typically produce the type of contamination that has been discovered. Although the evidence may only be circumstantial, the onus is on the government to prove that it did *not* contaminate the property. In many instances, this is very difficult, because the government's historical record is difficult to overlook.

In addition to the methods suggested here, there are other means of preventing a deal from terminating. The fact is, methods that have not yet been attempted may hold up in court and be within regulatory guidelines. In an arena as new as environmental law, the only restrictions on these types of agreements may be one's imagination and creativity.

6

Real Estate Development

In the business world, those who best anticipate changing business climates, market shifts, and future needs of consumers are the ones who continue to grow and flourish. Effective environmental management illustrates this "formula" for success because it calls for anticipation and contingency planning. The key is understanding the basic environmental issues and how they affect the real estate industry.

DEVELOPING CURRENT LANDHOLDINGS

Real estate development is one of the most basic aspects of the industry; one might say that without development there would be no industry. Unfortunately, real estate development is a major contributor to environmental problems. Consequently, some environmental groups and ordinary citizens may perceive developers as "the enemy."

Because the developmental process does create environmental problems that are very much issues of concern, much of environmental law directly affects the developer. The process of real estate development—whether the project in question is a single-family home or a hundred-story office building—is one that depletes the supply of natural resources. Wood, water, iron, aluminum, copper, and clay are all used in construction. Before any construction begins, the land may require grading. Earth and ground cover may be replaced with manufactured materials, which may change drainage patterns, volumes of run-off water, and ecological systems in the immediate area.

The use of power tools, motorized equipment, and other machinery requires electricity or the burning of fossil fuels. The use of raw materials requires harvesting or mining as well as manufacturing and other processes (all of which use power and fossil fuels). Grading and paving decrease natural vegetation and water absorption while they increase drainage and reflected heat in the immediate area. In many instances, wetlands and other fragile ecosystems are significantly altered or completely destroyed by development.

Completed developments increase pedestrian and vehicular traffic as well as the use of electricity, the production of wastes and sewage, the need for water treatment and associated chemicals, and the generation and release of hazardous substances (e.g., CFCs, PCBs). The use and disposal of paints, stains, cleaning fluids, pesticides, and fertilizers also increase once a project is completed and occupied.

This chapter will focus on those things that every developer should do to avoid environmental problems—from unnecessary delays to liability for remediation costs. *Note: For purposes of clarity, the words "owner" and "developer" will be used as synonyms here.* This material is not intended to be a comprehensive examination of environmental issues from the perspective of the project architect or engineer. Indeed, every development project involves dealing with design and construction issues that affect—and are affected by— the environment. Something as seemingly simple as the quality of the soil must be analyzed carefully (for compaction, porosity, etc.) to assure sufficient stability for the structure foundation(s) and proper drainage. Water run-off is another issue that warrants attention. Many such matters of design and construction are covered in state and local building codes. A competent architect or engineer should address such issues appropriately.

The evolution of environmental legislation has been based on scientific data and observed environmental problems rather than an industry-by-industry assessment of violations. Hence, the environmental legislation in place has had—and will continue to have—a tremendous impact on the real estate industry as a whole and development in particular. For this reason, it is essential to plan and prepare for environmental issues when developing real estate of any sort.

PRECONSTRUCTION ANALYSIS

Prior to any construction, there are a number of issues to be taken into account. These considerations are social, environmental, and contractual by nature and are described in the following sections.

Social Considerations

Like the loggers in the Northwest, oil companies, and the federal government, developers tend to be targets of citizens' groups and environmental activists.

The law allows for civil suits by those opposed to a project, and action on a site can be postponed until the complaint has been properly reviewed by the courts. Regardless of the nature or merit of any opposition, it must still be allowed due process.

Many people believe developers to be exceedingly wealthy and able to withstand repeated resistance and multiple lawsuits. In reality, such actions may seriously delay or even kill a project entirely. The possibility of a delay provides tremendous motivation to plan for every contingency in the earliest stages of project development.

If the planned development is the first of its type to be located in the area, there is a higher probability of encountering resistance. If people in the area have a history of raising objections to development, expansion, improvements, etc., resistance may be likely (even if there are projects in the area that are similar to the proposed one).

Inadequacies in public utilities or services such as fire departments, police, and hospitals could create problems with neighboring homeowners who might fear that development will result in a further decline in services. The presence of an endangered species in or near the area might also elicit a negative response.

The developer who recognizes the possibility of facing resistance should conduct significant research to assure that civil objections do not endanger the project. Environmental impact statements and prepared responses to objections drafted in advance, can not only ease the minds of those people who are raising objections but also create a positive image for the project from its inception. One of the most effective ways to sway the opinions of the opposition is to address community concerns quickly and in detail.

Environmental Considerations—The PSA

The goal of preconstruction environmental analysis is to identify pertinent issues and possible problems and to plan for contingencies that might arise. Essentially, the property's environmental status must be evaluated.

An ideal starting point is the Preliminary Site Assessment (PSA) or Phase I Site Assessment (Phase I) that was performed prior to the purchase of the property. However, many developers and corporations own land for years, and the land in question may have been purchased before the enactment of environmental legislation and the need for any prepurchase assessments. If an assessment has not been performed, a PSA should be conducted before any detailed planning is done.

A PSA can provide a wealth of information, not all of which is environmentally oriented. Aerial photographs, a site inspection, and a title history are all part of a PSA report. This material may reveal areas of the property that were backfilled or used as unregistered waste disposal sites. Such information is important when determining grading and soil compaction for foundations and parking areas (a reminder that the PSA reveals other concerns that

E X H I B I T   6.1

PSA Findings and Related Concerns

Items Noted	Questions Suggested from Notes
Backfilled land area	Where did the fill come from? Is the fill contaminated?
Prior or existing storage or fuel tanks (underground or aboveground)	Have they been removed? If so, when were they removed? If not, should they be? Did or do they leak? Has the groundwater been affected in any way?
Old dump site or landfill	What kind of waste was disposed there? Has it caused any contamination problems? Could it be a source of future problems?
Old pond or creek bed	Is it a wetlands area and how does this affect development? Was the pond natural or added by a developer? What did the pond contain? Is it a source of possible contamination?

are *not* related to environmental liability). *PSA Findings and Related Concerns, Exhibit 6.1,* lists a few examples of PSA findings and the kinds of questions that should be suggested by their presence.

Essentially, the developer is hoping to avoid surprises. This means making every effort to understand what lies below the surface of the land. In the Southeastern United States, for example, developers grading project sites have actually uncovered World War II vintage artillery shell casings and tank shells because the land previously housed military storage dumps. There have also been cases in which buried 55-gallon drums of unknown origin and contents have been uncovered. A site assessment can make the developer aware of conditions that indicate the potential for problems.

The PSA can also indicate potential problems with the existing structures on the property. This is especially important if the buildings are scheduled to be destroyed or removed during construction. Older buildings with concrete, pipe insulation, floor tiles, ceiling tiles, asphalt shingles, electrical cloth, etc., may contain asbestos-containing material (ACM). Demolishing ACM could create friable asbestos and a serious health hazard. Old transformers or machinery using hydraulic fluid may contain PCBs that should not be released during demolition. There are a number of considerations unique to destruction and/or removal that should be addressed by an expert.

Other areas of concern that may be identified by a PSA are locations of old wells, septic tanks, cesspools, underground storage sheds, and underground gas or other utility lines. Old oil pits, repair facilities, irrigation pits, and areas where wastes and trash have been incinerated may also exist. Finally, a PSA may uncover previous environmental violations or accidents. It is possible that state and/or federal agencies may have participated in these violations if they occurred when different laws were in place. If a governmental agency has been involved in the past, it is safe to assume they will monitor the situation with care in the future.

Special Assessments and Determinations

Several specific assessments and determinations should be made before detailed planning for a project begins. While there are those developers who wait until just before construction to address these issues, it is not a wise practice. Such investigations can generally be performed fairly quickly, and some may uncover information that can delay construction (and that is strong motivation for acting prior to the construction date). Some examples follow.

Determining Availability of Electrical Service. Many people are likely to assume that they have access to certain utilities. Environmental regulations have made this issue one that must be addressed prior to developing the architectural design for any project. In most instances, electrical service is readily available or easily accessed.

The possible presence of PCBs in electrical transformers is a consideration. It is important to determine the type of electrical transformers that are located on site. This generally requires a phone call to the local electrical utility followed by a written request for the information. If possible, it is wise to obtain copies of the service records for each unit on the property. *All information provided by the utility should be in writing.*

If electrical service is going to be brought onto the property during construction, it is important to insist on the right to choose the type of transformer that is to be used. While the costs associated with new, unused, "dry" (PCB-free) transformers are somewhat higher than the costs of "rebuilt" or "recycled" transformers, there are no PCBs in new transformers. By law, PCBs are no longer used in transformers; however, "recycled" transformers may or may not have contained PCBs at one time and, if they did, no utility will certify that they are completely free of PCBs.

Because of widespread awareness of the problems created by PCBs, many purchasers (especially institutional ones) will not buy a property that has "wet" (PCB-containing) transformers on site. The fear associated with PCBs and related environmental liabilities tends to influence business decisions, even though the risk of exposure to PCBs is very slight (to cause exposure, a transformer must develop a severe leak or explode and shower PCBs everywhere).

There are those developers who choose to investigate the use of alternative energy sources (e.g., solar, wind). Some may be motivated by a lack of access to conventional electrical utilities, others wish to pursue more environmentally friendly means of generating power, and still others might be investigating cost-cutting measures.

Identifying the Source of Water Supply. Another item that must receive special attention from the developer is water supply quality and availability. Does the project have municipal water service from the local water-treatment facilities, or does it rely on a well or wells dug into the groundwater underneath the project? Many developments are likely to have access to a municipal water system; however, small projects in more rural locations will have to rely on well water as their source. It is essential to determine where the water will be coming from and whether there will be sufficient volume and pressure. It may be prudent to consider future (increased) needs for water; this will involve special engineering and design and extra costs to prepare the project during its initial construction.

When a water supply is provided by some means other than a municipal utility, the potential for environmental problems increases precipitously. Water quality is a long-standing environmental concern and one that is closely regulated. Individuals are becoming more aware of the importance of acceptable water quality. More tenants are demanding to see written documentation of recent water-quality testing results before they will sign a lease.

When water is supplied to a project from a nonmunicipal source, it is necessary to obtain a series of permits. Permit requirements will vary from state to state and even from county to county. Research into the permitting process and requirements can most likely be expedited by the project engineer and/or the architect; the permits themselves can be obtained by the general contractor. It is important to be aware of these permits and their attendant fees when budgeting for a project.

One permit requirement is likely to be the installation of a series of permanent groundwater monitoring wells to facilitate periodic testing for contaminants. Water is tested for the presence of volatile organic compounds (VOCs) such as toluene, trichloroethylene, etc. Other concerns include the possible presence of heavy metals such as lead, mercury, and arsenic. Should the groundwater be so contaminated that it cannot be brought to drinking water standards, an alternative source of water must be found. This could pose a serious threat to the viability of the project.

Water monitoring is advisable even if the permitting process does not require it. Not only could the owner incur liability under environmental law, he or she might also face lawsuits from tenants and/or residents in the project.

Plumbing was routinely joined with lead solder and welding until the 1980s and the advent of PVC piping. At the writing of this book, some state and local building codes did not indicate lead joints as a code violation. When wording construction contracts, it is important to specify that lead may not be used in any plumbing or building service equipment because water that has stood overnight in lead-containing plumbing lines is likely to have a higher-than-normal lead content. During rehabilitation or redevelopment projects, this problem may be rectified by adding filters to all water end-sources (taps, fountains, etc.) in the building.

Assessing Sewer Systems and Understanding NPDES Permitting. In many projects, the most sensitive and most regulated utility service is sewage treatment and disposal. Monitored at the federal, state, and local levels, the discharge of sewage is a primary concern for regulatory agencies and is closely watched at all levels. This regulation begins with National Pollutant Discharge Elimination System (NPDES) permitting.

Projects that utilize municipal sewerage facilities and services are not exempted from regulations and permitting requirements. During construction, the project will go through several stages of permitting and design approval before it can be connected to the municipal sewerage system. Once the system has been connected, the regulatory agencies will monitor it on an ongoing basis, and inspections are usually done without advance warning.

In most buildings, sewage discharge will not be a major concern. However, in projects that have medical or dental professionals, architectural firms, photo developing operations, testing laboratories, and similar specialty uses, the tenants should be prohibited from disposing chemicals and other wastes into building drains.

The permitting processes are best left in the hands of those who specialize in them. Most engineering, architectural, law, and environmental consulting firms usually have someone on staff who specializes in wastewater permit applications at the local level. The job becomes more difficult when a project will not be connected directly to the municipal sewer, and effluent wastewater must be discharged into a pretreatment plant before it can enter storm sewers or other water removal systems.

Systems not discharging directly into federally regulated municipal sewerage lines are required to have special pretreatment facilities designed to handle waste types specific to the intended use of the project. These custom-designed systems must be maintained by specially licensed maintenance companies and are monitored very closely by state and/or federal regulatory agencies. They are required to have NPDES permits to operate.

The permitting process is part of the Clean Water Act and its amendments. NPDES permits are required for everything from small wastewater pretreatment plants (most common to larger real estate projects) to the discharges from chemical manufacturing plants. Sizable federal fines for permit violations are assessed every day the violation goes uncorrected; these fines are imposed in addition to any state fines for the same violation (those also can be significant). For this reason, internal monitoring procedures become critical for NPDES permit holders.

It is important to note here that the regulations distinguish between discharges *to* private pretreatment facilities and *from* them. The law states that discharges *to* privately owned treatment works are exempt from NPDES permit requirements; *discharges from them are not.* It can be very costly to assume that discharges from pretreatment facilities are exempt from NPDES permits.

NPDES regulations allow states with EPA-approved programs to monitor and enforce compliance. The guidelines used by the state in determining violations must be at least equal to those set by the EPA, but there is no limit to their stringency. Thus, if the state regulates a developer's NPDES-permitted site, the owner is assured of being in compliance with federal standards. *States with EPA-Approved NPDES Programs (1991), Exhibit 6.2,* lists those in place as of 1991 (at the time this book was written).

Whether through state or federal agencies, NPDES permitting procedures are very technical and involved. They are also very time-consuming; it may be months before permits are granted, even if submission is done correctly and there are no questions or other delays. An attorney or engineering firm specializing in these matters should be retained to obtain the permit and expedite the process.

Maintenance of the pretreatment facility should be performed by a licensed contractor specializing in treatment plant maintenance. When soliciting bids for the contract, references should be checked very carefully, and insurance coverage for liability and for errors and omissions should be deemed to be sufficient. Disclosure of the contractor's prior violations should also be required. On request, state environmental departments will supply a list of approved contractors, and they can verify violations by providing a list of notices of violation (NOVs) assessed against the contractor over the past several years.

Contractors who have committed violations should not necessarily be excluded from consideration. There are many types of violations—everything from administrative errors to failing to pay license renewal fees. Some violations may not be the fault of the contractor. For example, even though the owner ultimately controls the volume of waste being processed by the plant, the contractor will also be cited for a violation if the volume exceeds the plant's capacity.

Ultimately, all permits are in the owner's name and it is he or she who will incur any and all liability associated with the treatment plant. It may be a breach of contract when a maintenance contractor does not notify the owner or manager of a violation, but it is not a defense from liability for the owner. According to the law and the regulating agencies, it is the owner who is liable for expenses due to the presence of problems or incidents of noncompliance.

The two most common problems encountered with private treatment plants are the discharge of untreated or improperly treated wastewater from the plant and excessive volume of waste passing through the plant. Excessive volume may be described as more than is allowed by the permit or more than

E X H I B I T   6.2

States with EPA-Approved NPDES Programs (1991)

Alabama	Nebraska
Arkansas	Nevada
California	New Jersey
Colorado	New York
Connecticut	North Carolina
Delaware	North Dakota
Georgia	Ohio
Hawaii	Oregon
Illinois	Pennsylvania
Indiana	Rhode Island
Iowa	South Carolina
Kansas	Tennessee
Kentucky	Utah
Maryland	Vermont
Michigan	Virginia
Minnesota	Washington
Mississippi	West Virginia
Missouri	Wisconsin
Montana	Wyoming

Note: States *not* listed do not have EPA-approved state programs for NPDES permitting; however, most states will still have state permitting requirements that must be followed. Such state permits must be obtained in addition to the EPA permit.

can be treated effectively by the plant. While a permit specifies allowable daily volume, it is possible for daily discharges to be within volume discharge guidelines while exceeding the volume that can be properly treated (e.g., the chemical makeup of the discharge might have changed). Simple quality control programs can help one avoid such problems.

A third-party engineering or consulting firm should be contracted to provide quarterly or semiannual testing and inspections of the pretreatment plant. The service would test for materials present in the inflow water; it would also check pH (acidity, alkalinity), temperature, and chemical content of plant discharges. In addition, the daily volume should be calculated to assure that the volume being treated is within permit guidelines. A special inspection should be ordered each time a significant new activity takes place at the site (e.g., the property gains a major new tenant or a new type of tenant, a building is expanded, or another project is connected to the plant). This will provide an early indication of any new problems that need to be addressed.

Finally, it is important to remember that while the discharge *into* a private treatment system is not regulated by federal NPDES standards, state and local authorities may regulate them. In many instances, state NPDES programs will require a permit for flow into the system as well as away from it (state programs are allowed to be more stringent than federal programs). In addition, states that do not have their own NPDES programs may choose to regulate exempt discharges on their own.

Due to the complexity of overlapping federal and state laws on sewage issues, it is advisable to employ both an engineering firm and an attorney to handle the permitting process for a project. Time is always an important factor in real estate development, so the time saved by employing these professionals will certainly compensate for the costs.

Handling Wetlands Classification.   When a property (or a portion of the property) is classified as wetlands, that fact is critical to the planning of the project. Being classified as wetlands may determine whether the property can ever be developed. Such classification has a direct effect on all kinds of development—from commercial to residential to agricultural.

The process of classifying a property as wetlands is highly involved. Very stringent criteria must be met for a parcel of land to be classified as a wetlands area. In addition, there are four federal agencies involved in the process of permitting development in and around wetlands areas: the Army Corps of Engineers (COE), the Fish and Wildlife Service (FWS), the Soil Conservation Service (SCS), and the EPA. Obtaining a permit is a long and expensive process.

A definition of "wetlands" is part of the Code of Federal Regulations (CFR); this is the definition used by the COE (quoted in chapter 2). While the COE definition is the most common one, it is important to note that the Food Security Act of 1985 and the Emergency Wetlands Resources Act of 1986 also contain definitions of wetlands. Depending on the situation and the agency involved, any of these definitions could be used.

Agency interaction concerning wetlands classification is varied and complex. The COE has primary jurisdiction over wetlands determination under Section 404 of the Clean Water Act. The FWS and SCS also review permit applications and may handle wetlands classifications in some areas. The COE accepts input and comments on permit applications from the FWS and SCS as well the National Marine Fisheries Service (per the Fish and Wildlife Coordination Act).

Although a permit is granted from the COE and approved by all other agencies involved, it still must be reviewed and approved by the EPA. The EPA has final authority over permit issuance and may veto any permit approved by the other agencies. Add to this process the fact that the permit must comply with as many as four or five different environmental acts and it becomes even more obvious why the permitting process takes so much time. In order to decrease the amount of time involved, the COE, FWS, and SCS have specific time limits for issuing their responses. Unfortunately, there are no time restrictions on the EPA, whose final approval is always required.

In the event a property or a portion of a property is classified as wetlands area and a permit is sought and obtained, the conditions under which the permit is granted may still prohibit development. The permit may call for certain action to be taken when the land is changed in any way. Such prescribed action is likely to be expansion of other wetlands in the area or re-creation of the destroyed wetlands in another location. The costs for such activity can be significant, and may prove prohibitive.

One reason for determining wetlands classification prior to purchase is that many wetlands areas were converted to farm and agricultural usage prior to enactment of the laws and grandfather clauses exempted the landowners at the time the law was passed. Unfortunately, unless the clause is transferable to subsequent owners of the property, sale of the property may not only prevent further use of the area, but also require restoration of the wetlands to their original condition.

Protecting Endangered Species. The Endangered Species Act (ESA) sets forth guidelines for treatment of species listed on the endangered species or threatened species list. The Act in general provides for the conservation of endangered or threatened species and establishes cooperative responsibility of federal departments and agencies to further the goals of the ESA. Thus, most situations involving the ESA are extraordinarily time-consuming and very expensive.

The stated goals of the ESA are to provide methods of conserving ecosystems in which threatened and endangered species exist, establish a definitive program for doing so, and comply with various international treaties regarding this matter. The primary agency involved is the U.S. Fish and Wildlife Service (FWS).

In section 7 of the Endangered Species Act, federal agencies, licensees, and permitees are required to refrain from further endangering listed species *and their habitats.* Section 7 includes a list of procedures that must be carried out, especially by federal agencies. In most instances, the ESA will not apply because development tends to be done in previously developed areas. Its impact is felt when a project is on previously undeveloped land. When applicants are requesting a permit to perform activities in potentially critical habitats, it is the permitting agency's responsibility to prepare an environmental impact study (sometimes called a biological assessment). The assessment is not the responsibility of the individual requesting the permit.

All contracting and construction in the area of the study must cease during performance of the study. Not only does this delay the proposed project, but it may also delay unrelated projects that are underway. This often overlooked fact should be kept in mind when developing projects near an area that may someday require an environmental impact study.

Section 9 of the Endangered Species Act specifically forbids activities that can either directly or indirectly harm listed endangered or threatened species. This could apply to any individual or other entity within the United States or its jurisdiction. Specifically prohibited is the "taking" of any species of fish or wildlife that is listed as endangered or threatened. United States' jurisdiction includes territorial waters and the "high seas," which can impact development projects requiring landfill or located on coasts.

Significant to the interpretation of section 9 is the definition of "taking" an endangered species. According to the Act, "taking" is "to harass, harm, pursue, hunt, shoot, wound, kill, trap, capture, or collect or attempt to engage in any such contact." After an initial reading, one might not assume that this definition would conflict with development. Nevertheless, in the case of *Palila v. Hawaii Department of Land and Natural Resources* (1979, affirmed on appeal in 1981), the destruction of a critical habitat was determined by law to be a "taking." Critical habitat is commonly defined as environmental conditions in a specific area crucial to the survival of a listed endangered or threatened species. Hence, construction processes are considered destructive to wildlife habitat.

The only exceptions to section 9 of the Act are the "taking" of a listed species in defense of human life or by a federal agency that can prove an imminent threat to human life and suggest no alternative protection from that threat (e.g., a rabid wolf, a rogue grizzly bear). Due to the fact that the Act made a significant impact on the developer, Congress set forth a permitting process in Section 10 of the ESA whereby nonfederal entities may apply for permission to "take" listed species in otherwise legal activities. Originally the Act addressed only the manner in which governmental agencies were to deal with threatened or endangered species.

In the slow, expensive process of obtaining a permit, the application should include a biological assessment that identifies effects on listed species, mitigation and monitoring activities to minimize the impact, alternatives that were considered and ruled out (and the reasons why), and any other measures that should be taken (and why). In essence, these permits require a different type of environmental site assessment for the application alone; such an assessment is performed in addition to any other site assessments. Because the Endangered Species Act is highly complex, it is essential to employ an attorney specializing in the ESA and its permit processes, as well as a scientist or engineer specializing in environmental impact and the ESA.

When an environmental impact assessment is performed and the presence of a listed species or a critical habitat is identified, it may have a serious impact on the property's value and marketability. This is because redevelopment or additional development will be prohibited unless an exemption under the ESA is obtained or a habitat conservation plan is prepared and implemented. It is also important to understand that the issuance of a waiver or permit will not prevent civil suits and construction restraining orders from being filed by concerned citizens and environmental activist groups.

In the event that an environmental impact study must be performed, the following guidelines should be considered in contracting for the work.

1. The scope of the study should be determined prior to its commencement. This is done to assure that all sections of the ESA that apply to the situation are addressed, even if it is as yet undetermined whether compliance is possible.
2. A draft report should be made available to the developer and the developer's legal counsel to verify the accuracy of the contents. *The owner's representative or counsel should never attempt to change the substance of the report.* He or she should only check to see that all data are correct as presented.
3. Prior to issuing a final report, it is necessary to decide whether to include recommendations in the study itself or in a separate document.
4. The report submitted by the scientific and/or engineering contractor should not include speculation, assumptions of facts not supported by hard data, or legal conclusions.
5. The study should be performed during a season when the species in question is active and may be monitored. Otherwise, the report may focus on the habitat alone and include speculation regarding the species' actions within that habitat.

Under ideal circumstances, the ESA will not be a development issue. Unfortunately, it may become an issue in some unanticipated ways. Consider, for example, the problem some people in the city of New York have experienced when repairing, maintaining, and renovating high-rise buildings. At one time, special nesting sites were provided for falcons in New York because pigeons and other food sources drew falcons into the city to hunt. As a consequence, repair, maintenance, and construction activities that involve a disruption of falcon nesting places fall under the purview of the ESA.

In dealing with ESA-related issues, proper selection of attorneys and consultants is very important. Regardless of the competence of the experts, expenditures of time and money are inevitable.

Construction Contract Protection

During the construction phase of a large real estate project, the developer has very little day-to-day control of the subcontractors' actions, unless he or she is also the general contractor. Because this creates opportunities for shortcuts and environmentally unsound practices, it is wise to add a few contractual clauses to the standard American Institute of Architects (AIA) construction contract. These clauses are designed to protect the developer. Among the issues to be addressed are insurance, waste storage and disposal, recycling, fill dirt, and a general waiver. The following material provides some of the reasons for including such safeguards in a contract.

Insurance. The way to assure adherence to all contractual warranties and guarantees is to confirm that the contractor carries adequate insurance on the project and that the developer is named on the insurance certificate as an additional insured. This way the developer can go back to the underwriter at any time in the future should problems develop that are directly related to the contractor's activities (even if the contractor changes coverage after the project's completion).

The developer should establish an official company policy requiring contractors to have adequate insurance coverage and specifying dollar amounts of coverage (when appropriate). *The issue of insurance should not be negotiable with contractors.* Advisable insurance coverage varies by geographic location and the type of project; it is wise to consult an expert when determining the appropriate coverages. As this book was being written, the following were useful general insurance guidelines.

1. Workers' compensation insurance must be carried as required by applicable law but not less than $1 million per occurrence.
2. Comprehensive general liability insurance that includes property damage of not less than $1 to $2 million.
3. Professional errors and omissions insurance between $1 million and $2 million (it is better to err on the high side).
4. Motorized vehicle insurance to include personal injury, liability, and property damage in an aggregate amount of $1 million.
5. Insurance for special situations (e.g., blasting) should be acquired as needed and in amounts recommended by state and/or federal guidelines.

Waste Storage and Disposal. The storage and/or disposal of construction waste on site may be a liability if either is done improperly. Precise instructions regarding these issues should be included in all construction contracts.

The contract should specify that the contractors are liable for expenses incurred due to the improper storage of materials on site; the same clause would indemnify the developer from such liability. Improper storage can lead to spills and accidents. These types of incidents may have environmental ramifications; they may also result in excessive product use and/or additional cost to the contractor or the developer. Improper storage and/or disposal of waste may be a violation under OSHA; that can mean fines, construction delays, and negative publicity. Correct storage techniques are in everyone's best interest—including the general contractor's.

In the past, the practice of on-site disposal in on-site construction landfills was popular with both developers and contractors. It allowed the contractor to reduce the costs of construction debris disposal because dumpsters were not required for all waste and there were lower haulage or disposal charges. As soon as construction was completed, the landfill site was easily closed (covered). Some people continued this practice even when state and/or local ordinances discouraged or prohibited it because the laws were not actively enforced.

The construction contract should absolutely forbid the on-site disposal of construction wastes. Although a landfill on site may save some money for the contractor, the owner faces a liability risk in the future.

When on-site disposal is used, there is no way to monitor what is disposed in the property. Because there is also no guarantee that the landfill does not represent some risk (e.g., the ground sinking, chemicals leaching into the soil and/or groundwater, methane off-gassing), its presence is unacceptable.

Recycling.   The issue of construction waste is attracting the attention of environmentalists around the country. More and more, people are aware that large quantities of aluminum, copper, rubber, steel, paper, cardboard, and other building materials are being disposed rather than recycled. Because legislators at the state and federal levels are introducing and passing many recycling laws, it is only a matter of time before it is a requirement to recycle construction wastes.

The expense of recycling is less than one might think. Much of the waste can be separated at the source fairly easily. The costs of additional dumpsters, special containers, and the extra time required for separation can be recouped to a great degree (if not entirely) by using recyclers who purchase specific wastes. In some instances, recycling companies may supply their own dumpsters, etc., at no charge to the developer.

Not only is recycling a good thing for the environment, it is also a great way for developers to establish a positive image within the community. The process of recycling may eventually result in reductions in material costs as well as shipping and distribution costs (in the areas where recycling plants are located). Recycling can be required by special clauses in construction contracts and is easily monitored by construction managers.

Special machinery has been developed for construction processes such as demolition, where waste separation is much more difficult. One example is a giant shredder that is capable of grinding metal, brick, wood, steel, asphalt, and other types of construction debris into a "mulch." While this "mulch" is not recyclable, the construction debris occupies about 10 percent of its original volume. Volume reduction lowers the cost of landfill disposal of specific wastes and thus extends the life of available landfill sites. The mulch may also be incinerated at greatly reduced costs.

Fill Dirt.   It is common for construction projects to require that fill dirt be brought in for grading, landscaping, or other purposes. This is a relatively minor issue.

Nevertheless, contracts should require the contractor to warrant that any fill brought in from off site is free of environmental contamination. The contract should guarantee that the owner will face no liability for contaminated fill at any time in the future. In order to enforce the warranty, the precise location of all sites filled with off-site material on the property should be noted on the construction drawings and certified by the project manager in writing at the time it is brought in.

This may require the contractor to test the entire supply before use, test each load of fill brought to the property, or obtain certification from the supplier that fill is "clean." This may increase the costs of fill somewhat, but the incremental cost is minimal compared to the problems associated with contaminated soil. The ratio of cost to potential benefit is certainly acceptable.

It is also important for the contract to state that the contractor assumes responsibility for soil that is removed from the subject property to be used as fill elsewhere; it should not be the responsibility of the owner. The owner should be exempted indefinitely from liability as a potentially responsible party (PRP).

A simple question arises: If an environmental assessment is done and the soil tests clean before being taken to another site, why is it necessary to get a waiver of liability for future contamination? The answer is simple: Environmental law states that *anyone* who has contributed off-site material to a site that has been determined to be contaminated is considered a potentially responsible party and can be assessed a share of the cleanup costs.

Even when there is proof that the subject soil was not contaminated, the cost of attorneys' fees and court time may still be quite high. When the contractor is liable, those costs are not the owner's concern. The courts have generally upheld waivers that address such issues in clear, concise terms.

General Waiver.   A general waiver of liability for contractor-caused environmental problems is a must for all construction projects. This may be included in the "indemnity" or "warranty" section of the contract by inserting the phrase "including environmental liability, cleanup, or other environmental responsibilities" in the appropriate place(s) in the contract.

Also added to the warranty section should be the contractor's warranty that no asbestos-containing material (ACM) was used in the construction process. In light of asbestos-related legislation and the availability of materials that are not ACMs, this should be added to the contract if it is not already included. It should not be a negotiable issue.

Most standard form contracts cover the necessary items as standard clauses, especially the AIA-approved contracts. However, AIA contracts have not yet accounted for environmental issues in a manner that specifies such issues individually. The contract changes suggested here are relatively easy to insert; furthermore, they should not affect costs in any significant way. They assume that the owner is adequately protected from developmental liability involving the construction contractor with warranties that survive the completion of the project. As long as the courts tend to involve those with the "deepest pockets" in litigation, such warranties will be welcome contract additions for owners who encounter construction-related environmental problems after the project is completed.

Leasing Considerations

One of the most important things an owner or manager can do to provide protection from environmental liability is to implement a strict set of procedures for screening lease applicants and negotiating leases with prospective tenants (lessees). It is just as important to ascertain that no problems exist as it is to avoid creating new problems. In order to achieve both these goals, safeguards must be built into a leasing program and strictly enforced. The proper use of lease clauses can provide both owner and manager with proper protection.

A common argument against environmental clauses in leases is that such clauses are often noticed by potential tenants who invariably attempt to negotiate around them. While this may be true, it is essential to recognize that a tenant who will pay thousands of dollars in rent over the term of a lease could create environmental problems that cost the property owner hundreds of thousands of dollars.

Some leases do not have environmental clauses. As a result, it is also worthwhile to understand that lease clauses that are commonly used in the industry can provide some liability protection for the owner and manager. The key is knowing how to use them.

THE LEASE APPLICATION

Almost all management and leasing companies require a lease application from prospective tenants. The truth is that so many businesses find themselves in financial and/or environmental trouble, even the most well-known companies should be required to complete an application. It is wise to remember that applicants with solid credit may still have divisions or subsidiaries that have problems or might create them.

Most of this discussion concerning the application and screening process will not pertain to residential leasing. While it is absolutely essential to investigate environmental issues prior to leasing space in an industrial park, it is not necessary to conduct the same kinds of investigations prior to leasing apartments. An applicant for an apartment lease would not be asked to fill out a statement of proposed use, for example. Nevertheless, it is important for the owner and manager to reduce their exposure to liabilities that might be incurred as a result of residential tenant activities. Because such protection can be secured through the lease itself, issues that relate to residential properties will be addressed later in the chapter during the discussion regarding standard lease clauses.

In the case of certain tenants (especially industrial and, to some extent, retail and office), it is necessary to obtain information regarding potential environmental problems prior to leasing. Including a series of environmental questions in the lease application form is the first step toward securing such information. These questions should be brief (subsequent inquiries can be made later) and applicants should be required to answer them. When requested information is not applicable to the tenant's operation, it should be so noted. It is also important to give special attention to each applicant's statement of "use" to assure that it is sufficiently detailed to reveal possible areas of concern.

Description of Use

The portion of the application in which the prospective tenant describes the proposed use for the leased space should be detailed without being cumbersome. It should be written in such a way that the applicant does not have to make judgment calls concerning what information to share. An itemized questionnaire such as *Example Statement—Proposed Use of Premises, Exhibit 7.1,* is one way to handle this section of the application.

The information provided by the applicant can be used to estimate the potential for his or her business to create environmental liabilities for the owner and/or manager. When the risk of liability seems high, additional information should be requested from the applicant to better understand the extent of the risk. If the applicant becomes a tenant, all this information will help the property manager know what to look for during routine environmental inspections.

Some prospective tenants may be puzzled by some of the questions related to their proposed use of the premises (see exhibit 7.1). Most office tenants and many retail tenants will be unaware of such things as waste generator

E X H I B I T   7.1

Example Statement—Proposed Use of Premises

The proposed use of the premises is described as indicated below. Applicant acknowledges that any future change in the nature of the use must be approved by the owner prior to said change. (If more room is needed for answers, please attach additional sheets.)
1. Nature of use (general office, retail sales, storage/distribution, light manufacturing, etc.)

2. Applicant's SIC (Standard Industrial Classification) code, if applicable.

3. Applicant's waste generator number (if applicable) _____
4. Applicant's generator status (please check one)
   Large Quantity Generator (greater than 1,000 kg/month) _____
   Small Quantity Generator (less than 1,000 kg/month)   _____
   Not Applicable   _____
5. List chemicals to be used and/or stored on site that require OSHA Material Safety Data Sheets (MSDS). _____

6. List all permits required to operate the business other than state and local business permits. _____

7. List all waste disposal contractors used, other than general municipal trash disposal.

Adapted with permission from Trammell Crow Company (Charlotte Division).

---

status and material safety data sheets (MSDSs). This need not present a problem if a manager or leasing professional goes over the form with each applicant and crosses out those sections that are not applicable.

If the applicant has a waste generator number, it will be one of the most significant pieces of information derived from the application. All operations that generate hazardous or listed wastes are assigned such a number—especially operations that generate wastes requiring a special means of disposal. Once an applicant has provided a waste generator number, he or she must also include generator status, OSHA material safety data sheets (MSDSs), and waste disposal contract information on the application. (Note: A definition of MSDSs appeared in chapter 1 with an example.) If this information is not included on the application, it should definitely be requested. If the applicant insists that the information provided is complete without these details, the owner and/or manager should ask why the business has a generator number if no hazardous wastes will be produced or kept on site.

It should be noted that it may be necessary to require one or more material safety data sheets (MSDSs) even if the applicant does not have a generator number or special disposal contract. If a waste generator number is provided, however, it almost always means that the operation involves the use of one or more substances for which an MSDS would be required.

Environmental Questions

To maintain a system of checks and balances in the application process, the lease application should also include specific questions related to environmental issues. Although some environmental questions may seem to overlap inquiries made in the use section of the application, it is important to address environmental issues specifically and directly. Environmental questions may be grouped together on the application or they may be interspersed throughout the form. The point is that these questions must be asked. Like some of the questions in the "use" section of the application, environmental inquiries will not be applicable to all tenants. Nevertheless, it is absolutely essential to ask certain tenants—especially industrial ones—about environmental issues. Such questions should be a part of the application form.

Under environmental law, there are those operations that require special permits. These permits specify standards and provide for monitoring to assure compliance. Permits that are required by the Clean Air Act, Clean Water Act, etc., are pollution control or discharge permits. Such permits may be required to enable the tenant to perform certain necessary procedures, but they are not necessarily required for the basic operations of the business at hand. As a result, a reference to such a permit might not appear in the use section of the application. This makes a separate question regarding environmental permitting absolutely necessary.

A question regarding the use of regulated materials should also be included in the application, as should a request for a list of all substances used that require MSDSs. The applicant should be asked to explain any special requirements associated with materials that would be stored on site. It is important for the owner and/or manager to have all this information; a simple list of substances does not provide sufficient information to identify substances of special concern.

The application should ask whether any special handling, storage, or safety controls are required for the particular materials that will be kept on site. Fire codes may dictate the use of "explosion-proof" space for the storage of certain substances, or special ventilation may be required to prevent the accumulation of explosive or toxic fumes. The presence of some substances calls for additional fire prevention precautions such as special sprinkler systems. There are also those substances that pose environmental problems when they interact with certain other substances (even though they present no threat individually). A question concerning the on-site presence of potentially hazardous combinations should also be included in the application.

A specific question concerning the company's record of environmental violations and fines is a must. The assessment of environmental fines and other penalties can have a tremendous impact on an entire organization. In some cases, fines have pushed companies into bankruptcy and out of business. Incurring fines is something that will affect all divisions and subsidiaries and not just one portion of the company. Hence, a companywide compliance history is important. The lease application should ask for a companywide list of all fines assessed by environmental agencies and all notices of violation (NOVs).

The application should conclude with a statement in which the applicant attests to the completeness and validity of the information he or she has disclosed with a space for a signature and a date. The applicant's signature provides additional protection against liability. A signed lease application that outlines the tenant's self-described environmental profile will provide court evidence that the owner and/or manager made every effort to assure that the property would not become an environmental problem.

When lease application information indicates that the applicant might create environmental problems, a visit to the current site of the applicant's operations is vital. The condition of the facility and the manner in which the applicant conducts operations will indicate the type of tenant that the applicant is likely to become. It is wise to conduct an environmental inspection of the applicant's current space and operation as well (the applicant's permission should be obtained beforehand). From such an inspection, the owner and/or manager can gain a sense of the applicant's strengths and weaknesses.

Potential problems can be addressed in the lease itself, through specific rules and regulations and with special monitoring. A warning sign for every owner and/or manager is a prospective tenant who takes issue with all lease terms that relate to environmental issues.

SCREENING PROSPECTIVE TENANTS

Environmental law provides for the compilation of information regarding environmental issues at the state and national level. The National Priority List (NPL), Superfund, and RCRA all require certain lists to be kept and updated. Many hazardous waste sites not included on the NPL are recorded through the Comprehensive Environmental Response, Compensation and Liability Information System (CERCLIS) as well as various state and local agencies. Most states maintain a list of all large and small quantity hazardous waste generators (LQGs, SQGs) located within their boundaries. These lists are commonly organized by business name, generator number, and county and are usually updated quarterly; some states also cross-reference by address or zip code.

For a nominal fee, most states will provide an owner or manager with a computer printout of all the listed LQGs and SQGs in the state. While state listings are more likely to be accurate and up-to-date, one can obtain a copy of the federal RCRA listing by contacting an EPA office.

Once an owner and/or manager has a list of generators of hazardous waste on file (referred to as a generator list), it is easy to check all the applicants against it. Prospective tenants who complete applications giving false or partial responses should be questioned at length, or an investigation should be made to determine why the information was not provided. It is possible for some people to misunderstand the application. If this is the case, it may be an indication that the applicant does not have a complete comprehension of applicable law. Such misunderstandings are most common in retailing and among small business operators.

If the owner and/or manager still have concerns regarding an applicant whose name does not appear on the generator list, the applicant can be checked through state and federal agencies (such requests must be in writing). Because the procedures for requesting such a check vary from state to state, it is best to contact the appropriate state agency or department and the regional office of the EPA to learn the correct procedure. Unfortunately, dealings with governmental agencies are not always expeditious. Sometimes the timing of a lease deal may curb efforts to conduct an extra check on an applicant.

Even when a supplementary check reveals no evidence that the applicant has ever generated hazardous waste, the applicant could still cause problems as a tenant. This explains the importance of documentation of any extra investigation regarding the applicant and a signed lease application; it gives credibility to the owner's claim that "all appropriate inquiry" was made. Such evidence can make or break an environmental liability case. By performing a PSA or Phase I prior to purchasing a property, the owner has a good idea of the current environmental status or baseline of his or her property. An applicant screening process should focus on those prospective tenants who are actively generating hazardous materials; they are most likely to change the property's environmental status (as tenants).

THE ENVIRONMENTAL LEASE CLAUSE

The lease document controls the relationships between tenant and owner and tenant and manager. It is the most important document a manager has for enforcing such requirements as timely rent payment and proper maintenance of the property. The typical lease also provides key protections for both owner and manager; it should protect them from environmental liability as well.

A special environmental clause should be part of every lease in addition to those lease clauses that are standard in the industry (e.g., use, liability, inspection, estoppel). The intent is to protect both owner and manager from any liability associated with a tenant's environmental negligence. When used in conjunction with a prepurchase environmental audit and periodic written reports on environmental inspections, such specific lease clauses help the owner (and the manager) develop the best "innocent landowner" defense possible. In fact, the management contract negotiated between owner and manager should require an environmental clause in all tenants' leases. [Note: Those issues that are unique to property management—including the management contract—are addressed in chapters 8 and 9. While it is true that managers negotiate their management agreements prior to engaging in leasing activity, it is important to have a thorough understanding of the leasing process before management contract negotiations begin.]

Due to the sensitive nature of environmental issues and some lack of knowledge on the part of property owners in this regard, many leases still in use do not contain an environmental section. Many owners and leasing representatives prefer to ignore environmental issues when negotiating leases rather than work out the details of such clauses.

The first step toward developing an environmental clause for a lease form is to look at the property's loan documents. While reviewing a purchaser's proposal for property financing, most lenders ask for evidence of environmental language in the leases. Lenders are likely to require an environmental clause in addition to the standard lease clauses and may specify minimum acceptable standards for such a clause (this is especially true in the case of loans made after 1990). Such requirements must be met to avoid defaulting on the loan. Because the best defense is a good offense, a conservative lender will require an environmental clause that uses clear, direct language (see Appendix A, Example Lease Clause—Environmental).

Any environmental language incorporated into a lease document should be reviewed by an attorney to assure that it is enforceable and that all applicable local, state, and federal laws are addressed. Once a clause is added to the lease document, a legal opinion should be obtained regarding those points that are negotiable. Leasing agents and individuals authorized to lease a property should be informed of the negotiability of every part of the lease.

It is important to remember that no lease or other document will relieve the owner of absolute liability. For the manager, only prudent management practices and consistent efforts to avoid liability can reduce his or her exposure. It is necessary to make these practices routine and require others to act responsibly (through contractual obligations to do so). While property management may be less risky than property ownership or development, avoidance of environmental liability is an ongoing process that never provides guarantees. The courts have cited "reasonable influence" in the past to attach liability to otherwise "protected" parties. Once again, the tendency to include those with "deep pockets" will most surely mean that this will continue. It is crucial for the management company and the property manager to understand how to provide protection for themselves.

A good environmental clause will allow the owner some means of recovering the costs from the tenant responsible for a problem. While clauses with highly specific language tend to be more enforceable, they are also more likely to disturb applicants and become an issue of negotiation. An environmental attorney should be consulted before any points are negotiated away.

The issues commonly addressed in an environmental lease clause are: (1) definition of terms, (2) description of tenant activity, (3) indemnification of the owner, (4) establishment of tenant liability, and (5) conditions or actions that comprise default. The property's location may dictate the inclusion of additional issues (e.g., a recycling clause). The decision to omit any of the key issues noted here should be evaluated by the attorney.

Definitions

An environmental lease clause should identify the important terms used and include definitions of words and references to specific laws. The definitions most commonly covered are those for "hazardous material," "hazardous waste," "release," "treatment, storage, or disposal (TSD) facility," and "environmental laws." Of these terms, the most important is "environmental laws." A detailed list of what is referred to by "environmental laws" allows the phrase to be used throughout the lease without confusion.

In general, the term "environmental laws" is defined as: "A body of laws that includes the following: Comprehensive Environmental Response, Compensation, and Liability Act (CERCLA); Superfund Amendments and Reauthorization Act (SARA); Clean Air Act (CAA); Clean Water Act (CWA); Toxic Substances Control Act (TSCA); Solid Waste Disposal Act (SWDA); Resource Conservation and Recovery Act (RCRA); Occupational Safety and Health Act (OSHA); all amendments and additions to the aforementioned; and all other environmental regulations promulgated on a local, state, or federal level." Thus, an acceptable definition of the term "release" (as used in the lease) would be: "A discharge into the environment of any substance that is deemed to be hazardous under current environmental laws." Other definitions of terms would be handled similarly.

Tenant Activity

The environmental clause should address the activities that the tenant will perform on site. It is necessary to state that the tenant will not perform any activity that could result in a release of a hazardous material, discharge of a pollutant, or violation of current environmental laws. The clause should also state that the tenant will not engage in any activity that could qualify the property as a treatment, storage, or disposal facility under current environmental laws.

This statement of the parameters of the tenant's activities should include the provision that the tenant is solely responsible for complying with any and all current environmental laws and obtaining and maintaining all applicable licenses and permits required for business operations. Any notices of noncompliance or notices of violations must be shared with the owner and manager. Such notification should be made personally and in writing to assure communication within two business days.

Blanket Indemnity

The lease clause should include blanket indemnification of the owner and his or her agents for any violations of current environmental laws that are perpetrated by the tenant or for any suits or other actions directed against the tenant. It should provide a *hold harmless* statement (a declaration that someone is not liable for things beyond his or her control), protecting the owner and manager from liability for problems caused by the tenant. The owner and manager may also set insurance requirements for the tenant that would be stated in this clause. All of the tenant's insurance should list the owner and manager as additional named insured parties. Certificates of insurance should be required as proof of appropriate coverage.

Some tenants will demand their own written indemnification from liability incurred because of any conditions that existed prior to signing the lease. Such a tenant may insist that results from recent environmental testing or site assessments are stated in the lease to establish a "baseline" of existing environmental problems. This addition to the lease creates a means to identify those liabilities from which the tenant is indemnified. Although few owners automatically include a tenant indemnification in all leases, many owners are likely to respond positively to requests for such additions.

Tenant Liability

The environmental clause should set forth the tenant's strict liability for the costs of any environmental assessments, testing, remediation, fines, and attorney's fees that are incurred as a result of the tenant's activities. Such possible costs should be described in detail because the courts tend to honor contractual language that is highly specific. As previously stated, some tenants will insist on written indemnification from any liability for environmental costs that are a result of someone else's activities.

Default

The clause should state that violation of any environmental law will constitute a default of the lease agreement by the tenant. Remedies of such default should be stated. While the environmental clause may refer to a standard default clause already in the lease, it should add that the tenant's liability for costs incurred will survive the termination of the lease. This is an important point and one that is not negotiable because certain environmental problems may not be immediately discoverable.

USING STANDARD LEASE CLAUSES

Unfortunately for property owners and managers, some tenants may very well have current leases that do not include formal environmental liability protection in the form of specific environmental clauses. Consider the industrial tenant who has a long-term lease that predates environmental awareness or the residential tenant who is not likely to have an environmental clause in his or her lease. For this reason, it is important to understand that leases without specific environmental language can sometimes protect the owner's rights when environmental problems occur. This knowledge is extremely useful in many different situations.

It is essential to recognize that any advice concerning the use of "nonenvironmental" lease clauses in environmental situations does not replace the recommendation to include specific environmental language in leases. In truth, "nonenvironmental" clauses will not always apply successfully to environmental situations, but their possible applicability is something one might wish to pursue. Leases are likely to be interpreted according to the intention of the parties at the time of execution of the agreement; it may be challenging to derive new rights from a lease. Consequently, the development of a strategy to use a "nonenvironmental" lease clause in an environmental context should be done carefully and with the assistance of an attorney. In addition, state and local laws must be taken into consideration.

Certain basic clauses appear in most leases. Such "standard" clauses include use, alterations, inspection, liability, estoppel, and confidentiality. Different leases may assign varying names to these clauses, but most will contain clauses that are parallel in content. The following sections suggest ways that these lease clauses might be used to provide protection from environmental liability.

Use

Use clauses have historically been somewhat vague regarding the actual, day-to-day operations of the tenant on the premises. In some instances, the use clause may not even contain a description of the tenant's particular type of business. Instead, it might include a generic characterization assumed to fit the kinds of operations that are typically performed in the given building type. If this is the case, the use clause should be modified to include a description of the tenant's operation. "General office/warehouse" and "general retail sales" are inadequate descriptions that could characterize hundreds of very diverse businesses. A phrase such as "retail dry cleaning and laundry, including plant," however, provides a description that identifies the tenant fairly accurately. By providing this type of description for every tenant in the project, the owner is protected from changes in a tenant's business operations that may pose environmental problems.

Most use clauses will generally cover the following points.

1. The tenant is required to maintain any and all necessary permits and licenses.
2. The tenant must comply with all governmental laws and regulations at the tenant's sole expense.
3. The tenant will not emit any noxious odors, smoke, noise, etc., or perform any action that would harm the other tenants or the building.
4. When the tenant's use raises the costs of insurance, the tenant is liable for the entire amount of the increase.

Most managers do not read the use clause with environmental considerations in mind. Once considered from this perspective, however, such applications for the use clause become more obvious.

Unless the clause specifies the permits and licenses that are required (most do not), the use clause may be applied to environmental permits and licenses as well. It also gives the owner and manager the implied right to verify that such licenses and permits are indeed current and to require the tenant to update them as necessary. A violation of the clause is a technical default of the lease.

Most use clauses require the tenant to comply with all governmental laws and regulations and to correct any areas of noncompliance (at the tenant's sole expense). Again, unless specific laws are identified, this portion of the clause will apply to environmental laws as well as all others. Noncompliance is an enforceable default of the lease.

Noxious odors, smoke, noise, etc., are forbidden by most use clauses, as are actions that could potentially harm other tenants or the project. Regardless of the actual impact, environmental violations have the potential to affect not only humans and the environment, but also the integrity of the property's environmental status. Legal precedent has established that environmental violations constitute damage and loss.

Finally, the use clause will probably address the issue of tenants who add to the cost of the building's insurance and require such tenants to reimburse the increased insurance costs. Some leases may specify fire and extended coverage premiums in this portion of the clause and, if they do, it may be difficult to seek reimbursement on insurance related to environmental risk. If types of insurance are not specified, however, and the tenant poses sufficient risk to warrant the purchase of additional pollution or other environmental insurance, the extra cost of this insurance could be passed through to the tenant.

The problems encountered when seeking insurance reimbursements have to do with proving the risk sufficient to dictate extra coverage. The tenant may argue that environmental risk could have been anticipated in advance and appropriate action should have been taken during lease negotiations. Because both insurance underwriting and lease law are highly technical in nature, it is advisable to check with an attorney before trying to enforce insurance payment reimbursement.

There is some precedent for utilizing the use clause to address environmental issues. It is wise, however, to consult an environmental attorney before applying the use clause in this way. While it does provide environmental protection, the lack of specific environmental language makes legal action more difficult.

Alterations or Construction

There are many different names for clauses that deal with alterations made by tenants. The essence of such clauses, however, is fairly constant—they set guidelines for all alterations that the tenant wishes to make to the premises. An alterations clause may require the tenant to seek owner consent prior to making any alterations; it may also demand restoration of the premises to their original condition when the lease is terminated.

Although it may seem like a subtle interpretation, the environmental contamination of a property can be considered an "alteration." "Alteration" is generally defined as the act or procedure of making different or modifying. It can certainly be argued that contaminating a property is making a change and a modification in perception, value, and usefulness. It would be rather difficult to imagine a tenant requesting and receiving permission to contaminate a property. Therefore most contamination would be a violation of any lease that prohibited alterations without owner approval.

Such clauses often state that any alterations must be removed and the property returned to its original condition when the lease is terminated. Restoring space to its original condition excludes the necessity to compensate for "normal" wear and tear. Because environmental contamination is not recognized by law as "normal," it can be argued that the tenant should be required to cover the costs of remediation.

Again, the lack of specific environmental language in most alterations clauses creates the need for an attorney's services before any action is taken. Nevertheless, an alterations clause can be used to support valid claims against tenants who have contaminated the property and is a method for an owner to recover costs of remediation from a tenant.

Inspection

In many instances, there will be no visible indication from the exterior of a building that environmentally unsound practices are occurring inside it. It is the inspection clause that gives an owner and/or manager the right to view a tenant's space and observe operations. Under this clause, the manager has the right to conduct the interior portions of inspections. Although this clause has no particular use for assigning liability to the tenant, it creates opportunities for owners and/or managers to prevent problems from occurring. It is important to remember that an inspection clause may neither imply nor state the tenant's consent to the performance of environmental assessments. Nevertheless, inspection clauses do grant owners and managers the right to inspect the premises. During a standard inspection, the environmentally aware owner or manager may note indications of possible environmental problems.

Liability

The "liability" clause assigns liability to the tenant for damage to persons or property caused by the tenant. It generally provides for the collection of the owner's damages and attorneys' fees for any suits or other actions required as a result of the tenant's actions. Because the courts tend to define environmental damage as "damages" in the legal sense, the tenant may be held liable under this clause for costs that are the result of environmental problems. In most cases, liability clauses also state that proof of insurance must be made available to the owner and manager and that the owner and manager must be included as additional named insured parties.

Problems in collecting for environmental damages under the liability clause occur because most insurance policies specifically exclude pollution and environmental contamination from coverage and may not pay damages under those circumstances. For this reason, the high-risk tenant who signs a lease without an environmental clause should be required to carry insurance that does cover environmental problems. Given that the owner has legal recourse through both the use and the liability clauses of the lease, the need for special insurance should seem obvious to the tenant, but this is not always the case. As always, the owner and manager should require certificates of insurance to verify coverage.

Confidentiality

Most leases include a confidentiality clause that prevents tenants from discussing lease terms and other sensitive items with other tenants or outside parties. Some leases make the confidential nature of the tenant-owner-manager relationship reciprocal or binding on all parties while others do not. When environmental issues are involved, it is helpful to have a reciprocal clause.

Environmental issues are so sensitive that confidentiality regarding disclosures in this area should be required by one or both parties. When the issue of confidentiality is questionable, involved parties often prefer to risk penalties for nondisclosure rather than release sensitive information. This is especially true when a tenant believes trade secrets to be involved. There have been cases in which tenants have ignored requirements of the U.S. EPA just to protect such secrets.

From the owner's or manager's perspective, it is important that information regarding environmental problems is not freely given out to the general public. In many instances, a problem may be easily rectified with little or no potential for harm to tenants, the community, or the property. When a property is associated with environmental problems, the negative perception of that property may reduce its value. When disclosure it not required by law, it is always best to maintain the confidentiality of environmental problems that are not harmful.

As a result, a binding confidentiality clause for both environmental and nonenvironmental issues is a wise addition to a lease. Confidentiality clauses that are not reciprocal should be modified; ideally they should also include a special reference to the confidentiality of environmental issues.

Estoppel

The lease clause that requires the tenant to provide the owner and/or manager with an estoppel certificate offers unique possibilities in the environmental arena. Unlike the other so-called "standard" lease clauses that have been discussed in this chapter (use, alteration, inspection, liability, and confidentiality), estoppel clauses are not likely to be included in residential leases. Nevertheless, requiring the inclusion of estoppel clauses in industrial, retail, or office leases provides various opportunities for environmental protection. In particular, the vagueness of the language in most estoppel clauses provides a means to apply their contents to environmental situations (see Appendix B, Example Lease Clause—Estoppel).

The purpose of an estoppel clause is to give the owner and/or manager the right to request estoppel certificates from tenants. In this context, an estoppel certificate is a statement from the tenant certifying some aspect(s) of the status of the lease. Often the owner and/or manager prepares a certificate and sends it to the tenant to be completed (as necessary), signed, and returned within a specified amount of time. The tenant is thereafter prevented from claiming something other than that which is stated in the estoppel certificate. Because most estoppel clauses allow the owner and/or manager to request any necessary information that pertains to the lease, it provides a means to obtain critical information regarding environmental problems.

The estoppel clause paves the way for the owner and/or manager to procure a document as useful as it is unique—the environmental estoppel certificate. This is the name frequently given to those estoppel certificates that state environmental information. Such certificates are extremely useful for owners and managers who seek critical information and wish to protect themselves from environmental liability. Environmental estoppel certificates are also considered a worthwhile sales and marketing tool because they provide assurance to others who have interest in the property (e.g., prospective tenants who are concerned about other tenants in the project, potential purchasers of the property, and lenders).

Ideally, lease estoppel clauses would include a requirement for tenants to confirm the current environmental status of their operations on the leased premises. Failure to supply the estoppel certificate constitutes a violation of the lease and gives the owner and/or manager the means to evict the tenant if the situation warrants.

The owner or manager might request an environmental estoppel certificate from tenants or send them a form to be completed within a prescribed period of time. An environmental estoppel certificate should cover the information pertaining to the status of the lease *plus* additional declarations concerning the tenants' environmental compliance status (see Appendix C, Example Environmental Estoppel Certificate). The certificate may be condensed, expanded, or otherwise modified to fit the particular situation. There is no specific requirement to obtain one from every tenant in a multitenanted project unless otherwise stated in the lease. As with all documents, an attorney should review the certificate prior to its use to assure its applicability to the situation and its conformation to the appropriate state and local laws.

The first portion of the estoppel certificate should include the following.

1. An identification of the lease document by date, owner, and tenant.
2. The fact that the lease is currently in full force and effect.
3. An acknowledgment that the premises have been accepted by the tenant and that the tenant is currently in possession of the space.
4. The date through which rent payments have been made and a statement that the tenant is not currently in default.
5. An affirmation that the tenant is not currently involved in bankruptcy proceedings.
6. A statement that the tenant has procured all appropriate licenses and permits to operate the business located on the premises (and that they are current).
7. A declaration of the authority of the individual signing the estoppel certificate.

The following items may be added to the estoppel certificate to document environmental issues of concern for an owner or a potential purchaser. These are the items that make the difference between a standard estoppel certificate and an "environmental" estoppel certificate.

1. Certification that no local, state, or federal notices of violation (NOVs) of environmental laws have been received. NOVs received should be attached as a separate schedule.
2. A statement that no underground storage tanks (USTs) exist or, if they

do, copies of tightness tests and paid registration fees (if applicable) should be attached in a separate schedule.

3. A declaration that all waste disposal activities are performed in compliance with local, state, and federal laws.
4. Acknowledgment that the owner and manager do not participate in the day-to-day operations of the tenant's business.

Including these issues in an estoppel certificate offers many legal advantages. In particular, the certificate may become a source of protection from environmental liability. The items regarding NOVs, waste disposal, and USTs not only provide the owner and manager with the tenant's acknowledgment of responsibility for these areas, they also require the tenants to examine their operations and review their compliance status. Some prospective tenants may have a negative reaction to environmental language in an estoppel certificate. Nevertheless, it is ultimately in each tenant's best interest to assure compliance with environmental law.

Because the property owner already assumes absolute liability for environmental problems, a tenant's certification that no one else participates in business operations becomes a significant benefit for the property owner and manager. To some extent, this also protects the manager from being assigned status as an "operator." Any documentation available that distances the management company and the manager from operator status would prove valuable if a defense from liability is needed. (A more detailed discussion of the concept of "operator" appears in chapter 8.)

In addition, an environmental estoppel certificate will provide environmental information that might otherwise be difficult or even impossible to obtain. Copies of NOVs are rarely distributed voluntarily and a simple request for them might not produce results. Such documentation may be very useful in the event of legal proceedings; even copies of written requests for information (whether or not any information was received as a result) can be beneficial to owners and managers.

ADDING MONETARY SAFEGUARDS

Lease clauses are not always perceived as a sufficient way to address possible environmental problems. Whenever there is a question of environmental liability, the primary concerns are safety and cost. Remediation, investigations, attorneys' fees, and fines can add up to many thousands of dollars. The absolute liability of the property owner is a given, regardless of the care exercised in screening tenants and placing safeguards in a lease document. How, then, is additional protection provided?

The technical nature of environmental law and the number of necessary permits, manifests, licenses, etc., leads one to the conclusion that the potential for environmental problems always exists—no matter how diligent an applicant has been in the past. Given the changing nature of environmental law, the question of future violations becomes even more uncertain. The standards by which applicants are judged today may be inadequate tomorrow.

When an applicant's operations are clearly risky, certain "monetary safeguards" may be used to reduce the owner's exposure to liability. The most common such safeguards are security deposits, irrevocable letters of credit, and bonds. When determining the monetary safeguard that is best, it is important to quantify the potential exposure. This is extremely difficult because each situation or problem is unique and environmental costs expand unpredictably. Such determinations are often made by isolating those problems that the applicant has the potential to create and averaging typical costs associated with similar problems.

First, a determination of the type of exposure is required. Although environmental risk usually involves soil and vegetation, it is crucial to assess the applicant's potential for creating human health hazards. One should determine whether the applicant's business requires USTs and, if so, whether the substance being stored will spread to groundwater if there is a leak. Even when USTs are not involved, it is necessary to evaluate the possible effects of the applicant's operations on groundwater because groundwater contamination is one of the most expensive types of problems to correct. Because groundwater contamination is generally associated with specific types of activities (e.g., any type of underground waste disposal), it is usually possible to either confirm or eliminate the potential for creating groundwater contamination. Thus, historical data can help one arrive at a cost estimate for potential exposure to soil and groundwater problems. To estimate possible expenses, the owner or manager should consider the average remediation costs for similar problems and the likelihood of the applicant to create such a problem.

Increasing the tenant's security deposit is a safeguard that offers limited effectiveness and tends to meet with resistance from prospective tenants. Although a tenant may be willing to make a security deposit equivalent to three months' rent, it is doubtful that the amount will cover environmental costs. On the other hand, it is unrealistic to expect any tenant to set aside the average cost of contamination remediation for the term of a lease.

As a result, the use of bonds and letters of credit is becoming more and more popular with tenants and owners alike. Both of these options make more money available to the owner and provide about the same security while the cost to the tenant is much lower. Usually, when dealing with estimated exposure of less than $250,000, property owners will accept bonds or letters of credit that can be held with the lease. This provides a means to cover most cleanup costs for soil contamination as well as any fines. The cost to the tenant is such that a savvy applicant is willing to do this in order to make the deal.

When estimated exposure exceeds $250,000, the owner should require an irrevocable letter of credit. A financial institution is in a much better position to cover large expenses than is a bond company or underwriter. This does not mean that irrevocable letters of credit are free of risk; even large banks and insurance companies have had their problems. Nevertheless, such institutions carry much more weight in the industry and therefore are preferable when estimated risk carries a large price tag.

The truth is that most requests for increased security deposits, letters of credit, or bonds will be met with resistance from tenants unless the owner and manager have significant cause for concern (e.g., the tenant has a history of environmental violations). Even tenants with prior problems are likely to protest. This makes it all the more important to have a strict policy on the negotiability of these issues.

TENANT REQUIREMENTS

With their heightened awareness of environmental issues, prospective tenants have become increasingly demanding during lease negotiations. The applicant who has some exposure to environmental problems is more likely to have a series of detailed requirements that must be met before the lease is signed.

Prior to leasing space, some applicants may require certain information about the premises. Typical requests are recent test results (e.g., water and indoor air quality, electromagnetic field strength) and written policies (e.g., recycling, inspection). When this information is not readily available, testing may be necessary. This will increase both the time invested in leasing and the money spent pursuing the lease.

In the case of retail and industrial properties, prospective tenants may also require copies of PSA or Phase I results. Retail and industrial tenants may demand more information because of the variety of uses and tenant types in retail and industrial projects. A prospective tenant may also request a current statement of tenant compliance (this is usually an owner's statement that should not violate any confidentiality agreements in place).

In some facilities, especially office, retail, and special use (e.g., medical), tenants are more likely to be concerned with the issue of electromagnetic field (EMF) strength in the premises. This information may be obtained by contacting the local power utility and having them perform the test. Although debate continues regarding the health effects of EMFs, the effects on phone systems and computers are generally acknowledged and may be a major concern for some tenants.

When the property includes facilities for pretreatment of wastewater, prospective tenants are more likely to request copies of permits and inspections. This is understandable because CERCLA ties liability to contractual relationships, and tenants at sites with pretreatment facilities contribute to the effluents running through those systems. Failure to provide these results or a history of violations and compliance problems may result in the loss of leasing opportunities.

Prospective tenants are most likely to request indemnification from liabilities incurred through problems caused by the owner or another tenant when leasing space in properties where there are pretreatment plants, USTs used by other tenants, or situations that involve environmental compliance by someone else. This type of indemnification was discussed earlier in the chapter. In most instances, such a warranty against liability should not be a problem if the prospective tenant is neither controlling nor contributing to the issues in question. As always, an attorney should draft the document or clause to assure that it is properly worded.

Assuming that environmental laws continue to be enacted and these issues remain in the forefront of industry concerns, tenants will continue to become more knowledgeable in the area of lease requirements. When preparing a leasing plan, it is important to take this into account and prepare for those things that a prospective tenant is likely to demand and that a savvy owner should seek.

INSURANCE FOR LEASING PERSONNEL

In most instances, a leasing agent or real estate broker does not assume environmental liability for merely marketing a real estate project. Although misrepresenting the environmental status of a property might generate some liability, it would most likely result in charges of fraud or prosecution of a lawsuit on that basis. When the leasing agent represents the property to prospective tenants as the owner has represented it to the leasing agent, all information can be presented to applicants as "to the best of the agent's knowledge."

All the same, it is probable that an environmental lawsuit filed by a tenant will include the leasing company and the leasing representative among the defendants (lawsuits tend to include everyone). This may result in attorneys' fees, court costs, and other expenses, regardless of the final court decision. For this reason, it is advisable for the leasing company and agent to carry an errors and omissions (E & O) policy—in addition to other necessary policies—to cover costs associated with such proceedings. Frequently, the courts have determined that reasonable investigation was all that was necessary to determine potential environmental problems. If the court finds a leasing agent negligent in any way, E & O insurance will go a long way toward minimizing costs associated with such judgments.

THE LEASING PROCESS

One of the most readily available safeguards for maintaining a property's current environmental status is a program of leasing that includes environmental screening and the utilization of available lease protection through environmental lease clauses. While it is important to add an environmental section to leases currently in use, older leases without specific references to environmental issues may still provide some environmental protection.

Because the owner's liability is absolute, lease negotiations on environmental matters become very important. The use of an environmental attorney is an important part of self-protection throughout the leasing process. Equally important is the development and implementation of strict leasing policies. Any viable leasing program must have both elements.

While the owner and manager wish to protect themselves from liability, they must recognize that all the players in the leasing game have the same intent. Tenants will try to minimize their exposure. Leasing agents and real estate brokers are likely to be cautious. The minute an applicant walks through the door, leasing begins; it is a process to be taken seriously every step of the way.

8

Property Management

The management of existing facilities presents some rather interesting liability questions. When this book was being written, legal precedents were insufficient to define the parameters of a manager's potential liability. It was not truly clarified in the body of environmental laws.

Under Superfund, the types of parties who may be responsible for remediation or cleanup costs are: (1) parties who transported wastes to the site (sometimes called "transporters"), (2) parties who arranged for wastes to be disposed of or treated at the site (sometimes called "generators"), and (3) present and past owners or operators of the site. A substantial amount of Superfund litigation has been devoted to attribution of liability; many courts have ruled that there is "joint and several" liability under Superfund (i.e., the obligation may be enforced against all involved parties jointly or against any one of them separately). Furthermore, Superfund provides that "any person may seek contribution from any other person who is liable or potentially liable." In light of this information, one can perceive the environmental liability risks faced by property managers.

One issue of concern is whether the management company or property manager can be considered an "owner" of the facility. An owner who manages his or her own building certainly qualifies as an owner, as does a company that uses its own employees to manage properties it owns. Nevertheless, a great many properties are managed by parties with no ownership interest. For example, one can generally assume that a fee manager would not be considered an "owner." (Admittedly, a fee manager who acts as an *agent* of the owner faces the possibility of assuming ownership status—although this is unlikely.)

If a manager is not an "owner," is he or she an "operator"? Here is the crucial liability question. A manager who participates in the day-to-day business operations of the project could potentially qualify as an operator. This would appear to be the case for the manager of an apartment building who has constant involvement in its operations. However, the manager of a retail center that includes a print shop and auto repair business is not likely to have control over the day-to-day activity on site (other than what is allowed by the lease); such a manager could argue that he or she has not acted as an "operator" of the facility.

Historically, the courts have held that individuals or entities who could reasonably be expected to influence activities at a particular site can be held liable for environmental problems (in the case of problems that could have been prevented during their period of influence). The control a management company has over tenant activities could be sufficient to result in liability for environmental problems—especially if the lease document grants that control.

Confusion arises over the subject of contractual liability. A fee manager is likely to be operating under contract with the property owner. According to Superfund, those contracts that can lead to the assumption of liability are "land contracts, deeds, or other instruments transferring title or possession." While the main emphasis has been the transfer of title or ownership, a contract that gives the manager the right to act on behalf of the owner and as a representative of the owner's rights (i.e., as an agent) could be interpreted as a kind of transference of "possession" of the property and of the owner's interest in its day-to-day operations.

Regardless of the logic that is used to arrive at assessments of liability, past actions by environmental agencies and the courts have indicated a tendency to involve as many parties as possible. With this in mind, management companies should strive to protect themselves and their personnel from the threat of liability. Protection from liability starts with the development of a carefully considered management contract and involves the execution and documentation of environmentally sound management practices. Liability exposure is reduced by establishing thorough training programs for the property managers who are in turn responsible for training maintenance and other on-site personnel.

ENVIRONMENTAL MANAGEMENT TRAINING

The avoidance of liability is the primary goal of environmental management. One might see property managers as the front-line soldiers in the environmental trenches. Property managers must be properly trained to assure that appropriate action is being taken and that all activities are thoroughly documented. It is essential for property managers to have the knowledge to help them foresee potential problems and act to prevent them (inasmuch as prevention is possible).

There are various ways to provide environmental training. Many local real estate boards offer half-day seminars on such subjects as property inspection and contamination prevention techniques. The costs are generally quite reasonable and the benefits are immeasurable.

Community colleges and universities are sources of training. Some schools offer semester-long courses that teach procedures for preventing environmental mishaps and provide an overall background regarding day-to-day techniques and practices. Most common, however, are the one- or two-day educational seminars that are designed to improve community awareness. Such seminars may be taken at little or no cost. Many times these are sponsored by local businesspeople who specialize in environmental affairs and volunteer teaching time in return for the public relations value provided for their companies.

Producing a company handbook is another good idea. If the manual is a ring binder, there will be space for supplemental material so that it can be tailored to a specific property. A handbook provides a handy reference whenever it is needed. Manuals may include such helpful additions as photographs depicting things to look for and checklists to use during inspections. Another wise inclusion is a list of phone numbers that may be useful including environmental and other "hot-line" numbers. Most importantly, a handbook documents company policies and communicates the importance of environmental management.

Regardless of the method used, training is absolutely necessary to foster environmental awareness at all levels in the management company. The education can be general in nature (highly technical knowledge is unnecessary). Without such training, however, the management company may be unable to compete effectively for management contracts. In general, training should focus on three primary topics—negotiating management contracts, conducting property inspections, and understanding insurance.

THE MANAGEMENT CONTRACT

When negotiating management contracts (also commonly called management agreements), it is essential to assess the potential environmental liability associated with property management. While a fee manager does not incur liability as an "owner," he or she faces the risk of being deemed an "operator" or involved by contractual association. An owner's liability is not likely to be affected by the contractual agreements made with a property manager. The fee manager's liability, however, can be an issue that is addressed in and affected by the management contract.

Under common law and civil law, a property manager may be liable for "toxic torts." A "tort" is generally defined as a wrongful act, not involving breach of contract, for which a civil suit can be brought. There are two types of torts—those that involve property damage (property torts) and those that involve personal injury or damages (personal torts). The only way the manager can distance himself or herself from any environmental liability that the owner incurs is to address the issue of tort liability in the management contract.

The management contract is the most important defense a fee manager has against toxic tort lawsuits. The wording of clauses protecting the management company and the manager are critical; tort law includes everything except "breach of contract." If the manager and the management company are contractually excluded from environmental liability, only a breach of contract lawsuit can include the manager in environmental issues. Hence, managers should seek such an exclusion in the form of indemnification from environmental liability (see Appendix D, Environmental Issues Addressed in Management Contracts). Consultation with an environmental attorney is also recommended. Because states are allowed to enact laws that are more stringent than federal laws, a specialist in laws of the state in which the contract will apply should review the document. Additions and/or deletions may be necessary to comply with applicable regulations. Also, some owners may be less inclined than others to accept environmental clauses in management contracts. Frequently, negotiation is necessary. Nevertheless, managers and management companies alike should be aware of such clauses because environmental issues must be taken into account during contract negotiations.

The ultimate aim of the environmental section of a management contract is to protect the fee manager from liability for situations that are beyond his or her control. This means securing specific indemnity from toxic torts and other civil suits that could be brought against the owner. It also means contractually defining the manager's operational status. As previously noted, a fee manager's liability as an "operator" or "contractual" participant is a gray area; every attempt should be made to minimize this liability.

In general, many problems can be averted by careful preparation of the contract and avoidance of certain terminology. The professional capacity of a fee manager should never be referred to using the word "operator," and the terms "operator," "operate," and "operations" should be removed from the contract altogether.

Environmental law requires the manager to pay attention to specific tenant procedures that might endanger the environment or violate current regulations. The courts have little mercy for landlords and owners who ignore harmful or illegal practices. At the very least, an owner or manager should notify the proper authorities when activities seem suspicious.

Even though it may seem to the manager that he or she is awash in a sea of paperwork, it is best to notify the tenant *in writing* when operating procedures that appear to be environmentally questionable are observed. The tenant should be informed that if these practices are not modified or terminated altogether, the property manager will report his or her observations to the appropriate local, state, or federal agency. Under no circumstances, however, should the owner or manager act in any way that suggests he or she has the authority to change the tenant's operation. To do so would be tantamount to assuming operational control and thereby qualifying as an "operator."

For this reason, it is important for the management contract to include a specific definition of the fee manager's status that exempts him or her from operator status as defined by law. This should: (1) define financial responsibility, (2) establish all the activity required in managing the asset, and (3) indemnify the manager against liability being incurred as an "operator" because of the actions of tenants or other contractually associated entities (see Appendix D).

It is clear that careful wording of the management contract can help the management company and the property manager reduce their exposure to environmental liability. In addition to managerial indemnification, other points should be addressed contractually. The text that follows examines four such issues: establishing the environmental status of the property when the manager takes over, assuring that the owner complies with prevailing laws, requiring the owner to properly insure the property, and agreeing on a standard lease form that addresses environmental issues.

Environmental Status of the Property

Before a manager can complete the negotiation of a management contract, he or she must be familiar with the property. It is important to inspect the property to evaluate its condition; it is just as essential to do an environmental profile of the property. In the case of newly purchased or refinanced properties, chances are good that an environmental assessment has been done for the property. A copy of that assessment should be made available to the manager or management company upon request. While an in-depth site visit may not be possible, a general understanding of the property's condition may still be obtained from inspecting the property and/or reviewing the results of a PSA. In some cases, an assessment will not be available. Some management companies are willing to assume the cost of performing a PSA because they believe it to be a worthwhile expense. The owner who permits a management company to perform a PSA on his or her property is likely to insist on ownership of the PSA if no contract is signed with the management company; such an owner is also wise to obtain a statement of confidentiality from the management company. Obviously, owner's consent is necessary before any kind of inspection or assessment can be performed. When an owner refuses to allow such activity on his or her property (performed at the management company's expense), it may signal the existence of a problem.

Areas of primary concern in contract negotiations include the presence of asbestos-containing materials (ACMs), polychlorinated biphenyls (PCBs), and underground storage tanks (USTs), as well as tenants that qualify as large quantity generators (LQGs) or small quantity generators (SQGs) under the hazardous waste generator guidelines. It is important to discover these situations prior to entering into a management agreement so the manager can secure adequate environmental protection. A clear delineation of the current status of the property is essential.

Once the current status is established, this baseline serves as the standard for judging future environmental situations. Determining whether the environmental status of a property has improved or deteriorated may influence the outcome of toxic tort lawsuits. Thus, it is important to delineate current environmental status in the management contract and document future environmental issues as they occur.

Assume that ACMs, PCBs, or USTs are located on the property and one of the following situations exists: (1) they do not require removal, (2) the owner refuses to remove them (note: in the case of transformers containing PCBs, the utility may be the owner) or, (3) they are currently in use (a typical situation with USTs). Such situations demand that the management contract include the specifics of an operation and maintenance program that meets state and federal requirements. The contract should require the property owner to absorb the costs and perform periodic environmental audits of known problems.

Compliance with Regulations

Environmental law is fluid and constantly changing. What may be perfectly acceptable and legal today, may be a criminal offense tomorrow. Inasmuch as it is possible, the management contract should take the changing nature of environmental law into account. This means requiring that the owner absolutely comply with changes in regulations. Failure to do so should provide grounds for releasing the manager and the management company from contractual obligations based on owner default and breach of contract.

An example of regulatory change that affected the property owner rather than the tenant is the EPA storm water drainage regulation published in the November 16, 1990, *Federal Register*. The EPA changed storm water drainage regulations so that certain properties and property types were suddenly required to obtain NPDES permits for storm water draining from the property into public storm sewers. While most commercial leases will allow the costs of such permits to be passed through to the tenants, it is the property owner's responsibility to obtain and maintain the permits and to absorb all costs in the case of a residential property.

The cost of NPDES permitting can be high in some instances and the process generally requires the assistance of an experienced attorney and/or engineer. In the case of the storm water drainage regulation, the EPA allowed a set period of time (one year) for everyone to comply with the law. In such situations, some owners may have a tendency to procrastinate. The manager must assure that the owner attends to the process in a timely manner.

In the event the owner does not comply with a regulation by the appointed time, fines may be assessed against anyone associated with the property, including the fee manager and the tenants. Such fines can be sizable. It is easy to understand why a management firm should require the owner to comply with the law. Owners who violate this portion of the management agreement risk default on their part and breach of contract.

The owner compliance clause should be included in an environmental section of the management contract (see Appendix D) and should cover three basic areas: (1) definition of owner default, (2) notification and period in which to cure default, and (3) remedies available to the fee manager in case of owner default. The clause should add that default as defined by the conditions indicated will also be construed as a breach of contract. This protects the fee manager because it distances him or her from the violation and provides a means to recoup any costs associated with penalties resulting from the violation. Ultimately, it also protects the owner because it provides an extra incentive to comply with the law and to avoid the assessment of penalties.

Owner Responsibility for Insurance

Insurance is a topic that will be addressed later in this chapter; at this point, however, it is necessary to mention that insurance is an issue that must be referenced in the management agreement. The owner should be contractually required to maintain adequate insurance coverage on the property. The management contract should specify all the types of insurance that the owner must carry (e.g., property damage, comprehensive general liability, boiler, umbrella liability, and any other coverages necessary to adequately protect the property). It should also require the fee manager to be identified as an additional named insured party on all property policies.

Some management contracts call for the owner to carry errors and omissions (E & O) insurance for the property manager and, if ACMs are present, asbestos insurance for the property. In the presence of heavy industry, pollution insurance may also be required. Such coverage is advisable. These policies should also carry the fee manager as an additional named insured party and should disallow *subrogation* on environmental claims. Subrogation is the right of the insurer to attempt to recover amounts paid to the insured through a third party. Should subrogation be prohibited, the owner's insurer would be prevented from attempting to recoup payments through the property manager or the management company (as a third party involved).

A disallowance of subrogation is especially important in light of the size of environmental claims (often in millions of dollars). Because coverage under E & O insurance and asbestos insurance extends only to the limits of the policies, it is conceivable that both the owner's and the fee manager's policies could be needed to settle a lawsuit.

Finally, the management agreement should specify amounts of coverage. Should the owner request it, the fee manager's insurance policies may also include the owner as an additional named insured party.

Contents of a Standard Lease

The management contract should require the owner to include an environmental clause in certain types of leases for tenants (environmental lease clauses were discussed in detail in chapter 7; Appendix A provides an example of such a clause). It is absolutely essential for an environmental clause to be included in leases for high-risk tenants (e.g., all industrial tenants, some office and retail tenants). While most residential leases do not include specific references to environmental concerns, some may have simplified environmental clauses. The issue of an environmental lease clause should be discussed by the owner and the prospective property manager and addressed in the management contract. It is important for owners and managers alike to understand this crucial means of providing liability protection.

ENVIRONMENTAL INSPECTIONS

Once the manager takes over a property, ongoing environmental inspections are an important part of minimizing liability or avoiding it altogether. When a manager performs environmental inspections, he or she is extending the owner's effort to make "all appropriate inquiry" to uncover problems and providing the owner with additional evidence for making an "innocent landowner" defense (should it be necessary). Even though inspections may be required by lenders during the purchase or refinancing of a property, no one is likely to require the manager to inspect the property. The manager's environmental inspections will be fairly simple in nature and require little specialized training. While such inspections do not provide the technical data of an environmental site assessment, they are invaluable.

There are two types of environmental inspections that the property manager can perform. (Note: It is important to emphasize that these inspections are not to be confused with those more involved inspections, studies, and/or assessments that would be performed by an environmental consultant or engineer.) The exterior inspection covers the outside of the building, the roof, and all grounds. Exterior inspections should be done two to four times a year. The interior inspection covers the tenant spaces as well as any common areas, storage spaces, or other parts of the building not used by one specific tenant alone. Office buildings generally will not require tenant space inspections because day-to-day office activities rarely create environmental problems. Nevertheless, *inspection is necessary for those tenants who lease space in an office building for something other than general office use* (e.g., photographic processing, photocopying, dry cleaning, food service, etc.). Regardless of the type of operation, interior tenant space inspections should be limited to once or twice a year because tenants can be very sensitive about environmental issues. *Types of Businesses Known to Generate Hazardous Wastes, Exhibit 8.1,* lists some of the types of tenant operations that signal the need for interior inspections.

An environmental inspection should be as standardized as possible. Specific procedures, checklists, report formats, and means of documentation should be developed and followed. Having set requirements for every inspection reduces the chances of making an error or omitting an important item.

Separate checklists should be developed for exterior and interior inspections, and they should be customized for different types of properties (a shopping center versus an apartment building versus industrial facilities, etc.). Checklists that have been developed for a specific property type can be tailored to meet the needs of the individual property by adding a separate "comments" section on the checklist form. All such checklists should be reviewed by an environmental attorney who should be asked to add or delete items and assure that use of the list does not compromise the management company legally.

Any checklist item that could possibly trigger regulatory reporting requirements should be discussed with the attorney to determine whether it should remain on the list. When one considers the highly technical nature of environmental laws and reporting procedures, the removal of an item from the checklist makes sense (although at first, such action may seem to run counter to the whole purpose of an inspection). In truth, the average person conducting a basic inspection is not sufficiently knowledgeable to fathom the intricacies of environmental law. Consequently, a written record of any inspection conducted by the property manager should provide *general* information; *anything that could be construed as speculative is inappropriate.* A tenant environmental checklist need not be overly detailed (e.g., it is not necessary to list every Material Safety Data Sheet [MSDS] that a tenant has on site; it is sufficient to note that the tenant has MSDSs).

Consider the following example: A medical supply company tenant ships kidney dialysis fluid in 55-gallon plastic drums. During a routine inspection, the property manager discovers two empty dialysis fluid drums in back; they are marked with the word "leaking." There are no damp areas of earth, but it has been relatively warm for a number of days and there is no way to know how long the drums have been there. Such a discovery poses two significant questions: (1) Were the drums placed where they were found while leaking

E X H I B I T   8.1

Types of Businesses Known to Generate Hazardous Wastes

Acid manufacturing, storing, or distributing
Aircraft maintenance
Aluminum manufacturing
Architectural drawing or drafting
Automatic car washes
Automobile dealerships
Automobile servicing or refueling
Auto wrecking or salvage
Battery manufacturing, storage, distribution, recycling, or disposal
Boat repair
Bowling alleys
Car painting
Car rental
Chemical manufacturing, storage, mixing, or distribution
Computer manufacturing or assembly
Concrete contracting
Construction services and supplies
Delivery companies
Dry cleaners or retail dry-cleaning plants
Electrical repair or rewiring
Electrical transformers, generating stations
Electronics manufacturing
Electroplating
Engraving
Farms of all types
Fast food restaurants
Feedlots or slaughterhouses
Fertilizer storage or manufacturing
Fleet servicing or fueling
Food processing
Food service
Funeral services
Furniture manufacturing
Gasoline stations
Glass manufacturing
Gravel or stone pits
Home supply sales or product manufacturing
Hospitals
Janitorial supplies storage, manufacturing, or use
Junkyards
Laboratories
Landscape equipment sales and maintenance

Laundries
Machine shops
Meat-packing plants
Medical offices
Metal finishing
Newspaper printing
Nuclear power plants
Oil change or muffler replacement shops
Paint and body shops
Paint mixing, manufacturing, or storage facilities
Paper pulping or manufacturing
Paving contractors
Pesticide storage or manufacturing
Petroleum refining, storage, or distribution
Pharmaceutical manufacturing, storage, or distributing
Photocopying services
Photography
Plastics manufacturing, painting, or assembly
Plumbing
Printing
Publishing
Railroad yards
Restaurants
Roofing contractors
Shipping
Sign companies
Solid waste treatment
Steel storage and distribution
Tape and adhesive manufacturing
Taxidermy
Telecommunications manufacturing and assembly
Testing laboratories
Textile manufacturing
Tire repair or sales
Tire storage, distribution, or disposal
Tobacco processing
Trash removal services
Trucking
U.S. armed forces
Wood painting
Wood preservation
Wood products manufacturing

and full, or only after they were empty? (2) Is dialysis fluid classified as a hazardous or regulated substance?

If one of the checklist items is "Improper Disposal of Medical/Laboratory Chemicals," the inspector may violate a reporting requirement every time he or she notes such improper disposal and fails to report its presence to the appropriate regulatory agency. This oversight might be revealed during an inspection review by the regulatory agency in question. If nothing is wrong, the management company, the tenant, and the environmental agency will have wasted their time. If the review reveals that a problem was not reported, the management company could be in serious trouble—and all because of using the word "improper" to describe the disposal of chemicals on an inspection checklist. Deeming disposal "improper" is a judgment beyond the average person's ability. An attorney would recognize the problems presented by such wording.

A better solution would be to list the checklist items as "Empty Storage Containers" and include a "comments" section to provide information regarding location and labeling of any containers that are found. It is also prudent to follow up such a discovery with a letter instructing the tenant not to leave drums in the rear of the building, regardless of the contents. A copy of this letter should be kept on file.

In any environmental inspection, it is important to be able to interpret certain visual evidence. It also helps to understand the different types of hazardous wastes that are generated by certain types of businesses. An often overlooked source of information during any inspection is the labeling of hazardous materials. The labels on containers for hazardous materials indicate those properties of the contents that make them unsafe (e.g., flammability, toxicity, corrosivity, radioactivity, explosivity, etc.). By noting the labeling of hazardous materials on site when performing inspections (both inside and outside any buildings on the property), the manager becomes aware of the types of substances that are kept on site and can verify proper handling conditions. For example, when a manager notices a container that has a label indicating that the contents present a fire hazard if heated above 73 degrees Fahrenheit, he or she should assure that the tenant is providing a refrigerated storage area for the substance. Simply by asking to see the refrigerated area, the manager lets the tenant know that he or she is aware of the substance.

The National Fire Protection Association (NFPA) has a system for identifying hazardous materials. Their symbol is one large diamond that is divided into four smaller diamonds. Red at the top signifies flammability; blue on the left signifies health hazards, yellow on the right signifies reactivity (explosiveness); and white at the bottom covers other types of hazards, particularly corrosivity. Numerical ratings in the colored diamonds indicate the degree of hazard. In the white diamond, capital-letter abbreviations indicate specific hazards. *NFPA Rating for Hazardous Materials, Exhibit 8.2,* depicts this symbol. (Sometimes labels on shipping containers will show a large single-

E X H I B I T   8.2

NFPA Rating for Hazardous Materials

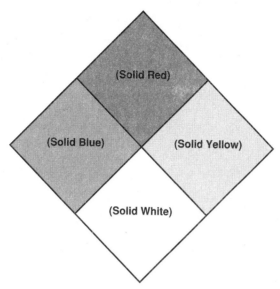

Source: National Fire Protection Association, Quincy, Massachusetts.

In the diamond symbol, the top three (colored) diamonds may each contain a numerical rating from one to four (a zero or no number signifies no applicable rating) to indicate the severity of the hazard posed. The bottom (white) diamond will either be blank or include an abbreviation that indicates a specific property of a material such as corrosivity (COR), acidity (ACID), or alkalinity (ALK). Some materials have multiple hazard designations (e.g., flammable and corrosive).

colored diamond to indicate hazardous contents—for example, red for flammability—in compliance with U.S. Department of Transportation labeling requirements. These are generally comparable in information content to the NFPA designations.) The manager who makes notations of such symbols observed on container labels, wall signs, etc., is recording valuable information during his or her inspection.

Armed with such general knowledge, a checklist of things to look for, and the commitment to conduct environmental inspections regularly, the property manager is ready to begin.

The Exterior Inspection

It is important to do exterior inspections in stages. The first stage should be an inspection of the outside of the physical structure itself including the roof and roof drains. The second stage should be an inspection of the grounds immediately adjacent to the building as well as the parking lot. The third stage should extend all the way to the property line. For many properties, the inspection will not continue beyond stage two because of limited acreage. Some properties in outlying areas are larger and may provide enough space to encourage night dumping in a relatively isolated area of the property.

Example Environmental Inspection Checklist (Exterior), Exhibit 8.3, includes the types of things that a property manager should look for when he or she is performing exterior inspections. Supplementary material is provided in Appendix E, Indications of Possible Contamination (a list of warning signals to help the property manager perform an effective exterior inspection) and Appendix F, Visual Examples of Possible Environmental Contamination.

Structures.   There are numerous indications of potential environmental problems on and around structures. Some are more obvious than others; even the most experienced professional cannot identify them all. Indications observed on the outside of the physical structure can be some of the most difficult to recognize. The manager must learn what to look for.

The appearance of certain irregularities on the exterior of the building should be taken into consideration. Items of note include stains or sooty accumulations on the walls, accumulation of dust or powdery material that is suspicious in color or quantity, and pipes that extend through a building wall without being attached to anything external. Their presence could indicate such things as careless or improper disposal, wind-dispersion of powdery residue or ash, incineration of waste, and/or insufficient filtration for gaseous emissions.

One should inspect the roof very carefully, especially the areas near ventilation stacks and HVAC units. Exhaust vents and ventilation ducts that are coated with soot may signal that burning is taking place without proper filtration. Greasy buildup near vents from restaurant operations indicates malfunctioning or inadequate grease traps on cooking machinery. Staining (especially colored stains) on and/or around vent pipes may mean that paint or solvent vapors are escaping to the atmosphere. Ventilation ducts that are heavily rusted or eroded may signal the presence of oxidizers or strong acids. Excessive patching or other signs of repairs in HVAC system equipment or ventilation ducts may indicate other problems.

Visible indications on the building that are suspicious in nature should be noted on the inspection checklist, and the appropriate tenant should be contacted. All conversations with the tenant and explanations from the tenant should be confirmed in writing to document management's efforts to minimize or prevent environmentally unsound practices.

Adjacent Land.   Most visible indications of potential environmental problems will be found on natural areas of the property rather than on the building itself. This is because vegetation is more sensitive to hazardous substances

EXHIBIT 8.3

Example Environmental Inspection Checklist (Exterior)

Property: _____ Prepared by: _____ Date: _____

1. Underground storage tanks. Yes ____ No ____
   Aboveground storage tanks. Yes ____ No ____
   Indicate location and contents of each one (if contents are unknown, this should be stated). _____
2. Areas of dead or dying vegetation. Yes ____ No ____
   Location and description: _____
3. Disposal, trash, or waste treatment facilities. Yes ____ No ____
   Location and description: _____
4. Ponds or water tanks. Yes ____ No ____
   Location and description: _____
5. Oily or discolored water on or around the property. Yes ____ No ____
   Location and description: _____
6. Areas that are free of vegetation (i.e., those *not* intentionally cleared).
   Yes ____ No ____
   Location and description: _____
7. Areas where land is stained, discolored, or oily. Yes ____ No ____
8. Vent pipes protruding from the ground. Yes ____ No ____
   Location and description: _____
9. Any unusual or unpleasant odors (especially those that could be described as chemical or gas-like). Yes ____ No ____
   Location and description: _____
10. Electrical transformers. Yes ____ No ____ Wet ____ Dry ____ Unknown ____
    Owner _____ Location: _____
11. Abandoned structures. Yes ____ No ____
    Location and description: _____
12. Discarded construction materials. Yes ____ No ____
    Location and description: _____
13. Discarded machinery or vehicles. Yes ____ No ____
    Location and description: _____
14. Machinery and/or vehicle repair facilities. Yes ____ No ____
    Location and description: _____
15. Storage area for 55-gallon drums or other large containers. Yes ____ No ____
    Location and description: _____
16. Presence of railroad tracks or loading areas. Yes ____ No ____
    Location and description: _____
17. Piping or hoses running out of any structures. Yes ____ No ____
    Location and description: _____
18. Disposal of containers (broken or unbroken; metal, plastic, or glass; empty or not empty). Yes ____ No ____
    Location and description: _____
19. Burned area on site. Yes ____ No ____ Approximate size _____
    Location and description: _____

Note: A sketch of the site should be attached and each problem noted on this form should be marked with its corresponding entry number. A checklist such as this one should allow sufficient space to note all appropriate information.

Adapted with permission from Trammell Crow Company (Charlotte Division).

than manufactured materials are, and will show the effects of exposure more quickly.

Accidental spills and improper dumping or disposal are the most common causes of environmental contamination. Indications of such activities include stained patches of soil, burned vegetation, dead or sickly vegetation in the midst of healthy plant life, and cleared areas where there is no obvious indication of need for the clearing.

More obvious (and more traceable) signs of improper storage or disposal are empty or partially empty containers, absorption materials spread over an area of ground (to soak up liquids), old batteries, or an obviously recent excavation. When specific containers are found, it is relatively easy to determine their ownership if the manager knows the types of materials used by each tenant. Once identified, the tenant should be contacted immediately, and all communications should be documented by keeping copies of correspondence and written notes of telephone and personal conversations. In some instances, it may be necessary to hire a consultant to examine the substances that have been discovered and determine if it is necessary to report the findings to the appropriate regulatory agency.

It is also necessary to inspect areas on the property away from the main buildings, especially those where machinery is used or materials are stored. When examining such an area, one should be concerned whenever any of the following are observed: staining on the ground (soil surface) or pavement; uncovered storage containers and any pools of unidentified liquids close to them and/or absorption materials distributed in the area around them; residues from power-washing; and storage containers that are overturned, rusting, and/or damaged. These items should be noted on the inspection checklist and brought to the attention of the appropriate tenant.

When inspecting areas containing fuel-dispensing facilities and machinery, it is important to note the visible evidence as well as what is suggested by what is *not* seen. The *absence* of monitoring wells in an area of underground storage tanks (USTs) indicates that a possible leakage problem may be undetected. The fact that oil and gas dispensing equipment is *unused* may be determined from a lack of obvious traffic or ground (soil) disturbance, but undetected problems may still exist. Aboveground storage tanks may suggest the presence of underground tanks that have been abandoned and are no longer tested or maintained. Indications of the potential for soil contamination include stains near piping to exterior equipment, stains beneath aboveground storage tanks, and stains around oil and gas dispensing equipment. Exterior generators, air compressors, and other machinery may show signs of leakage or that spillage has occurred during maintenance. Large areas of recently disturbed ground or repaired asphalt in the area of USTs may indicate the removal of an older tank that could possibly have been leaking.

Other Areas.   Very large sites often include isolated areas, away from the developed sections, where "hidden" activities could take place; these should be areas of concern. To be noted are areas where wastes are being dumped (i.e., where one observes the presence of household, municipal, or construction materials), trash has been burned, and pits or ditches have been created. Such activities can create nuisances and eyesores; they also have the potential to result in environmental problems. Steps should be taken to prevent future dumping and to clean up any existing environmental problems.

Adjacent properties containing real estate projects that are visible from the property line should also be inspected. Concerns off site include storage facilities (buildings) and outdoor drum-storage areas located immediately adjacent to the property line. Staining on and around these areas could indicate careless storage and handling techniques and the potential for contamination to leach onto the owner's property. Finally, the existence of USTs—both visible and suspected—should be noted.

The Interior Inspection

A much more sensitive issue is the inspection of interior spaces. Just as good tenant communications are important prior to performing an environmental site assessment, the same good communications are essential before conducting regular inspections. Tenants should not be made to feel threatened or accused, nor should they be led to believe that the manager suspects any problems. Managers should address the issue of inspections in a positive manner. Despite growing awareness of environmental issues and the importance of protection from liability, some tenants will be offended by regular inspections of their spaces. Tenants who have a history of violations are likely to be particularly sensitive.

For this reason, inspections of tenant spaces should be done along with all other building inspections—with the same frequency and the same degree of scrutiny. In truth, most environmental problems will manifest themselves outside a tenant's space, except for problems resulting from the improper disposal of substances in building drains. Nevertheless, it is important for the manager to take a look at interior space on a regular basis. A form such as *Example Tenant Environmental Checklist, Exhibit 8.4,* is an invaluable aid during the inspection and provides a written record of all findings. Such an individualized form creates a record of each tenants' status over time and helps managers to avert potential errors of attributing one tenant's level of compliance with that of another tenant.

When performing interior inspections, it is important to avoid a highly technical approach. Attempting to suggest how a tenant should store or dispose hazardous substances might mean qualification as an operator. However, *it is important to record the conditions and activities as observed* and to confirm in writing that it is the tenant's responsibility to assure that storage, use, and disposal activities are in full compliance with applicable local, state, and federal laws.

Items deserving special attention are interior transformers that appear to

E X H I B I T   8.4

Example Tenant Environmental Checklist

Tenant: _____

Performed by: _____ Title: _____ Date: _____

1. Hazardous waste generator status: SQG _____ LQG _____ Not listed _____

2. Hazardous substance "diamond" rating (NFPA classification): Red _____ Blue _____
   Yellow _____ White _____ (White will be an abbreviation rather than a number)

3. Material safety data sheets (MSDSs) on site: Yes _____ No _____ N/A _____

4. Waste disposal contract(s). Hazardous: Yes _____ No _____ Contractor _____

5. Explosion or fire containment rooms: Yes _____ No _____ Contents: _____
   _____

6. Accessible fire control equipment: Yes _____ No _____ Type _____
   (FE = fire extinguisher, HS = halon systems, SS = sprinkler system)

7. Evidence of substance handling. Comments made here should note indications of frequent spills, the presence of open containers not currently in use, general cleanliness of space, appearance of floor drains and sinks, etc. _____
   _____

8. Electrical transformers in tenant's space.
   Yes _____ No _____ Wet _____ Dry _____ Unknown _____ Age _____

9. Additional comments: _____
   _____

Note: A similar type of checklist should be prepared for the other interior areas of the building(s).

Adapted with permission from Trammell Crow Company (Charlotte Division).

___

be leaking; storage areas that are dirty, difficult to enter, and/or show signs of spillage; unattended open containers in high-traffic areas; cluttered workstations and other issues related to housekeeping. Regardless of the potential for environmental problems, disorderly work conditions can be a threat to the safety of employees and may cause damage to the property.

Visible indications of improper disposal into drains are rusted or deteriorating floor drains; stains in sinks and toilets and around floor drains; corroded plumbing fixtures and multiple plumbing leaks; and various odors (pleasant and unpleasant) emitting from drains. These discoveries should be called to the tenant's attention in writing, with a statement that explains the assignment of liability to the tenant and a request to dispose of waste in another way.

Special use tenants, especially in high-rise office buildings, are more difficult to monitor effectively. Medical and dental offices and photography studios may dispose of certain substances in drains, but because of the particular odors associated with the operation as a whole, it may be difficult to determine distinctive smells at particular drains. Architectural firms use inks and chemicals in plans, drawings, blue print machines, and copiers; these may also be difficult to identify in a drain.

The dumping of chemicals and other substances down the drain is a common cause of environmental problems. Regulatory agencies strenuously object to such practices, so tenants should be discouraged from them. In truth, many tenants who dispose of chemicals in this way are not conscious of any wrongdoing and will alter their behavior when asked to do so.

One of the most important—and effective—aspects of the interior inspection is the fact that it alerts tenants to management's commitment to prevention of environmental problems. By conducting regular inspections, the manager calls environmental issues to the tenants' attention and consistently emphasizes the fact that the tenants will be held liable for any problems they create. In many instances, this is all it takes to keep tenants in compliance.

INSURANCE

After establishing and enforcing good management policies, the most common way to protect a real estate investment is to purchase insurance. During an evaluation of the property's insurance, one should determine that the coverage will protect the interested parties (the owner, the management company, and the manager) from liability in the event of environmental problems.

It is wise to evaluate the financial stability of insurers. Many insurance companies will provide copies of their annual reports on request. Some state insurance commissioners compile insurance shoppers' guides. One can also utilize insurance reporting services such as A.M. Best Company in Oldwick, New Jersey. Such services provide ratings of such things as the quality of the insurer's underwriting results, economy of its management, adequacy of its reserves, ability of its capital and surplus to absorb unfavorable operating results, and soundness of its investments. Insurers are generally rated on a scale from C (fair) to A+ (excellent).

The Owner's and/or Manager's Insurance

To assure adequate coverage, every property owner should perform periodic reviews of his or her insurance policies with a representative of the insurance company. It is important to have written confirmation that environmental losses are covered, regardless of the property's status. Understandably, properties with known or suspected environmental problems will be classified differently than properties without problems; in such cases additional insurance must be purchased to maintain the same level of acceptable coverage.

Even properties with no determinable evidence of environmental problems may have insurance policies that specifically exclude environmental liability from coverage. The costs of testing, remediation, and cleanup are so high that most insurance companies have begun to exclude any coverage for losses of this nature. Fortunately for the property owner, several court decisions have forced insurance carriers to cover losses that are related to the environment. Nevertheless, obtaining appropriate coverage is a far better practice than relying on a court ruling in one's favor.

Coverage for environmental problems generally falls under a standard comprehensive general liability (CGL) policy. Thus it becomes crucial to know how the current insurer interprets the coverage under CGL; this makes the meeting between the owner (or his or her representative) and the insurer all the more important. During that meeting, issues of concern should be addressed, and the insurer should provide clear interpretations of the policy; these interpretations should be confirmed in writing. Should an insurer refuse to document such a discussion, it is a warning that one's policy may be deficient. There are two primary questions that should be asked when determining whether environmental problems are covered under the existing policy and that the existing coverage is sufficient. They are as follows.

1. Does unintentional contamination or the discovery of previously unknown contamination of the environment constitute "property damage" as defined and covered by the policy?
2. Do site investigations, attorney's fees, and remediation costs constitute "damages" as defined and covered by the policy?

Clearly, the desired answer to these questions is yes. Environmental losses should be covered as long as the problem was not knowingly and willfully created by the owner or the owner's agents or employees. What the owner wants is assurance of the following.

1. "Property damage" should be defined as physical injury or damage to tangible property. The environment consists of soil, air, water, etc.—all of which are tangible and, therefore, the owner's property when within defined boundaries of the owner's land.
2. The costs of restoring tangible property to an environmentally and/or legally acceptable level should be covered as "damages" in the same way costs associated with restoring property damaged by fire are covered. Generally speaking, "damages" are defined as monetary compensation for an injury or loss of value to property.

It is important to recognize that almost every CGL issued since liability became a serious concern for property owners has a pollution exclusion. The language of pollution exclusions varies widely; there is no single industry standard. In general, such exclusions limit or omit coverage for pollution-related situations and specifically exclude pollutants that are the responsibility of the owner, tenants, or other parties involved with the property. The definition of "pollutant" is usually derived from environmental law.

While it is worthwhile to note that a pollution exclusion is intended to be all-inclusive and thus relieve the insurer of environmental liability, it is also important to know that there are definite legal precedents for the disallowance of this exclusion in certain instances. Regardless of legal precedent, this exclusion should be negotiated, even if a higher premium is required. The objective should be to protect the owner as much as possible from exposure to liability from unexpected or unintentional environmental problems.

In some circumstances, the title insurance on the property should reimburse the costs associated with environmental contamination and remediation. That is the case for owners who, at the time of closing their property, purchased title insurance containing "pollution law" coverage. However, in October 1984, the American Land Title Association changed the policy form to exclude laws, ordinances, and government rules and regulations regarding environmental problems with properties.

For both property owner and manager, a comprehensive errors and omissions policy will offer some protection from those environmental problems that occur after they have taken over the project. While the liability remains with the property owner, errors and omissions coverage will provide protection for owner, manager, tenant, or maintenance caused liability (up to the limits of the policy). An errors and omissions policy covers losses caused by human error as well as ignorance of environmental laws, rules, regulations, etc.; it will not cover losses that result from gross negligence. Errors and omissions coverage is considerably less expensive than pollution insurance. Coverage in the aggregate amount of $2 million is generally sufficient for the average property, but each situation needs to be evaluated individually.

The Tenants' Insurance

Tenants must be properly insured and required to name the owner and property manager as additional named insured parties in all policies. The owner and property manager should avoid being named as "certificate holders" because this only means that they have copies of the certificates. Certificates of insurance should be required from all tenants to verify that sufficient coverage has been obtained and that lease requirements are satisfied.

So-called "claims-made" insurance should be disallowed in the lease. Claims-made insurance is relatively inexpensive. This type of coverage is available to industrial tenants as well as consultants and engineers. While it is perfectly valid insurance, it only covers claims made and reported during the current insurance contract year. Any claim made after the policy termination date is no longer covered. So, if the carrier cancels environmental insurance offerings or the policy-holder changes insurers or discontinues coverage, it is no longer possible for the insured party to make a claim against the "claims-made" policy, regardless of whether the damage occurred while the policy was in effect.

Every manager should develop a tenant insurance tracking system for the tenants on the managed property. Such a system would involve the use of "tickler files" to remind the manager that tenants' policies are due for renewal. Tenants whose operations pose the greatest environmental risk should be monitored most carefully. While insurers will usually inform owners and property managers of cancellations or changes in tenants' insurance policies (if tenants require their insurers to do so to comply with the lease), every experienced property manager knows that insurance carriers sometimes fail to make such notifications.

Specific Environmental Coverage

At the time this book was being written, insurance designed specifically to cover environmental problems was as difficult to find as it was expensive. So-called pollution insurance was often cost-prohibitive. Nevertheless, it was becoming more common and more affordable.

There are companies that offer environmental insurance to consultants, engineers, and other interested parties such as property owners. The coverage is expensive, so much so that an owner would probably not wish to purchase it unless he or she owned property leased to a chemical company or other similar industrial tenant. It is especially important for industrial tenants and environmental consultants to list the owner and/or manager as additional named insured parties in their environmental policies. This should be verified through certificates of insurance. The owner should also check the policies to assure that they are not for claims-made insurance.

When asbestos is known to be present (regardless of its condition), it may to desirable to purchase asbestos insurance. Asbestos insurance can provide protection from liability incurred through an asbestos operations and maintenance (O & M) program as well as an asbestos removal program. Asbestos insurance is well worth having whenever asbestos is known to be present in the building.

As insurance companies become more familiar with environmental issues, they will be better equipped to assign risk factors to the different areas of potential environmental liability. This situation should continue to improve, and as it does, owners and managers should be able to reduce their exposure to risk by acquiring appropriate insurance.

9

Management Policies
and Procedures

One doesn't have to read many newspapers, watch television often, or listen to much radio to be aware that environmental issues elicit strong reactions from people. In many instances, these reactions can be emotional, especially when an entirely unexpected environmental problem is discovered. The key to successful environmental management often involves keeping emotions in check, making decisions carefully, and staying informed.

An immediate or emergency response is rarely called for after the discovery of a spill, improper disposal of waste, or other environmental problem. Furthermore, immediate disclosure of available information (which is likely to be incomplete) may result in problems with and even panic among employees, tenants, and the community. It is important, however, that employees and tenants who may be in a position to make such a discovery are informed about the nature of possible problems and made aware of the proper reporting procedures. Property owners and managers should know what information to share and who needs the information. This requires basic training about the most common environmental problems.

Most management companies, managers, and owners have established procedures to be followed in emergencies. Procedures that are recommended in the event of a fire will naturally differ from those advised for a bomb threat. In the same way, recommended responses to environmental problems will vary from appropriate actions for other types of emergencies. When developing certain environmental emergency procedures, it may also become necessary to perform specific assessments of potential health hazards.

BASELINE RISK ASSESSMENT

The owner or manager of an occupied property with potential environmental problems should determine the actual human risk involved by hiring a consultant to perform a baseline risk assessment (RA), sometimes called a health endangerment assessment. The purpose of this assessment is to determine the human health risks associated with exposures to certain contaminants. The EPA manual that provides guidelines for performing these studies is called *Risk Assessment Guidance for Superfund: Volume I, Human Health Evaluation Manual.* This extremely technical manual is written for use by environmental engineers; it is not something property managers need to have.

A risk assessment is not required for every property; the need for such an assessment should be determined while emergency procedures are being developed and as potential contaminants are identified. Formal risk assessments are very involved, requiring complex calculations developed by the EPA and making assumptions from the data that result. They are also expensive and time consuming. Nevertheless, when a risk assessment uncovers minimal risk, it can provide valuable documentation that can be used to address owner, tenant, and employee concerns.

A risk assessment, when performed, commonly generates a five-section report. First, the specific problem being assessed should be identified and tested; information concerning sampling and test results would appear at the beginning of the report. Next, the potential exposure pathways (the means by which the average person would become exposed to the substance[s] in question) should be isolated. If it is determined that human exposure is *highly unlikely,* the report should summarize these results, state the reasons that led to such a conclusion, and end.

For those situations that present the potential for human exposure to one or more hazardous substances, the third part of the report should detail the characteristics, toxicity, and potential effects of each substance. A fourth section should explain the assumptions that were made during the study and how they relate to the calculation, and the actual calculation itself should be presented in detail. The fifth and concluding section should be a summary.

EMERGENCY PROCEDURES

Certain emergency procedures concerning environmental discoveries should be included in the standard emergency procedures manual for each property. Each procedure developed should involve five primary steps: evaluating the problem, notifying the appropriate parties, hiring qualified professionals, performing an assessment, and choosing and implementing an appropriate response plan.

1. *Evaluating the Problem.* Emergency procedures should prescribe methods for evaluating the degree to which employees, tenants, and the property itself are in peril from a particular environmental problem. Only in very rare instances will an environmental problem pose an immediate threat to the safety of a property or its associated personnel (such a problem might be contaminated drinking water). Determination of the hazards involved and their immediate threat is the first priority after any discovery.

2. *Notifying the Appropriate Parties.* Once a discovery is made and the immediate hazard has been determined, the notification process should be initiated. Specifications concerning notification should include the identification of those who should be informed and when, the order and manner of notification, and the individual responsible for distributing the information. Again, because of the complexity of applicable laws, an environmental attorney should assist in the development of notification guidelines for environmental emergencies. If an owner or manager misinforms or fails to inform the appropriate parties when a problem exists, penalties may be assessed by state and federal agencies.

Due to the complexities of environmental law, the notification process will vary with the problem. Different situations will call for unique notification procedures. In general, however, the property manager is likely to be the primary contact and the person responsible for carrying out the established procedures.

When a problem is discovered, the property owner should be notified immediately and continually updated as the situation develops. Notification procedures should also identify individuals within the management company who should be informed and updated on a regular basis. These parties will most likely be notified along with the owner (although this may not always be the case). *Even when several parties have been identified for immediate notification, the owner should always have top priority.* During the initial briefing on the situation, the owner should be given a summary of what has occurred and the actions that will be taken. When the owner knows how the management team is dealing with the problem, he or she is more likely to have confidence in the way the situation is being handled. As a rule, there is no reason to withhold information from any of these people—even incomplete information—because "emergency team" members should know as much as possible.

Continual updates of all team members should be regular and timely. When the attorneys and consultants make certain determinations regarding the situation, it may become necessary to notify the authorities (i.e., governmental agencies), lenders, and tenants. There is no reason to notify the authorities unless the situation or the law requires it. State law must be considered as diligently as federal law, and notification decisions should be made by an attorney. When notification is deemed necessary, it should be handled by an attorney in order to maintain protection provided by attorney-client privilege.

Many loan documents drafted after 1990 require lender notification when environmental problems are discovered (an older document may or may not include such a requirement). Notification of the lender should be left to the owner unless responsibility is specifically delegated to the management company in writing (e.g., in the management contract). The procedure should be handled by an attorney, and the management company should be willing to assist with any necessary details. It may be wise to wait until information is complete before reporting to a lender. Lenders are extremely sensitive to environmental liability and may use anything they are told regarding the discovery of a problem to implement policies regarding the property and the loan. It is generally unfair to the lender to provide partial or inconclusive information.

Tenants usually are the last to be notified. The advice regarding lenders also generally applies to dealing with tenants—it is unfair and unwise to provide tenants with incomplete information. Tenants are usually the least knowledgeable about environmental matters and the most likely to react emotionally. There is one notable exception to this "rule": *Any policy to withhold information from tenants does not and should never apply in cases in which immediate danger is present.* In such instances, all tenants in the project become a first priority for notification due to safety issues. Any notification of the tenants should follow applicable legal requirements, and tenants should be provided with the most complete information possible.

In the environmental arena, there are numerous cases in which tenant notification is not required by law, nor does such notification provide any discernable benefit to the tenant (or the landlord). It may be best to refrain from notifying tenants in such situations. This prevents unfavorable tenant reactions as well as damage to the public image of the property. Again, it is important to be certain that the safety of tenants or their employees is in no way threatened. It is just as important to provide the tenants with information when they request it.

3. *Hiring Qualified Professionals.* The third step of most emergency procedures is to hire qualified environmental consultants and engineers. Specialized attorneys might also be called on at this time. To expedite the process, the procedures manual should provide the names of qualified experts who can be used (specifying the field of expertise of each person). For example, such a list is likely to include one set of

names for asbestos-related problems and another set of names for leaking underground storage tanks (LUSTs).
4. *Performing an Assessment.* Assessments should be done as quickly as possible. The extent or severity of the problem should not dictate the reaction time—the faster a solution is devised, the faster mitigation of the problem may begin.

The assessment can begin as soon as initial notifications have been made and attorneys and environmental professionals have been brought on board. The first priority is to determine any actions that are called for by environmental laws and regulations and whether notification of environmental agencies and/or civil authorities must occur. When such determinations are made, notification should follow legal guidelines.

It is important to understand the reporting requirements for each particular situation. In some instances, the law may require disclosure of the problem within twenty-four hours of discovery; in others, the time frame may be thirty to sixty days, and in some situations notification is not required at all. In the event the law allows for some time to elapse before reporting is mandatory, it is wise to use all the available time to quantify the problem. The more accurate and detailed the information provided to a governmental agency, the less involved the agency is likely to become during the assessment and/or response recommendation processes. Such action also establishes a good rapport with the agency and creates confidence that the situation is being properly addressed.
5. *Choosing and Implementing a Response Plan.* When assessments are complete and several alternative solutions have been recommended, a course of action should be chosen by the owner. All concerned parties should assist in the decision-making process; considerations should include cost, safety, and regulatory guidelines and requirements. As soon as the owner selects a particular course of action and the plan has been approved by the appropriate regulatory agency, it should be implemented expeditiously.

Although this chapter describes specific situations and suggests appropriate environmental policies and procedures for each, it is necessary to remember that policies should never be written in stone. Policies and procedures should be changed as laws, available information, and public attitudes change. It is also essential to understand that responding to an environmental problem is a fluid process, rather than a phased or staged one. For example, when hazard determination is in progress, the notification procedure should have already begun. Once a problem is discovered, the process should not stop until the issue is completely addressed.

The text in this chapter is intended to assist the management company and manager in developing appropriate policies and procedures for a variety of environmental problems. Management companies should customize environmental procedures to suit their own management philosophies and do so with the advice of their environmental attorneys. It is also helpful to have at least one individual in the company who has received additional training in environmental matters to act as a central control figure in the event a problem is discovered.

A property's emergency procedures should prescribe responses to the most commonly discovered environmental problems. These include the presence of asbestos or underground storage tanks (USTs), inferior indoor air quality, illegal disposal of waste, groundwater and soil contamination, and National Pollutant Discharge Elimination System (NPDES) and storm water discharge violations.

Asbestos

The presence of asbestos is a high-profile issue. Information concerning asbestos is readily available to owners, managers, and tenants. Purchasers and lenders performing environmental site assessments are likely to check for the presence of asbestos. Consequently, the sudden discovery of asbestos can be quite a surprise to all involved.

Maintenance personnel and building service and construction contractors are most likely to discover asbestos-containing materials (ACMs). Maintenance employees should know the policies in place regarding asbestos. These people should be taught how to identify potential ACMs. They should also understand that something that looks like asbestos may not necessarily be asbestos; only laboratory testing can confirm (or negate) such an opinion. When confronted with potential ACMs, everyone involved should exercise the utmost discretion; it is essential to avoid unnecessary alarm. Maintenance personnel should be trained in both the proper techniques for dealing with a potential ACM and the appropriate response and notification procedures if the presence of asbestos is confirmed.

Hazard Determination.   Risks associated with asbestos can be assessed using three key pieces of information: (1) the type of asbestos, (2) the amount of asbestos (a figure that includes airborne asbestos), and (3) whether the asbestos is friable. When assessing risk, it is important to understand that the risks to janitorial, maintenance, and construction personnel are usually always greater than any threat posed to other building occupants.

As noted in chapter 4, asbestos may be found in many areas of a building and in many forms. When insulation or similar material is made of an unknown substance that is found to be physically damaged, it is always a suspected ACM. Material that produces a fine dust when touched may also be an ACM.

To identify an unknown substance and assess any hazard it might present, it is necessary to contact an environmental consulting firm to perform sampling and testing. In the case of a suspected ACM, this will mean drastically reducing any activities that could cause additional destruction of the material and isolating the area as much as possible. It is very important to minimize human activity in the immediate area to prevent exposure. Building evacuation, however, is unnecessary except in the event of an obvious, direct, life-threatening situation. The initial hazard assessment should determine the immediate danger.

Notification.   Notification of building tenants is the most sensitive area in a situation involving asbestos. Occupational Safety and Health Act (OSHA) regulations govern the notification of employees and dictate workplace precautions. Most laws dealing with asbestos do not specifically address the issue of tenant notification. Thus, it becomes subject to legal interpretation, and the environmental attorney involved should make recommendations.

When dealing with asbestos, it is essential to have a policy that addresses those instances in which tenant notification is not legally required *and* safety is not compromised. Such a policy should be made at the highest level of the company and with advice from legal counsel. Under *no* circumstances should a property manager be given the responsibility to inform tenants about asbestos at his or her discretion. It is similarly unwise to make decisions on a case-by-case basis. A stated policy should be determined before any asbestos is discovered.

The EPA recommends notification of building workers, maintenance personnel, and tenants. It suggests distributing written notices and holding meetings to inform everyone about the situation and discuss any real or perceived threat to project occupants. The EPA reasons that tenants should know how the problem affects or does not affect their particular area of the building. They also believe that tenants who are aware of a problem are less likely to unknowingly add to it. These points should be considered when developing a policy.

Assessment and Follow-up.   Recommendations will usually call for implementation of an operations and maintenance (O & M) program, complete removal of asbestos from the project, or a combination of the two. These decisions should be made on a case-by-case basis; each asbestos problem is different and should be judged accordingly. Issues to be considered include safety, cost, publicity, marketing, and O & M staffing and training. Although the manager should make a recommendation to the owner, such decisions are the owner's to make.

Once chosen, the plan should be put into place. Usually an engineer will undertake the project, control it, and monitor its progress. It would be difficult for a property manager to direct such a project; what is more, project supervision creates a liability risk. Here, the environmental rule of thumb is simple: Hire a professional.

Underground Storage Tanks (USTs)

Under most conditions, the discovery of a previously unknown UST will not present immediate, life-threatening risks. Hazard determination should be fairly routine. Nevertheless, it is important to remember that there are exceptions to every rule and a UST can present some surprises. It is important for the environmental engineer to perform an initial assessment to assure that there are no immediate concerns.

Hazard Determination.   Generally, an abandoned UST may be assumed to be leaking a substance that is contaminating the surrounding soil. The existence and extent of contamination can be determined by testing the substance within the tank, the groundwater beneath it, and the soil around it. If the tank contains a highly explosive substance, it may present an immediate danger. In such a case, safety measures should be taken immediately.

Notification.   State and federal laws (including Superfund) address the issue of reporting requirements for leaking underground storage tanks (LUSTs). The attorney handling the situation should be able to provide a specific list of state, local, and federal agencies to be notified. Notification should be made by the attorney to assure attorney-client privilege.

Usually, tenant and lender notification is less complicated in situations involving USTs than in those that involve asbestos or other environmental problems that are perceived as extremely hazardous. People are not as sensitive to this issue. Tenant and lender sensitivity heightens, however, when a LUST may affect a well that supplies water used for drinking (by humans or livestock) or irrigating crops. In such instances, reactions can be strong.

It is necessary to have a company policy in place to dictate a notification procedure for those cases in which the law or the situation does not call for notification of tenants. Again, this policy should be made at a corporate level and not left to the individual property manager. The guidelines should be examined by an attorney, stated in writing, and enforced.

Assessment and Follow-up.   Immediately after determining the hazards associated with a UST, an environmental engineer should begin assessing the extent and nature of the contamination. The assessment should determine whether soil and/or groundwater have been contaminated and, if so, how far the contamination has spread. Once this is complete, recommendations may be prepared. When underground tanks present some hazard, there really are no alternatives—the engineer should recommend removal of the tank or tanks. He or she should also provide guidance regarding any steps that might be taken *beyond* tank removal (i.e., remediation or cleanup). Such recommendations should take all applicable laws into account. The difference between remediation and cleanup should be investigated, and cost versus benefit considerations should be examined. A final choice should be made using the advice of both the environmental engineer and an attorney.

Implementation of the plan should be *monitored* by the property manager while being *controlled* by the environmental engineer. This protects the management company and the property manager from liability incurred as a result of any UST removal, remediation, or cleanup. If groundwater has not been affected, soil contamination is the primary concern and generally a simple problem to handle. Regardless of the complexity of the project, an environmental engineer should be in charge; reporting, testing, and documentation requirements call for specialized knowledge, and an error could create a liability problem.

Indoor Air Quality (IAQ)

Indoor air quality is a complicated issue. First, it is difficult to determine whether a problem exists. When a problem is suspected, it is necessary to decide whether tests should be performed and, if so, what tests. Poor IAQ is rarely discovered by accident—one must go looking for it. This underscores the importance of understanding the human symptoms associated with inferior IAQ.

Hazard Determination. A determination of the hazards associated with substandard indoor air quality begins when a problem is either suspected or specifically identified. When problems are suspected, their existence must be confirmed before a risk assessment can be made. While poor indoor air quality may be indicated by unpleasant odors, it also may not be detectable by human senses. Symptoms of illness associated with inferior IAQ include headaches, fatigue, respiratory problems, eye and throat irritations, allergies, and nasal discomfort in addition to colds and flu-like illnesses. This is why poor IAQ is sometimes known as sick building syndrome (SBS). Those people most likely to be affected by poor IAQ are asthmatics, people with allergies, contact lens wearers, senior citizens, children, and pregnant women. When a property manager becomes aware of unidentifiable odors in a building or an unusually high incidence of human symptoms that may be related to IAQ, he or she should consider testing.

When an environmental engineer performs tests to investigate possible IAQ problems, he or she is likely to examine the ventilation capacity, condition, and cleanliness of the HVAC system; observe on-site activities such as smoking, housekeeping (especially those involving certain solutions and cleaners), and storage (particularly of such materials as paint thinners and solvents); measure temperature and humidity levels in the area; study building components such as carpeting, dyes, and adhesives; look for dust in open areas; and check for molds and mildew. What is more, poor indoor air quality does not have to be a result of something inside a building. Industrial pollution, vehicle exhaust fumes, and radon may enter a building from outside and affect IAQ.

The most serious risks are related to asbestos and radon. Asbestos is not generally a threat to building occupants unless damaged ACM has released fibers into the air. If the concentration of these fibers is beyond the level established for safe exposure, there is a real health concern, and the environmental engineer should immediately inform the owner and property manager and recommend a solution. Elevated levels of radon should also trigger immediate notification of the owner and/or manager by the engineer along with a recommended response.

One of the most severe health problems associated with IAQ is Legionnaires' Disease. This respiratory disease takes many forms, from pneumonia to a much less severe sore throat and cough. It has been linked with the presence of a bacterium (a species of Legionella) in vapors from such sources as cooling towers, evaporation condensers, shower heads, water faucets, and hot water systems. The Legionella microorganism is one of many airborne biological agents (others include fungi, dander, pollen, bacteria, etc.).

Notification.   Notification of a governmental agency is rarely required with IAQ problems except when significantly elevated levels of controlled or hazardous substances (e.g., asbestos, radon) are involved. It is important for an environmental attorney to assure that notification is *not* required under the Clean Air Act (CAA), Resource Conservation and Recovery Act (RCRA), or any state or local laws. Notification is absolutely required if any occupant(s) of a building or project contract Legionnaires' disease. In such cases, action should be taken immediately—including informing the local health department. It is essential for tenant and employee safety to be the primary concern.

It is wise to communicate with tenants regarding any air quality problems discovered. For the most part, tenants and their employees will suspect there is a problem because of the physical symptoms they have experienced. Good tenant relations are fostered by informing the tenants that both the owner and manager are aware of the situation and are trying to remedy it. What is more, tenants can often provide assistance because they can share information regarding likely problem areas. Many different things affect IAQ, and tenant use is one of them.

Assessment and Follow-up. It is essential to use an environmental engineer when evaluating IAQ in buildings. The engineer may use several methods other than air sampling to investigate the problem; in fact, it is possible to discover a problem without sampling at all. An engineer is best qualified to do this type of investigation because such things as HVAC systems and humidity control are highly technical.

When performing air quality studies, it is important to limit the testing to those concerns that have been identified. Unusual tests are usually expensive and generally a waste of time and money unless they relate to a suspected problem. At the beginning of the assessment, it is necessary to determine those substances that should be sampled and their location. As soon as sampling is complete, an experienced engineer can provide the owner with recommendations.

Generally, there are three basic solutions to air quality problems—source control, ventilation, and air cleaning. Source control may involve removing the origin of the problem (e.g., prohibiting smoking within the building, removing carpeting that serves as a breeding ground for microorganisms); reducing the problem (e.g., training housekeeping and maintenance staff to suppress dust, controlling release of contaminants); sealing or covering the source (e.g., downsizing the openings to storage areas so that odors and fumes are less likely to escape); or modifying the environment (e.g., disinfecting moldy areas, controlling the humidity).

Similarly, there are many ways to change ventilation. Options include increasing outside air usage, controlling air pressure within the system, altering air distribution, or making changes in system design.

Air cleaning is most commonly used in addition to ventilation and source control. A combination of these three types of action is almost always an effective way to combat IAQ problems. Air cleaning equipment can be very useful when one is attempting to control dust, bacterial growth, or a pollutant from outside that enters through air systems. There are three major air cleaning technologies available. Filtration to remove particles from the air involves the use of devices ranging from a very simple particle-catching filter or screen to high-efficiency particulate air (HEPA) filters. A HEPA filter is capable of removing submicron particles. Gases or vapors can be removed by adsorption or absorption. (Note: Absorption is the passage of one substance into or through another while adsorption is the adhesion of molecules of gas or liquids to a surface.) The use of activated charcoal is a good example of such a system because volatile contaminants adhere to the surface of the powdered carbon (this adsorption process effectively removes large gas molecules only). Electrostatic air precipitation has met with much success in removing fairly small particles from the air. An electrostatic air cleaner (EAC) applies an electrical charge to particles that pass through it, causing them to be attracted to a plate that carries the opposite charge. The collected material is then removed from the plate, which must be cleaned regularly.

Illegal Disposal of Wastes

Contrary to popular belief, those people who leave 55-gallon drums on an empty lot at night or pump materials down out-of-the-way sewers are not the only individuals guilty of illegal waste disposal. In truth, almost everyone is guilty of illegal waste disposal at one time or another. Of course, the average person "commits" an illegal waste disposal relatively infrequently and the volume of waste involved is fairly small. The volume of waste illegally disposed by industries is huge by comparison.

As the size of properties and the number and variety of their tenants increase, the real estate industry is being more carefully monitored by regulatory agencies. Big properties provide more opportunities for someone to dispose of regulated materials improperly. Examples of substances that can be disposal problems include film developing chemicals, photocopier fluids and toners, blueprint making chemicals, pesticides, paints, paint thinners, cleaners, solvents, oils, dry-cleaning fluids, and hydraulic fluids. Each commercial property type—retail, office, medical, manufacturing, or other industrial—will have a different tenant mix that creates its own problems.

Illegal disposal of wastes can only be discovered by conducting regular property inspections (see exhibits 8.3 and 8.4). Those tenants who generate hazardous wastes (or are likely generators) should receive special attention. Nevertheless, it is necessary to examine the space leased by all tenants—even responsible tenants with the best of intentions may violate environmental law unknowingly. Because most tenants do not volunteer information regarding their disposal methods, regular inspections are all the more essential. Once a violation is discovered, the responsible party should be monitored carefully. Tenants who were unaware of the illegality of their actions do not usually require the kind of close watch called for by those tenants who were willful violators of the law.

Hazard Determination.   As soon as a waste disposal problem is discovered, an environmental consultant or engineer should investigate it and determine the immediate hazard, if any. Determination of the threat to people in the area and the environment is top priority. Discovery of danger to those in the area should be followed by immediate notification.

In many cases, hazard determination will suggest changes in tenant disposal techniques that will stop the problem. When the situation is more serious, assessments and recommendations should be made immediately after the hazard is determined.

Notification.   When illegal or improper disposal is an issue, the notification process becomes very important and should be done correctly to avoid serious problems in the future. Hence, an environmental attorney should be consulted immediately after discovery of illegal disposal practices. Because each state has its own laws and regulations on notification procedures, the attorney should have a base of experience in that state.

In addition to notification of the owner, management personnel, and engineers, it is absolutely critical to provide the attorney with as much information as possible so that he or she can determine when (and if) regulatory agencies should be notified and which agencies to notify (federal, state, local). Disposal of a particular substance in a certain way may be considered more serious than another disposal violation; immediate notification of the appropriate regulatory agency may be required. When 24-hour notice is required, the clock starts ticking the moment the discovery is made.

The property manager or management company environmental expert should have the authority to direct the attorney to notify the proper agencies. Because time may be critical and each situation is almost always different, it is wise to give the attorney the authority to proceed at his or her discretion. Most attorneys will not act without proper authorization in circumstances such as these.

Assessment and Follow-up. When a significant problem is discovered and governmental agencies must be notified, it is quite possible that the alerted agencies will perform their own assessments and make recommendations. In such cases, the owner and manager assume relatively inactive roles in examining the problem. Assessments would be made by agency personnel or contractors, and their recommendations are not likely to be negotiable.

It is beneficial for the owner to know the identity of the party who has been disposing wastes illegally. This knowledge provides some protection from liability, although it does not eliminate the risk. If the responsible party is unable to pay for remediation or cleanup, for example, the owner may be liable for the costs. Nevertheless, owners are more protected in situations in which the responsible party has been identified. Hence, it is critical to note the vehicle license plate or company name when spotting a "midnight dumper." One warning: It is not wise to confront illegal disposers alone. This is something that should be handled by the appropriate authorities. Fortunately, most property managers will never encounter a situation that would require this type of caution.

In a situation in which no regulatory agencies are involved, it is important to have the assessment done as quickly as possible. Again, it is helpful to know who is responsible because it aids identification of the substance(s) being disposed. When problems are addressed expeditiously, immediate remedial action may prevent more serious problems in the future.

In truth, the problem of illegal disposal of waste is one that few owners or managers will have to confront. What is more, those waste disposal problems that are encountered are rarely a result of intentional violations of the law—it is often the case that the responsible party has been acting in ignorance. Disposal requirements vary from one state to another. In New Jersey (where recycling is law), it is illegal to throw away certain items (e.g., aluminum cans, newspapers), while such activities are not restricted in other states. Tenants who are new to the area may simply be unaware of the prevailing state or local laws.

Contaminated Water Supply

Theoretically, a brand-new building should be free of water supply contamination. While this may or may not be the case, it is essential for the owner and manager to understand that any discovery of water supply contamination should be followed by immediate corrective procedures. While lead may be the most notorious of water contaminants, there are many other chemicals and heavy metals that can adversely affect the safety of drinking water.

More and more tenants are requiring building water testing (or documentation of recent tests) prior to signing or renewing their leases. Water supply tests are not particularly expensive; regular testing can build good tenant relations and serve as a marketing tool during leasing.

Hazard Determination.   A water supply that is suspected to be contaminated must be tested. Such testing most often involves looking for volatile organic compounds (VOCs) and heavy metals (lead, chromium, etc.).

VOCs are generally compounds of carbon and hydrogen, by themselves or with certain other elements (e.g., chlorine). These organic compounds all participate in atmospheric photochemical reactions. This means that various solvents, cleaners, and other materials containing these chemicals can break down in sunlight and cause noxious or toxic fumes. VOCs enter the water supply by leaching and transfer processes (e.g., flow of storm water runoff over a contaminated surface). The most common VOCs have chemical names that end in "ene" or "ane" (e.g., toluene, methane, and trichloroethylene).

VOCs are considered hazardous and toxic by the EPA, which has established maximum contaminant levels (MCLs) of human tolerance for them. Some of these guidelines for exposure are quite low. In general, VOCs with names ending in "ane" are less toxic than those ending in "ene." Nevertheless, any discovery of a hazardous VOC is cause for concern. MCL measurements are generally quoted in parts per million or parts per billion. In the language of such measurement, a trichloroethylene (TCE) concentration in water of five parts per million is the equivalent of five molecules of TCE for every million molecules of water (this does not necessarily reflect current state or federal MCLs for TCE). The EPA establishes MCLs by attempting to measure the amount of a given substance that a person *could* ingest over a finite time to generate a one-in-one-million chance of getting cancer as a direct result of the exposure. Discovery of a VOC concentration above the MCL almost always calls for notification of the appropriate regulatory agencies.

Heavy metals are the pollutants most people know about. They enter the water supply from pipes, containers, and equipment as well as improper disposal procedures. While the most familiar is lead, elevated levels of other heavy metals such as chromium, iron, mercury, cadmium, arsenic, etc., are just as hazardous. Human consumption of these metals may lead to learning disabilities, birth defects, cancer, leukemia, blindness, or even death. The discovery of heavy metals in a water supply is definitely cause for concern.

Notification.   Many states have set MCL levels that are lower than the federal guidelines. This means that some discoveries must be reported to the state but not to federal agencies. After the discovery of water supply contaminants that exceed state or federal MCLs, tenants should be notified without delay. Such contaminants are an immediate health hazard and all appropriate parties should be informed.

Assessment and Follow-up.   When water supply problems are discovered, a detailed Phase II Site Assessment (Phase II) should be done immediately (see chapter 4). The goal is to protect tenants and employees from any health risks, determine the source of the contamination, and develop and implement a good remediation plan. To protect tenants and employees, certain water treatments can be used immediately to alleviate contamination; these treatments may even turn out to be the recommended solution.

The easiest way to handle heavy metal contamination is to install a water filtration system. Filtration can even address VOC problems to some extent. Equipment ranges from inexpensive faucet-connected screen filters that can be purchased in a hardware store to complex ozone filtration systems and charcoal filters. In many situations, water filtration will be part of the recommended solution, even though it is just as important to address the source of the problem.

Once a course of action has been chosen, there is usually a requirement to present it to the appropriate regulatory agency for approval. Thus, the engineer and attorney involved must prepare a report detailing the nature of the problem, the source of the problem, and the alternatives for remediation. After examining the report, the agency may accept the proposal, reject the proposal and request another, or dictate a specific alternative course of action. If it does the latter, the owner and manager have little choice but to follow the agency's directions.

National Pollutant Discharge Elimination System (NPDES)

NPDES regulations were designed to monitor and control the discharge of municipal and industrial wastes into the nation's waterways. Currently, NPDES regulations are more likely to address sewage and wastewater pretreatment because RCRA addresses many other waste disposal issues. Properties that do not have access to public water and sewerage systems are most likely to have NPDES problems. Such properties tend to have on-site treatment plants or privately owned treatment works. These treatment facilities are monitored regularly by a state regulatory agency with EPA approval or by the EPA itself. Similarly susceptible to problems are properties with tenants who are required to pretreat certain substances before discharging them directly into a publicly owned treatment works (POTW).

Hazard Determination. Because states can enforce more stringent regulations than those imposed at the federal level, the contractor investigating the problem must be familiar with the requirements of the particular state where the violation occurred.

There are several different types of NPDES violations; all deal with the discharge of waste. One should understand the cycle of discharge in any given property to gain a sense of where (and when) these violations might occur. The cycle described here is based on wastewater discharge into a privately owned treatment works. Assume wastewater is first discharged into a retention basin, the contents of which are transferred into a treatment facility where the wastewater is chemically treated to meet the NPDES permit standards. After treatment, the wastewater is emptied into a system of pipes that conveys it to a public sewerage system. If no public sewerage system exists, it may be piped into a creek, river, or other waterway.

Problems with such systems will most likely take the form of: (1) violations occurring in the transfer to and treatment within the privately owned treatment works, (2) contamination of the discharge piped from the facility after treatment, and (3) excessive volume of waste (inappropriate facility size). When the chemical makeup of these discharges does not conform to the requirements established by the NPDES permit, it is time to take notice. In terms of state and federal concerns, violations involving discharges from the facility pose the most serious problems.

Discharge to and Treatment Within the Facility. Generally speaking, NPDES permits are issued and treatment facilities constructed prior to lease-up. As a result, the limitations stated in the permit are often based on assumptions that may or may not reflect the actual tenant profile after the project is leased. Because an NPDES permit will designate certain chemical limits for discharge from the treatment facility, the facility will be designed to treat specific types and mixes of wastes from the tenants. One can easily understand how the addition of one or two unexpected tenant operations can create the potential for an NPDES violation. When problems are encountered, waste content should be checked; it is quite possible that the chemical treatment program may require adjustment to accommodate a previously unexpected tenant operation. If the treatment facility itself cannot handle the influx, it is possible that an added pretreatment station may be necessary.

Discharge from a Treatment Facility. Regulations are most likely to apply to discharges *from* waste treatment facilities. These will be monitored by state and/or federal agencies. As a result, treatment facility discharge should receive the most attention; regular monitoring is a must. The system should be free of problems as long as the composition of the discharge is within the limits established by both the law and the permit. When this is not the case, the potential for fines and other penalties will outweigh any costs associated with determination of the cause of the problem and remediation.

Size of Facility. The most expensive kind of problem associated with waste treatment (and pretreatment) facilities is insufficient capacity (i.e., a facility that can no longer handle the volume of wastes passing through it). An unexpected industrial boom in an area, expansion of a project, or a change of use can create such a problem. Even though most managers are becoming more environmentally aware, the issue of waste treatment facility capacity is frequently overlooked. An overloaded facility is likely to release some untreated wastewater—an obvious violation. Such a problem can only be remedied by expanding the treatment facility or reducing the amount of waste that goes through it.

Notification. Like the notification processes described for other environmental problems, notification concerning NPDES violations should comply with company policies and the law. An environmental attorney should determine the exact notification procedures and timing for state and/or federal agencies.

Assessment and Follow-up. As soon as the discharge is determined to be a problem, the assessment serves to identify the reasons for the problem and what can be done about it. Plans of action to be considered might include expanding the existing waste treatment facility, adding pretreatment facilities for certain tenant discharges, and altering chemical treatment procedures within the facility.

When the engineer has determined the plan that he or she believes to be most advisable, a recommendation should be made to the owner and the management company. As soon as a plan has been selected by the owner, its implementation will be initiated *after* receiving approval from the regulatory agencies involved. Prior approval of the regulatory agency is especially important in light of the fact that a new NPDES permit will have to be issued to reflect the changes that have been made.

A Word about Storm Water Discharge

Federal storm water discharge regulations have affected real estate owners and managers. It is a topic deserving attention from the property manager, who should understand the prevailing regulations in his or her area. Proce-dures for dealing with storm water discharge requirements vary by state. A copy of the regulations may be obtained directly from the EPA office in the manager's area of the country. City and county building standards depart-ments may also be of assistance.

Basically, businesses with certain standard industrial classification (SIC) codes are required to obtain storm water discharge permits. Such permitting provides a way for state and federal agencies to locate and monitor opera-tions that may utilize outside storage, leave waste in commercial dumpsters, or expose certain substances to the outdoor elements.

An environmental attorney or engineer should determine whether each tenant in a project is potentially a storm water discharge risk; tenants should be notified of the necessity to obtain applicable permits. It is the tenant who must comply with requirements; the owner and manager should avoid taking any actions that might lead to classification as an "operator" under the law.

Both NPDES and storm water discharge problems are highly complex and are best left to the experts (engineers and attorneys). The important thing to remember is that *any major change in a project should be a reason to assure waste treatment facility compliance with the NPDES permit and the law.* Under no circumstances should a property manager try to estimate the effect of a change without consulting experts.

REHABILITATION OF EXISTING PROPERTIES

Just as property managers should have guidelines for dealing with environ-mental problems that may be encountered, they should also establish proce-dures that help them address those environmental concerns that are related to rehabilitation projects. Like other issues that are affected by environmental regulations, the rehabilitation of properties must be addressed on a case-by-case basis. Each project will be unique in some way. The property manage-ment firm or property manager developing rehabilitation guidelines must also be mindful of the variable nature of state and local laws. Regulations and building code specifications will vary for properties in different locations.

Sometimes rehabilitation projects are executed by necessity rather than by choice. The introduction of new government required upgrades (GRUs) may create mandatory rehabilitation projects. GRUs vary by location; in earth-quake-prone areas, for example, building alterations may be required when building codes are changed to increase building safety.

If a recently purchased property is to undergo rehabilitation, it is likely that any environmental assessments done in conjunction with the purchase would identify potential problems. In the absence of clear guidance from an earlier assessment, an environmental engineer may recommend such evaluation. Environmental studies may be a requisite to obtain financing. The various types of assessment are detailed in chapter 4.

Every rehabilitation project should involve the assistance of an environmental engineer with local experience in the type of rehabilitation to be undertaken. Significant rehabilitation should begin with a detailed review of the existing property, the proposed changes, and the site assessment report. In this way, potential problems are taken into consideration before the rehabilitation is underway.

The range of environmental problems that might be encountered during a rehabilitation project is far too vast to discuss in a few pages. This section will address those issues that are most frequently encountered. One thing is certain: Whether property managers are faced with the presence of asbestos or HVAC systems that are insufficient, there are likely to be challenges related to the environment that must be confronted during any rehabilitation.

Asbestos

Asbestos is a primary concern during rehabilitation, especially when dealing with older properties. Fiber board, panelling, insulation, concrete, and roofing materials are all possible ACMs. Depending on prevailing laws, it may not be possible to continue an asbestos operation and maintenance (O & M) program during a rehabilitation project. Although the federal government and the scientific community acknowledge that some asbestos O & M programs are preferable to asbestos removal, state law may require asbestos removal in a building when extensive construction will occur. Such laws may include variances for occupied properties to prevent disruption of operating businesses. It is necessary to understand all asbestos-related regulations prior to the consideration of a rehabilitation project.

HVAC Systems

Some rehabilitation projects will call for the utilization of existing systems such as those for air circulation and ventilation. Such a plan should be examined very carefully to assure that proposed alterations do not affect indoor air quality negatively.

While heating equipment in an older building may have substantial capabilities, there is a chance that the air conditioning system will be insufficient. Another point to be considered is whether alterations can be detrimental to the existing heating elements. The most common indoor air quality problems are associated with poor air circulation, poor ventilation, high humidity, hot and cold spots, condensation in ducts, and accumulation of mildew and dust—and all of these types of problems can be created during a rehabilitation project.

After completion of plans and designs for a system change (alteration or replacement), an IAQ specialist and environmental engineer should jointly examine the proposed changes to highlight potential problem areas.

Mechanical, Electrical, and Boiler Rooms

It is essential for an environmental engineer to inspect the mechanical, electrical, and boiler rooms of any property that is being considered for re-habilitation. First, it is necessary to check insulation materials used in these areas for ACM. Lead-based paint on floors and walls is another source of problems. In older buildings, mechanical, electrical, and boiler rooms were designed for equipment that is likely to be outdated and insufficient today. It is most important for the building's ventilation system to have adequate capacity and the ability to remove toxic and hazardous fumes before they are circulated into the building.

Electrical rooms create an additional concern—the potential for PCB-containing transformers. Remember that older transformers are "wet" (PCB-containing) unless the PCBs have been replaced; new transformers must be PCB-free. Local or state law may require removal of PCBs during a rehabilitation project. It is wise to have all transformers on site tested before beginning a project.

Basement

Basements have the potential for the kinds of contamination already discussed—asbestos, lead paint, PCBs—and they also may contain radon. Radon usually enters a structure through its basement. Prior to rehabilitation, it is important to perform radon testing, especially in older buildings with poor ventilation. If the basement is also used for parking or deliveries, testing for carbon monoxide (CO) should be done as well.

Plumbing Systems

Plumbing systems are likely to be in pretty good shape. The wrought-iron or metallic piping used in older buildings is less likely to be affected by the natural settling of the building than is the PVC piping often used in new construction. However, many of the piping systems installed prior to the late 1980s contain lead solder or joint seals. As previously noted, the presence of lead and/or other heavy metals in drinking water can create a health hazard. Rehabilitation may require testing of drinking water.

Tenant Construction (Existing Improvements)

Additions and alterations made by tenants are also a concern. Constantly changing occupancy in a commercial building may result in repeated demolition and subsequent tenant improvement construction. In such cases, governmental agencies tend to prefer one-time removal of hazardous materials. While many existing structures may not require updates every time environmental laws change (grandfather clauses may deem their condition acceptable), a rehabilitation project may be considered new construction—a situation that can negate the applicability of the grandfather clause. State laws vary and some may specify the types of materials that are to be used in rehabilitation projects. Changes are not always necessary, however. For example, concrete that contains asbestos is not usually considered a problem, and replacement during rehabilitation is not usually required. An environmental engineer's examination and assessment is very important to assure that regulatory requirements are met.

Change of Use

Some rehabilitation projects are designed to both renovate a property and alter its use. For example, a developer may wish to convert a warehouse into retail space. As is the case with any rehabilitation, change of use projects present the possibility of being confronted by environmental problems. Because change of use projects often involve newly purchased properties, an environmental audit is likely to have been performed recently and the report of that audit would identify important considerations relative to the change of use. In the context of long-standing ownership, environmental assessment may be necessary or appropriate (see also chapter 4). Anyone undertaking a change of use project must consider issues that relate to the previous use of the property. Perhaps earlier tenants were large quantity generators (LQGs) of hazardous waste. Perhaps activities at the site required the use of underground storage tanks (USTs). Suffice it to say, it is essential to understand the activities that have taken place in any structure prior to the development of a plan for rehabilitation.

THE CHALLENGES OF ENVIRONMENTAL MANAGEMENT

Inspections are a major part of a successful environmental management program. Problems should be discovered and terminated before they become significant. The only way a manager can achieve this goal is to inspect the property regularly. Notification procedures for environmental problems should be developed and strictly followed by the owner, management company, manager, attorneys, and engineers (as well as any other involved parties). In some instances, environmental law (state or federal) may include notification requirements. Notification of governmental agencies should be handled by a qualified environmental attorney who specializes in such activities.

The key to environmental management often lies in understanding the three basic steps that should be taken when confronting any problem: (1) determination of the hazard, (2) notification of the appropriate parties, and (3) assessment and follow-up. Just as important is understanding the appropriate ways to communicate with tenants on these issues. To avoid classification as an "operator," the owner and/or manager should never provide tenants with instructions regarding compliance with permits or laws. While this will not guarantee protection against liability, it can significantly reduce the liability exposure of the management company and the manager.

10

Other Points
to Consider

Throughout this book, numerous environmental issues have been discussed in the context of the real estate industry. In chapter 1, some of the most commonly encountered—and frequently talked about—environmental problems were introduced and defined in general terms. Chapter 2 provided a broadbrush look at the scope of environmental legislation in place. With that foundation of information, the focus of the text narrowed. An examination of industry-specific issues included a look at the potential for liability and the unique components of different types of environmental site assessments. The typical concerns of different individuals (e.g., buyer, seller, owner, developer, and manager) were also explored. Now, before concluding this text, it is wise to take a look at four related subjects that deserve discussion: determining the qualifications of professionals, handling public relations, dealing with the ethical implications of some environmental problems, and understanding the role of the environmental manager.

WORKING WITH ENVIRONMENTAL PROFESSIONALS

No one person will have all the right answers for environmental problems. The savvy property owner or manager knows where to find the information he or she needs and the kind of expertise that will be most helpful for the specific situation faced.

With *any* environmental problem—suspected or verified—experienced, professional consultation on a legal, technical, and financial basis is essential. While cost must be scrutinized, experience is just as important a consideration. The most valuable professionals are those who are continually in contact with environmental problems because changing laws and their associated rules, regulations, and court interpretations require constant monitoring. While most people seek these qualifications when selecting an environmental attorney or engineer, they do not always consider environmental issues when looking for lenders, insurance companies, management companies, accountants, and others. The more environmental experience an organization has, the more likely it is to handle a problem situation properly and expeditiously.

It is important to understand the expense of environmental problems. In general, any situation labeled "environmental" is likely to be more expensive than other, seemingly similar problems. To some extent, one could argue that inflated environmental costs have simply become "the norm" and, as such, are accepted by the general public. Higher costs are also a reflection of increased liability exposure; any party associated with an environmental problem faces relatively large potential risks.

Hiring the right team of experts begins with an understanding of the evaluation process. For purposes of this discussion, each professional or company under consideration will be referred to as "the contractor." To qualify such a contractor, one should generally have a complete understanding of: (1) the contractor's upper level personnel (specifically, their education and experience), (2) the services and support that are obtainable through their staff, (3) the contractor's specific areas of regulatory expertise, (4) whether the contractor is approved by the federal and/or state EPA (lists are available), and (5) the type of insurance the contractor carries, coverage amounts, and identity of the carrier(s). One should also obtain a list of associated companies that offer additional services through the contractor. References are an absolute necessity.

Choosing a contractor may not involve consideration of every one of the points previously cited. For example, most attorneys and lenders will not be agency approved because they do not provide environmental consulting services (rather, they are likely to hire their own consultants). All the same, it is important to know an attorney's or a lender's experience with and policies regarding specific environmental issues.

Evaluating an Environmental Attorney

When selecting legal counsel, it is important to realize that bigger is not always better, even if a legal firm handles environmental cases exclusively. Because state laws often differ from federal laws, it is quite possible that a small firm that generally deals with local cases may have more of the necessary expertise to handle an in-state problem than a national firm that handles cases across the United States. In some instances, out-of-state owners who employ a national law firm may wish to have that firm engage a local firm to assist when special situations arise.

When choosing a law firm or an attorney, federal and/or state approval is rarely applicable. Similarly, insurance information is rarely a concern because attorneys face liability risks in all of their cases (environmental and nonenvironmental alike) and are subject to state licensing requirements for insurance.

Screening legal experts starts with learning essential facts about their education and experience. The demand for attorneys who specialize in environmental matters is fairly recent. Consequently, attorneys who have educational backgrounds in science, engineering, or industrial hygiene are tremendous assets. Also of note are attorneys whose primary continuing legal education has involved environmental law. Experience with environmental litigation is essential—every environmental problem discovered has the potential to end up in court. The more experience an attorney has, the better, especially if his or her experience relates directly to the problem at hand (five year's of experience might serve as a minimum guideline). An often overlooked asset is the availability of additional services through the firm or attorney. The ability to respond to a problem quickly may be tied to having adequate resources. Conversely, inadequate support and administrative staff may create time constraints.

Regulatory expertise and specialization in certain types of environmental law are important issues that should be discussed. A diversified environmental law firm may have attorneys who specialize in different laws such as Superfund, RCRA, the Clean Air Act, etc. When this is the case, there tends to be an additional source of information (i.e., informal discussions between attorneys). "Specialists" are very helpful when one is faced with a specific problem. What is more, attorneys who specialize in addressing one particular type of environmental problem (e.g., leaking underground storage tanks) are often well versed in a wide spectrum of environmental laws.

References are important and should always be checked. Most firms maintain a list of clients to use as references and will provide this list on request. Such a reference list should include information concerning the clients' needs and the results obtained; if this information is not provided automatically, it should be requested. (Note: It is important to recognize that due to the confidential nature of some environmental cases, this information may not always be supplied.)

Cost is naturally a concern; most firms will provide a copy of their fee structure. It is not unusual for the fees of individual attorneys to vary widely. Be advised that one cannot assume that more money will secure a better-quality attorney. Cost should be the last consideration when trying to decide between two similarly qualified firms.

It is also worthwhile to consider using more than one law firm for environmental issues. To reiterate: No single individual will have all the right answers. In many situations, it is worthwhile to get a second opinion. Different situations call for individuals or firms with unique fields of expertise.

Evaluating an Environmental Consultant

Generally speaking, an environmental consulting firm is made up of environmental engineers, geologists, and other scientific specialists who perform environmental audits or assessments of properties and provide emergency services in the event a problem is discovered. Most consulting firms will be diversified and can handle a wide range of assessments and investigations. Some will be highly specialized to focus on particular situations.

Similar to screening a law firm or attorney, choosing a consulting firm should involve obtaining information about personnel, available services, and regulatory expertise. References, too, are still important. In the case of environmental consultants, most states maintain lists of state-approved contractors and consultants (copies of these lists are made available on request). It is also important to secure insurance information and to obtain a list of associated companies and additional services available. Many consulting firms will have corporate brochures that detail their credentials (personnel education and experience, support staff, resources, primary and adjunct services, etc.). These promotional pieces usually contain valuable information and are worth keeping on file for future reference.

The education and experience of the company's management is very important. The fact that so many environmental assessments involve scientific and technical evaluation means that a strong educational base is necessary to assure accurate interpretations and conclusions. It is just as essential to have practical experience in addition to the base of education (specifically, experience with the particular problem that needs attention; preferably in the same state where the problem has occurred).

Availability of services and support varies from one firm to another. Some may have their own laboratories for sample analysis or their own rigs for drilling monitoring wells; others may not. Different firms may have unique types of scientific specialists on staff. To some extent, the importance of such services will depend on the situation at hand. While firms that offer more services may charge higher fees, their ability to achieve results quickly may outweigh any consideration of costs. In general, such "in-house" services result in greater efficiency. All the same, there are those who believe that it is preferable to hire a firm that does *not* do everything internally. At issue is the question of probability of error. While an independent laboratory would have the consulting firm looking over its shoulder, the consulting firm that does its own testing doesn't always have the same kind of mechanism to "keep it honest."

Regulatory expertise is a very important part of environmental consulting. Working in this area continually assures up-to-date knowledge of required procedures and practices. Having a good rapport with governmental agencies is often undervalued; positive relationships with regulatory agencies can make a significant difference when dealing with environmental problems. For this reason, many consulting firms have personnel on staff who are former employees of state, federal, or local regulatory agencies; their knowledge may expedite some processes (e.g., obtaining permits). Regulatory expertise is derived from regular interaction with governmental agencies while performing various types of assessments. Therefore, a list of current and recently concluded projects should be requested from each firm under consideration. An ideal candidate would provide several references from assignments that are similar to the one to be undertaken.

One of the most important qualities of an environmental consultant is his or her ability to streamline processes through personal contacts in the field. Acquaintances with industry people combined with a solid foundation of experience-based knowledge can allow a good consultant to avoid some of the "red tape" associated with environmental problems. The owner who hires a consultant may be dealing with an environmental problem for the first time. Consultants encounter environmental problems on a daily basis. In doing so, consultants learn *who* they need to know as well as what they need to know.

Insurance coverage is critical for environmental consultants because there are so many opportunities for errors that could cost thousands—even millions—of dollars. In addition to standard liability, comprehensive, all-risk, and other insurance coverages, a consulting firm should be bonded and have errors and omissions (E & O) insurance providing a minimum of two to three million dollars in coverage. The firm should be able to supply a copy of the insurance certificate and be willing to include the client as an additional named insured party. It is also wise to qualify the underwriter of the E & O insurance. While it may be difficult to determine an underwriter's exact strength (i.e., ability to pay claims), knowing the name of the company makes certain information accessible (assessing the financial stability of insurers was discussed in chapter 8). If the underwriter is small, privately held, or relatively unknown, some additional security should be required. Unfortunately, there is no such thing as a guarantee that an insurance company will always be able to pay claims.

A consultant's ability to obtain or arrange for additional services and supplies is extremely important, especially in an emergency situation. One could be confronted by an environmental problem at any time, and ability to respond quickly can mean eliminating or mitigating such things as damage to the property, threats to human health, and fines.

Evaluating a Lender

The existence of contamination should not be the sole determinant of whether a property is bought or sold. Nevertheless, it can be difficult to convince some property owners, prospective purchasers, and lenders of this fact. The knowledge that a $500,000 loan can become a $5,000,000 liability tends to bring out the most conservative tendencies in lenders and purchasers alike.

In truth, real estate sales transactions are taking more and more time (an environmental problem may add 90 to 180 days to a due diligence period). As a result, it is all the more important for owners and purchasers to be knowledgeable about lenders *before* they are involved in a deal; knowing each lender's policies regarding loans on problem properties may help to speed the process. It is entirely realistic to assume that each lender has specific policies for environmental issues, and these are policies that warrant examination. Such policies vary from lender to lender. Generally speaking, the larger the lending institution, the more conservative the environmental policies. Larger institutions are more aware of potential liability and the fact that those with "deep pockets" are rarely protected from risk. Some lenders may refuse to make loans available when contamination is even suspected, while others may have no policies regarding environmental issues in their lending guidelines. In fact, most lenders fall between these two extremes. A worthwhile "rule of thumb" is to avoid lenders that have no policies for environmental issues.

In a very real sense, it is necessary to evaluate a lender before applying for a loan. When investigating a lender, three primary things should be examined: (1) exclusions, (2) restrictions, and (3) additional requirements.

Lender Exclusions.   Some institutions will exclude specific environmental problems from their loan portfolio. In other words, any property with certain environmental problems will not be considered for a loan, regardless of its cash flow or potential income. Even though laws, health hazard assessments, and public attitudes may change, it may take a very long time for a lender to revise its policy. Some common exclusions are as follows.

1. *Asbestos in buildings.* Actually, when asbestos is discovered, purchasers will frequently back out of a deal before the lender does.
2. *Contaminated groundwater.* Many lenders refuse to even consider properties with groundwater contamination because the cost of remediation and/or cleanup can be extremely high.
3. *Elevated lead and heavy metals in tap water.* Although such problems can often be remedied by installing filters, some lenders avoid them.
4. *Radon and indoor air quality (IAQ) Problems.* Many lenders do not accept properties with these problems because of the cancer risk associated with radon and the difficulty and expense associated with quantifying poor IAQ.

Lender Restrictions.   Lenders willing to make loans on problem properties may place certain restrictions on these loans; they do so to reduce their exposure to risk. By decreasing the loan-to-value ratio (i.e., the amount of money borrowed divided by the cost or value of the property purchased, expressed as a percentage), a lender provides a smaller portion of the capital for a property and lowers its potential for loss. Loan-to-value ratios may vary a great deal, depending on the nature of the environmental problem. When a lender does lower its loan-to-value ratio, the buyer must either put up more cash, get the seller to lower the price or take back a second note, or find another lender willing to grant a second mortgage. It is advantageous to the primary lender when the seller takes back a note on the property. This means that the original owner is still involved with the property and may share any future liability. It may be difficult for the purchaser to find a second mortgagee because other lenders are also likely to be apprehensive about properties with environmental risk.

One is likely to encounter a higher debt coverage ratio (i.e., net operating income divided by annual debt service) when applying for a loan on a property that has potential environmental problems. The lender that demands a debt coverage ratio as high as 2.0 to 3.0 for a problem property may accept a ratio of 1.5 to 2.0 for a less-risky property. This allows the lender to make loans with greater confidence. When the lender has secured a higher debt coverage ratio, any costs associated with environmental problems on the property are less likely to deplete cash flow to the extent that the mortgagor can no longer cover debt service.

Lenders are becoming less and less likely to grant assumable loans—especially loans that do not require lender approval of a new mortgagor. Although such mortgages are rapidly becoming a thing of the past, a few words are warranted because of their special environmental significance. When a lender has granted an assumable mortgage, a buyer can assume the seller's old loan (sometimes without lender approval). From that point forward, the lender can no longer seek recourse from the seller (i.e., the original mortgagor) if the buyer (who has assumed the loan) defaults. One can see how an assumable loan would take away much of the lender's ability to control environmental liability.

From the seller's viewpoint, having an assumable loan may mean that funds are immediately available for financing the sale. Primary loan approval is avoided and the closing of the sale is expedited. What is more, due diligence periods may be shorter because environmental issues are investigated at the buyer's discretion. With an assumable mortgage that does not require lender approval, there is no lender looking over the buyer's shoulder and requiring certain environmental site assessments prior to loan approval. If the buyer is satisfied that the property has been sufficiently scrutinized, that is enough. Any buyer taking over an assumed loan should act as if he or she were the lender and insist on a Preliminary Site Assessment (at the very least). Admittedly, this will increase the cost of an assumable loan, but it may save a great deal of time and money in the future.

Lender Requirements. In addition to (or even instead of) restrictions on a certain loan, most lenders will have additional requirements that must be satisfied or agreed to by the purchaser. Environmental testing in the form of a Preliminary Site Assessment (PSA) or a Phase I Site Assessment (Phase I) is becoming routine practice prior to the purchase and sale of real estate. Lenders with specific concerns about a property may require additional testing before loan approval, including IAQ testing, groundwater sampling, and even a Phase II assessment (regardless of the outcome of the PSA or Phase I). In light of testing results, lenders may demand cleanup, remediation, or routine inspections to monitor the situation. Some lenders require a cleanup fund to be maintained in escrow or provision of additional collateral. These requirements will be part of the loan agreement.

Bad experiences with environmental problems in the past make a lender much more likely to require extra testing. The fact that such tests are rarely done at the lender's expense emphasizes the need for a purchaser to be aware of the lender's policies.

Some institutions may be willing to forego some or all restrictions on a loan in return for additional collateral. The kind of supplementary collateral sought is usually land or facilities that have been tested previously, with no indication of problems. This gives the lender a sense of confidence because the second property provides a means to collect on the debt if environmental problems make loan payment impossible for the owner.

Other institutions require the seller to put funds in escrow to be used in the event of future problems (a practice that is becoming more and more common). The amount required is usually equal to the estimated cleanup cost for the problem(s) in existence (funds placed in escrow are from the proceeds of the closing). These escrow funds would be released to the seller at a predetermined annual rate. For example, a $2.5 million escrow might be established because of groundwater contamination with the agreement that $500,000 would be released to the seller each year that there are no costs associated with the problem. In this example, both the lender and the buyer are provided with a source of funds to draw on if, within the next five years, they have to deal with environmental problems.

Lenders may specify that remediation and/or cleanup must take place before closing. This is common when dealing with a type of problem that can be remediated in a straightforward manner (e.g., soil contamination or asbestos). A long-term remediation program might be impossible to complete before closing (e.g., some groundwater contamination remediation projects can take years).

Lenders may also mandate annual property inspections to be performed during the term of the loan. Sometimes property managers are allowed to conduct these inspections as long as they submit completed inspection forms to the lender (such forms are either developed or approved by the lender). Other lenders require inspections to be performed by an outside party (e.g., a professional engineer or consultant). Regardless of who conducts the inspections, written reports of the results should be provided to the lender on a regular basis, as specified in the loan documents.

Restrictions may be written into the environmental section of the loan document, along with such things as requirements for environmental lease clauses and specific procedures for tenant screening and lease approval (as discussed in chapter 7). It is very important to have this section of the loan document reviewed by an attorney and understood by everyone involved in the management of the property; failure to fully comply with loan requirements constitutes a material breach of contract and default of the loan.

In summary: It is invaluable to have information regarding exclusions, restrictions, and requirements for a select group of lenders. Knowing a lender's policy up front can only speed the loan-approval process. Most lenders have written environmental guidelines for their own use, and they may be willing to provide a copy to a borrower. If this information cannot be obtained in writing, a short interview with a loan officer can provide a sense of each lender's range of acceptable (environment-related) terms for their loans.

PUBLIC RELATIONS (PR)
AND "GREEN" MARKETING

In many respects, the real estate industry as a whole is perceived as opposed to environmental protection. The so-called "media," the public, and environmental groups have been known to treat real estate professionals as though they were some kind of "enemy"—especially if those professionals are developers. Whether real or imagined, this industry image makes it absolutely necessary for the real estate professional to have good public relations and so-called "green marketing" skills.

As real estate-related activities become more environmentally friendly, it is important to publicize that fact. It is true that the real estate industry has a major impact on the environment (through the generation of waste alone). Consider the example of a building manager who develops and implements a voluntary recycling program; this is a change that should be made known to the public (who would otherwise remain unaware). Although extra time and money may be spent on the implementation of an environmentally friendly program, the positive opinions engendered are likely to provide a significant payoff.

In addition to developing a recycling program, other things can be done to foster goodwill in the community. Such plans include replacing chemical fertilizers and pesticides with "organic" or nontoxic substitutes, recycling construction wastes while a project is being built or renovated, and recycling or replacing CFCs during HVAC maintenance and servicing. When money has been invested in the environment, a press release may be used to alert various media to the change.

Claims made in the process of "green" marketing should be specific and significant. General assertions that "we're the most environmentally friendly development in town" are vague, unprovable, and suggestive of untruth to the listener or reader. Statements should never be made if there is any risk that they could be refuted—green marketing can be turned into a PR problem very easily.

The following guidelines are intended to help owners and managers develop messages that will generate good public relations on the environmental front.

1. First and foremost: *Publicize only those activities that can be demonstrated to be environmentally friendly.*
2. Publicize environmentally friendly activities that are unusual to the community.
3. Publicize environmentally friendly activities that are voluntary and involve major expenditures or major policy changes.
4. Publicize other environmentally friendly activities that are voluntary.
5. Refrain from publicizing environmentally friendly activities that are required by law—this draws attention to possible noncompliance in the past.
6. Refrain from publicizing vague or unprovable claims.
7. Refrain from publicizing activities that are of questionable impact or value.
8. Refrain from initiating argument or debate with citizens' or environmental activists' groups. A simple "no comment" may be the most effective response to questions and accusations from critical factions. (Public opinion is more likely to be turned *against* a real estate organization than for it.)

QUESTIONS OF ETHICS

The very complexity of environmental law allows for certain choices and interpretations that create issues with ethical implications. Certainly there are a multitude of ethical considerations related to the vast array of environmental issues; this section will examine a few such questions.

What are ethical actions? One might say that they are actions that conform to certain widely accepted morals or standards of behavior. However, words like "morals" and phrases such as "accepted standards of behavior" carry their own ambiguity. Just as the words "ethics" and "ethical" are difficult to define, judgments concerning ethics and ethical issues can be difficult to make. As is the case with other issues that are subject to interpretation, it is wise to establish policies or guidelines for dealing with questions of ethics. At the same time, it should be acknowledged that ethical issues are rarely clear-cut; case-by-case decisions may be necessary. Indeed, it would be inappropriate to suggest any definitive answers to ethical questions or ethical "rules of thumb."

Suffice it to say that almost every environmental problem encountered will pose some kind of question of ethics. What follows is a look at some basic issues for consideration as well as a few specific examples of situations that real estate professionals might encounter.

The important issues to weigh when faced with questions of environmental ethics are effectively the same as those that should guide other ethics-related decisions. It must be remembered that environmental issues elicit emotional responses; this makes extra caution advisable. Here are some of the questions that should be explored when faced with a decision concerning an environmental problem.

- How does it impact the short- and long-term health and safety of the people in the area?
- Does this action create the potential for liability in the future?
- Are there any obligations to the community that should be considered?
- Does it violate the letter or spirit of the law?
- How will reputations be affected by the action being considered (e.g., of the property, its owner and staff, and any associated companies)?
- Does the action violate any policies of the owner or the management company?
- What kind of publicity will this action generate and how will such publicity be handled?
- Is everyone comfortable with this decision (i.e., could this action weigh heavily on someone's conscience now or in the future)?

The last question on this list is the most vague; admittedly, everyone has different sensitivities in matters of conscience. Nevertheless, it is important to acknowledge that some person or persons must assume responsibility for any and all actions taken—and while responsibility may have legal and fiscal components, it may have emotional ones as well.

The next step is to put this advice into context. Here are three examples of "environmental" situations that pose ethical questions. These are the types of problems that should signal a need to consider the questions that have just been cited.

1. A potential buyer who has little knowledge of commercial real estate and less of environmental law is looking for a personal investment. A property has been located that seems appropriate, and the current owner has an assumable mortgage that does not require lender's approval.

    During the prepurchase property inspection, the prospective buyer discovers an old repair shed that has long since been abandoned. Outside the shed there is a gasoline pump marked with a sign that lists the price of gasoline as $.34 per gallon and another sign that simply states "Contains Lead, For Use as a Motor Fuel Only." Through personal reading, the prospective buyer is aware of the problems presented by lead in groundwater and soil. The prospect asks if the repair shed and gasoline pump have ever been brought to the attention of the proper authorities and, if so, whether there is cause for concern. The present owner has in fact reported the presence of the repair shed and gasoline pump to the state agency, but this was done several years ago. At that time, the state agency representatives expressed little concern and stated no requirements for filing an official report. Provided the gasoline pump remains "inactive," there are no regulations that require the owner to do anything more regarding its presence on this particular property.

The issue of *how* to answer the buyer's question can be interpreted as an ethical matter. Legally, the owner (or owner's representative) can respond by stating the fact that the situation was reported and, at that time, no additional action was required. One question remains: Should the owner point out the fact that one could reasonably suspect some kind of contamination as a result of the presence of the gasoline pump?

2. Asbestos has been discovered in a property managed by ABC Management. In this property, insulation used as pipe wrapping in the mechanical rooms is made of an asbestos-containing material (ACM). ABC manages the property for XYZ Real Estate Investment Trust (XYZ REIT); this particular management contract generates about $500,000 in annual revenue for the management firm. The property where asbestos was discovered is a high-rise office building that was built between 1973 and 1974. It is 90 percent leased, and approximately one-third of the existing leases will expire within the next twelve months.

The insulation material containing asbestos is undamaged and in excellent condition. An environmental engineer has estimated that removal would cost approximately $1 million; the engineer recommends the implementation of an operation and maintenance (O & M) program that would cost about $50,000 per year. In this particular case, the location and condition of the asbestos does not trigger any local, state, or federal community or tenant notification requirements.

Whenever asbestos is discovered in a managed property, it is ABC Management's policy to always notify owners, contractors, and tenants—*in that order*. When XYZ REIT is alerted to the situation, however, it refuses to allow ABC Management to notify tenants because of the concern that those whose leases are due to expire will not stay. XYZ REIT threatens to terminate the management contract if ABC Management fails to heed their instruction. Furthermore, the REIT says it will file a breach of contract lawsuit for each tenant who does not opt for lease renewal after receiving notification of the presence of asbestos.

In this case, the property management company is faced with a question that could be construed as an ethical one. XYZ REIT is not asking ABC Management to do anything illegal. All the same, ABC will be acting against its policy to inform all involved parties. Should the company comply with XYZ REIT's wishes?

3. John Smith, the environmental manager for ABC Management Company, also serves as property manager for an office building that is located on the site of an old industrial park. Mr. Smith is aware that tests performed around the site have revealed groundwater contamination (these tests were all performed about a half mile away from the office building). To date, no environmental assessments have ever been performed on the office building site itself, but Mr. Smith reasons that it may well have the same type of groundwater contamination as its surrounding neighbors. Because environmental assessments or tests have never been performed, there is no concrete evidence to support these suspicions.

Suddenly, a private investment club offers to pay cash for the property. Understandably, the present owner of the office building is eager to complete such a deal. As a result, the vice president of property management for ABC Management asks Mr. Smith to inform the buyers that, *to the best of his knowledge,* the property is not contaminated.

Here, Mr. Smith is faced with a consideration of an ethical nature. As stated, he has no absolute proof of contamination on the office building site. If he obliges the request of his supervisor, he is making the assumption that an unsubstantiated suspicion is not part of his *knowledge* (or, stated another way, that knowledge per se is made up only of verified facts). Should Mr. Smith share any of his speculation with the prospective purchasers, or should he do as his vice president asks?

Many situations that involve environmental problems can create ethical questions for people in the real estate industry. There are no concrete answers to the questions posed. All such decisions should be made carefully and with the assistance of appropriate professionals. It is always essential to consider health and safety issues; these matters may dictate any decisions that must be made.

THE ROLE OF THE ENVIRONMENTAL MANAGER

As environmental issues become increasingly complex, real estate firms and management companies will recognize the need for staff members who are environmental operations managers. It is very difficult to outline a precise job description for the environmental manager because company needs will vary. The needs of a brokerage company will differ from those of a development company, institutional investor, property management firm, etc.

Levels of environmental training vary widely from professional to professional. Some people have college degrees in "environmental affairs" or a related major. Others have attended environmental seminars or courses offered by colleges, universities, and private industry sources. Some law courses are particularly applicable to this field of expertise. As the need for environmental professionals continues to increase, educational opportunities are likely to become more widespread. In the interim, the experience that an environmental manager has is just as important as his or her education.

The environmental specialist in the field of real estate should have some industry experience to fully grasp the connection between environmental issues and real estate. When one person is the designated "environmental manager" for a management company, the information he or she has obtained through experience is readily available to the company's other employees. An environmental manager may wear other hats and perform additional duties (e.g., as site manager, construction manager, property manager, etc.) because environmental issues will probably not occupy him or her full time. Although large companies and institutions may require separate divisions for environmental management, this is not usually the case with small and moderately sized companies.

As a general rule, the environmental manager should coordinate activities, provide information, know the appropriate resources for assistance (e.g., environmental engineers, consultants, attorneys, etc.), and have a general knowledge of environmental laws (local, state, and federal) as they apply to the company's operations. As a coordinator, the environmental manager should work with purchasers, lenders, sellers, attorneys, and consultants to schedule environmental assessments and assure that the appropriate parties receive the information that has been collected. The environmental manager should accompany consultants on property tours, tenant visits, and other on-site activities to assure the completeness of the information collected. Not only does this offer the manager an opportunity to learn more about assessments and inspections, it also tends to make the whole process easier (e.g., tenants are less likely to resist inspection when a manager is present). Familiarity with applicable local and state laws is another requirement for an environmental manager; he or she should have a working knowledge of the primary federal laws (which in fact form the basis for most other environmental laws). The environmental manager should maintain a list of qualified attorneys, consultants, engineers, and insurance companies as well as files of lender information. A list of local, state, and federal agencies should include names and phone numbers of contacts. It is also a good idea for the environmental manager to develop a library of reference material that might include books of common chemical terms, environmental dictionaries, copies of prevailing laws, and collected newspaper and magazine articles regarding related topics. He or she should maintain a file of all the environmental reports written about company properties; this assures that such documents are easy to access because they are all in one place.

In fact, one of the purposes of having an environmental manager is *centralization*—of information collected and shared, of actions considered and taken. While the company is cultivating the environmental manager's knowledge through focused experiences, it is more likely to implement environmental policies that are consistent and carefully considered.

In addition, the environmental manager is able to anticipate problems common to a particular location or property type. Not only does the environmental manager help the company deal with existing environmental problems, he or she helps them to avoid future ones.

As environmental issues continue to have an impact on the real estate industry, the need for trained professionals will become even more pronounced. Having an environmental manager on staff is just one step toward addressing environmental problems effectively; no one can replace the expertise offered by engineers, consultants, attorneys, and other specialists.

This text has tried to demonstrate that *every* real estate professional can benefit from a foundation of knowledge concerning environmental issues. In truth, effective handling of environmental problems often involves hiring the right professionals for the job and timing their involvement appropriately. Nevertheless, the first step toward developing such a skill is the acquisition of some basic environmental knowledge.

APPENDIX A

Example Lease Clause—Environmental

(a) **Definitions.** For purposes of this lease: (i) "CERCLA" means The Comprehensive Environmental Response, Compensation, and Liability Act of 1980, as amended; (ii) "Hazardous Material" or "Hazardous Materials" means and includes, without limitation, gasoline, crude oil, fuel oil, diesel oil, lubricating oil, sludge, oil refuse, oil mixed with wastes and any other petroleum-related product, flammable explosives, radioactive materials, any substance defined or designated as a "hazardous substance," under CERCLA or any other federal, state, or local environmental law; (iii) "Release" shall have the meaning given such term, or any similar term, in CERCLA; and (iv) "Environmental Law" or "Environmental Laws" shall mean any "Superfund" or "Superlien" law, or any other federal, state, or local statute, law, ordinance, code, rule, regulation, order or decree, that regulates, relates to, or imposes liability or standards of conduct concerning any hazardous materials as may now or at any time hereafter be in effect and as amended from time to time, and all regulations promulgated thereunder or in connection therewith, including, but not limited to: CERCLA; the Superfund Amendments and Reauthorization Act of 1986 ("SARA"); the Hazardous and Solid Waste Amendments (HSWA); the Clean Air Act ("CAA"); the Clean Water Act ("CWA"); the Toxic Substances Control Act ("TSCA"); the Solid Waste Disposal Act ("SWDA"), as amended by the Resource Conservation and Recovery Act ("RCRA"); and the Occupational Safety and Health Act of 1970 ("OSHA").

(b) **Use.** Tenant hereby covenants and agrees that: (i) no activity shall be undertaken on the premises, nor shall any activity be undertaken within the building if the premises are less than the whole building or on the land on which the premises are situated by Tenant or its agents, employees, or contractors, which would in either event cause (A) the premises, building, or land to become a hazardous waste treatment, storage, or disposal facility regulated or subject to regulation under any Environmental Law, (B) a Release of any Hazardous Material into the environment at, on, in, under, above, through, or surrounding the premises, building, or land, or (C) the discharge of pollutants or effluents into any water source or system, which would require a permit under any federal law, state law, local ordinance, or any other Environmental Law pertaining to such matters; (ii) Tenant shall at its sole cost and expense comply with, and ensure compliance by all other parties with, all applicable Environmental Laws relating to or affecting the premises, and Tenant shall keep the premises free and clear of any liens imposed pursuant to any applicable Environmental Laws arising out of Tenant's use of the premises; (iii) Tenant shall, at Tenant's sole cost and expense, obtain and/or maintain all licenses, permits, and/or other governmental or regulatory actions necessary to comply with all applicable environmental laws and Tenant shall at all times remain in full compliance with the terms and provisions of the permits; (iv) Tenant shall immediately give Landlord oral and written notice in the event that Tenant receives any communication from any governmental agency, entity, or any other party with regard to Hazardous Materials on, from, or affecting the premises or the operation of Tenant's business therein; and (v) Tenant shall, at Tenant's sole cost and expense, conduct and complete all investigations, studies, sampling, and testing, and all remedial, removal, and other actions necessary to clean up and remove all Hazardous Materials on, from, or affecting the premises or, where resulting from acts or omissions of Tenant or its agents, employees, and contractors, affecting the building and/or land, in accordance with all applicable Environmental Laws and to Landlord's satisfaction.

(c) **Indemnification.** Tenant hereby indemnifies Landlord, its agents, partners, and assigns and agrees to hold Landlord, its agents, partners, and assigns harmless from and against any and all liens, demands, suits, actions, proceedings, disbursements, liabilities, losses, litigation, damages, judgments, obligations, penalties, injuries, costs, expenses (including, without limitation, attorneys' and experts' fees), and claims of any and every kind whatsoever paid, incurred, suffered by, or asserted against Landlord and/or the premises, building and/or land for, with respect to, or as a direct or indirect result of: (i) the Release or presence from, in, on, over, or under the premises of any Hazardous Materials, regardless of quantity, within the control of Tenant; (ii) the Release or presence from, in, on, over, or under the building or land of any Hazardous Materials regardless of quantity where caused by Tenant or its agents, employees, contractors, or vendors; (iii) the violation of any Environmental Laws relating to or affecting the premises or Tenant within the control of Tenant; and (iv) the failure of Tenant to comply fully with the terms and provisions of this contract; provided, however, that nothing contained in this contract shall make Tenant liable or responsible for conditions existing prior to the commencement of the term of this lease or first occurring after the expiration of the term of this lease except where caused by Tenant or its agents, employees, or contractors.

(d) **Violations/Noncompliance.** In the event Landlord suspects, in its reasonable opinion, that Tenant has violated any of the covenants contained in this contract, or that the premises, building, or land are not in compliance with Environmental Laws for any reason, or that the premises, building, or land are not free of Hazardous Materials for any reason, Tenant shall take such steps as Landlord requires by written notice to Tenant in order to confirm or deny such occurrences, including, without limitation, the preparation of environmental studies, audits, surveys, or reports. In the event that Tenant fails to take such action, Landlord may take such action and shall have such access to the premises as Landlord deems necessary, and the cost and expenses of all such actions taken by Landlord, including, without limitation, Landlord's attorneys' fees, shall be due and payable by Tenant upon demand therefor from Landlord as additional rent hereunder. Further, Landlord reserves the right at any time and from time to time to enter the premises following reasonable advance notice thereof to Tenant (except in cases of emergency) in order to perform periodic environmental studies, audits, surveys, and reports and in order to determine whether Tenant is in compliance with the terms of this contract.

(e) **Insurance/Underground Storage Tanks.**

1. In the event that additional insurance in the form of pollution insurance, liability insurance, or any other type of insurance is required specifically due to Tenant's occupancy, all costs of procuring and placing said additional insurance is the Tenant's sole cost and responsibility. Failure to purchase and maintain such insurance naming the Landlord as an additional named insured party shall constitute a breach of this contract and a default of this lease. Policies known as "Claims-Made" policies are hereby deemed to be unacceptable for these purposes.
2. Should Tenant's use require Underground Storage Tanks (USTs), which are either installed or otherwise exist in, on, around, and under the property or premises, maintaining such tanks and the associated permits, registration, and all associated liability shall be the direct responsibility of Tenant and shall be done at Tenant's sole cost and expense. In the event Landlord must expend funds with regard to a UST(s), Tenant shall reimburse Landlord the actual amount of such expenditures plus a *[state percentage in words (and numbers)]* percent administrative fee.

(f) The obligations and liabilities of Tenant under this environmental lease clause shall survive the expiration or earlier termination of this lease.

Reproduced with permission from Trammell Crow Company (Charlotte Division).

APPENDIX B

Example Lease Clause—Estoppel

Tenant agrees from time to time to provide Owner or Owner's designee with a signed estoppel certificate stating that this lease is in full force and effect, the date to which rent has been paid, the unexpired term remaining on the lease, and other such matters pertaining to the lease, as requested by Owner or Owner's agent. Tenant must deliver this certificate within *[specify number of days in words (and numbers)]* days of receiving written request. It is understood and agreed that Tenant's obligation to furnish such estoppel certificates in the allotted time is a material inducement to Owner's execution of this lease. It is further agreed that Tenant's failure to sign and return an estoppel certificate that Owner or Owner's agent has delivered to the tenant will be treated as confirmation of the statements contained therein.

Reproduced with permission from Trammell Crow Company (Charlotte Division).

APPENDIX   C

Example Environmental Estoppel Certificate

To: *[Insert owner's legal name and management company name]*
Regarding: *[Cite property address]*
In connection with the above-named property of which the premises are a part, Tenant certifies and represents to Landlord as follows:

1. The undersigned is the Tenant specified in the lease on the premises dated *[insert date lease was signed]* by and between *[insert name of landlord as identified on the lease]* (Landlord) and *[insert name of tenant as identified on the lease]* (Tenant). Tenant has not assigned, transferred, encumbered, or hypothecated any interest under the lease, and has not entered into any sublease, concession agreement, or license covering all or any part of the premises.

2. The lease is in full force and effect as of this date and Tenant is the sole operator in charge of the activities performed therein.

3. Tenant has accepted the premises and is in full occupancy and possession thereof. All space and improvements described in the lease have been furnished, constructed, and completed in accordance with the lease requirements and Landlord has otherwise reasonably satisfied all commitments made to induce Tenant to enter into the lease. Tenant is not aware of any inaccuracies in the square footage for the premises described in the lease.

4. Tenant certifies that Tenant is current in the payment of base rent as of the last day of the month this Estoppel Certificate is dated. Tenant is current in the payment of all additional rent and any other charges due under the lease. Tenant is not in default under the lease, and no fact or condition exists which, after notice or passage of time or both, could ripen into a default.

5. Tenant hereby further certifies as follows: (a) Tenant is not subject to any action under the federal bankruptcy law or any insolvency laws or other laws for consolidation of indebtedness or the reorganization of debtors, nor is Tenant insolvent in any sense; (b) Tenant has not received any notice of prior assignment or transfer of the lease or of the rents or amounts therefrom by Landlord; (c) the individual executing this Certificate on behalf of the undersigned has the power and authority to execute and deliver the Certificate.

6. Tenant (a) presently is not engaged in and does not permit, (b) has not at any time in the past engaged in or permitted, and (c) has no knowledge that any third person or entity has engaged in or permitted any operations or activities upon, or any use or occupancy of, the premises, or any portion thereof, for any purpose which includes the presence of any petroleum products or hazardous substances (as the same may be defined or regulated under any federal, state, or local environmental law), except for common janitorial and office supplies. Specific hazardous materials that are typical for companies in the business in which Tenant engages must be specified in an attachment. Tenant has obtained and maintains in full force and effect, all necessary permits, licenses, and authorizations required for the operation of Tenant's business at the premises. Tenant is currently in full compliance with all covenants, conditions, and restrictions affecting the premises and any governmental permits or licenses issued relative to the premises, including any laws, covenants or permits relating to environmental matters.

7. Tenant hereby certifies that it has not received any correspondence or other contact relating to the issuance of any Notices of Violation (NOVs), nor received any Notices of Violation (NOVs) from any federal, state, or local governmental agencies with regard to any petroleum substances, hazardous substances, or other regulated substances

or materials within the past five (5) years except as noted in the "Exhibit" attached hereto. Copies of such NOVs are on file and are accessible to Landlord within 48 hours of a written request for the same.

8. Tenant certifies that there are no underground storage tanks (USTs) located on the premises except as listed on the attached exhibit, and that appropriate tests are regularly performed to establish the integrity of such UST(s) and copies of such are available to Landlord within 48 hours of a written request for the same. Tenant also certifies that all local, state, and federal registration requirements and fees for said USTS are current and in compliance with all appropriate laws and regulations.

9. Tenant hereby certifies that all materials, wastes, and other substances are disposed of in compliance with all applicable local, state, and federal laws and appropriate disposal documentation and manifests are on record and available for Landlord's inspection within 48 hours of a written request for the same.

10. Tenant hereby certifies that Landlord, its agents, partners, employees, and assigns do not in any way participate in the day-to-day decisions or operations of Tenant's business, nor is Landlord involved in any ownership interest of the operation, nor does Landlord have any authority or responsibility, implied or otherwise, to determine the policies, procedures or methods used in the utilization, storage, or disposal of any supplies, products, stock, materials, or other substances associated with Tenant's business or operations, hazardous or otherwise. Tenant also certifies that Landlord acts solely as a commercial real estate Landlord and only performs in the capacity specified in the lease document referred to in this Estoppel Certificate.

The undersigned makes the statements herein for the benefit of the Landlord with the intent and understanding that this Certificate may be relied on by buyers, lenders, governmental agencies, courts, and other parties associated, their heirs, successors and assigns.

Tenant: _____
By (name): _____
Title: _____
Date: _____

ALL ATTACHED SCHEDULES ARE TO BE INITIALED

A P P E N D I X   D
Environmental Issues Addressed in Management Contracts

This appendix provides management companies and managers with a list of the types of environmental clauses that should be included in management contracts (also called management agreements). Specified clauses serve only as examples and do not make allowances for particular state and local laws that may have an impact on their contents. Like any legal document, a management contract should be reviewed by an attorney and environmental clauses included in it should be reviewed by an attorney specializing in environmental affairs.

It is also necessary to note that some owners may resist the inclusion of environmental clauses in a management contract. In such instances, negotiation is necessary. The management company or manager should seek legal advice regarding those issues that are negotiable and those that are not.

Nevertheless, management contracts that contain certain environmental representations and warranties as well as an environmental indemnification are better contracts for the management company and the manager. The well-informed manager understands the types of environmental clauses that should be requested during contract negotiations.

The following representations and warranties can be found in management contracts.

1. Disclosure related to past uses of the property by the owner, past owners, and tenants, including the presence of storage tanks and petroleum.
2. Disclosure related to the presence of hazardous material on the property including PCBs and asbestos.
3. Disclosure of chemical usage on the property in the past, by the owner, past owner, and tenants.
4. Disclosure and explanation of past waste disposal practices by the owner, past owner, and tenants.
5. Disclosure stating that neither owner nor (to the owner's knowledge) any tenant has received any notices or correspondence from regulatory agencies, including notices of violation of any environmental, health, or safety laws or proceedings affecting or impacting the condition of the property.
6. Disclosure of all environmental problems or potential environmental problems of which the owner is aware, including those that are a result of off-site activity.
7. Disclosure of the current status and maintenance of permits in compliance with applicable laws and regulations.
8. Agreement regarding the inclusion of an environmental clause in tenants' leases.
9. Agreement regarding owner compliance with prevailing environmental laws and the procurement of all required environmental permits and licenses.

In addition, an environmental indemnification clause should be included in all management contracts. An example of such a clause appears on the following page.

Environmental Indemnification. Owner agrees to indemnify, defend, and hold Manager and its partners, officers, employees, and agents harmless from any claims, judgments, damages, penalties, fines, costs, liabilities, or losses, direct or indirect, known or unknown, including without limitation, attorneys' fees, consultants' fees, and expert fees, which are incurred or arise during or after the term of this Management Agreement from or in any way connected with the presence or suspected presence of hazardous substances existing or present on, under, about, or affecting the property prior to or after the execution of this Agreement, including, without limitation, (i) hazardous substances present or suspected to be present in the soil, groundwater, surface water, air, or soil vapor on, under, or about the property; (ii) hazardous substances that migrate, flow, percolate, diffuse, or in any way move onto or under the property; (iii) hazardous substances present on, under, or about the property as a result of any release, discharge, deposit, injection, leaking, pouring, leaching, emitting, pumping, emptying, dumping, spilling on, under, or about the property; and (iv) any misrepresentation or breach of warranty, covenant, representation or undertaking by Owner under this Agreement. Without limiting the generality of the foregoing, the indemnification provided by this paragraph specifically shall cover costs (including attorney and consultant fees) incurred in connection with any investigation of site conditions existing prior to or after the date of execution of this Agreement or any act, including, without limitation, studies or reports as needed or required, remedial, removal or restoration work undertaken voluntarily by Owner or requested or required by any federal, state, or local governmental agency.

For purposes of this section, "hazardous substances" shall mean any hazardous, toxic, radioactive, infectious or carcinogenic substance, material, gas, or waste which is or becomes listed or regulated by any federal, state, or local environmental law or governmental authority or agency, including, without limitation, petroleum and petroleum products, PCBs, asbestos, and all substances defined as hazardous materials, hazardous wastes, hazardous substances, or extremely hazardous waste under any federal, state, or local law or regulation.

Owner or agent thereof hereby acknowledges and agrees that Manager, and its partners, officers, employees, and agents is not an "operator" of either the property or the tenant operations thereon and is not an "operator" as defined by any current or pending state, local, or federal environmental laws. Owner hereby agrees to defend Manager, and its partners, officers, employees, and agents from any actions occurring as a result of the management of the property.

In the event Owner defaults under any terms or conditions of this clause, it shall be deemed an environmental default and as such shall be deemed to be a material default of the terms and conditions of this Agreement; it shall be considered a breach of contract and shall be subject to all applicable legal remedies. In the event of default under this clause, Manager shall be able to terminate this Agreement with *[specify number of days in words (and numbers)]* days written notice of default hereunder.

In the event a regulation or legislative act requires a change in compliance procedures or practices, Owner hereby agrees to comply within the allowable legal time limit or such extension periods as may be available or granted. Owner shall be solely responsible for compliance and shall indemnify Manager, and its partners, officers, employees, and agents for any breach or failure of Owner or property to comply. Failure to comply within the statutory time limit shall constitute a material breach of this Agreement and Manager shall be able to terminate this Agreement with *[specify number of days in words (and numbers)]* days written notice of default. Manager, and its partners, officers, employees, and agents shall be indemnified against any actions initiated with regard to Owner's failure to comply or any other default under this clause.

Adapted with permission from Trammell Crow Company (Charlotte Division).

A P P E N D I X   E

Indications of Possible Contamination

The following list is intended to provide some guidelines regarding the types of things that may signal the potential for environmental problems on a property. It is also worthwhile to note that the presence of any one of these "indicators" on an adjacent property may also be cause for concern.

1. Gasoline or propane dispensers may indicate an underground storage tank (UST); it is wise to check for stains from spills or leakage.
2. Aboveground storage tanks can be an indication of previous problems with underground tanks, or they may become a site for contamination caused by tank leakage or loading spills (again, it is prudent to look for stains).
3. Historical use by industrial or commercial facilities.
4. Historical use by any governmental organization (federal, state, or local), especially involving such activities as machine repair and refueling.
5. Past history of oil, gas, or mining operations.
6. Areas of dead or sickly plants in otherwise normal vegetation coverage; areas without plant growth that are surrounded by healthy vegetation.
7. Developments built on previous landfill or other disposal sites.
8. Old waste treatment, waste storage, or chemical storage areas.
9. Ponds or water tanks containing drainage pipes.
10. Cleared areas that exist for no obvious reason or purpose.
11. Unpleasant odors or unusual odors of any kind.
12. Vent pipes protruding from the ground (these generally indicate some form of gas release process and may indicate a landfill area).
13. Oily or discolored staining on the ground.
14. The presence of electrical transformers (they may contain PCBs).
15. Buildings constructed or rehabilitated prior to the late 1970s are the most likely to include asbestos-containing materials (ACMs).
16. The presence of a wrecking yard, a salvage yard, or abandoned machinery.
17. The presence of a metalworking or machine shop.
18. Areas where woodworking has been or is being done.
19. The presence of 55-gallon drums, whether marked or unmarked, empty or containing something. The accuracy of labeling on large drums (or any other types of containers, for that matter) should never be assumed.
20. Blown-in, "fuzzy" insulation in walls and ceilings and around pipes.
21. Waste dump sites (for municipal wastes, tenant wastes, construction materials, etc.).
22. The presence of an oily substance in the water of nearby streams and ponds.
23. Areas with discarded items (e.g., tires, oil cans, metals, etc.).
24. Areas where trash has been burned.
25. Areas where substances are suspected to be "washing" or "migrating" from neighboring properties.
26. Off-site tank farms bordering the property.
27. Interior storage areas that are dirty, untidy, inaccessible, or inadequately equipped with fire protection.
28. Interior work areas that are dirty, untidy, inaccessible, or inadequately equipped with fire protection.

29. Open containers indoors.
30. Corroded or discolored floor drains.
31. Stained sinks, toilets, or drains.
32. Special use facilities (e.g., medical office, dental office, photography studio, restaurant, dry-cleaning establishment).
33. Ash or powder accumulation.
34. Burned areas.
35. Retention basins or ponds that are not natural.
36. The presence of absorption materials on the ground.
37. Darkly stained areas of ground adjacent to parking lots or concrete pads.
38. Greasy accumulation on ground or parking lot.
39. Lack of monitoring devises near underground storage tanks (USTs).
40. Staining around exterior transformers.
41. Staining on power poles and/or the ground beneath elevated transformers.
42. Metallic substances on the ground.
43. Storage of old batteries on unprotected ground.
44. Rainbow-colored substance on top of any water on or around the property.
45. Rusting containers in outdoor storage areas.
46. Stained concrete in outdoor storage areas.
47. Residue from powerwashing.
48. Indication of any piping leaks.
49. Leaks or staining around emergency generators or air compressors.
50. Newly repaired areas near suspected UST sites.
51. Stains on walls near entries, exits, or other building openings.
52. Pipe extending through a wall and not attached to exterior machinery or tanks.
53. Dust or powder accumulation around doors and/or windows.
54. Areas where brick appears to be worn smooth or concrete is grooved or eroded.
55. The appearance of oily or greasy residue inside the lips of downspouts.
56. Staining on roof near exhaust vents.
57. Greasy build-up near ventilation apparatus.
58. Heavy rust on ventilation or outside air ducts.
59. Ventilation or outside air ducts that are deteriorated.
60. Areas of excessive roof patching near a particular roof penetration.
61. Hazard "diamonds" posted on walls (i.e., the National Fire Protection Association symbols for hazardous materials).

APPENDIX   F

Visual Examples of Possible Environmental Contamination

Top. Substandard storage area management. Stains on the walls indicate poor handling of materials (e.g., spillage); stains located high on the wall might suggest intentional dumping. The hazardous materials "diamond" posted in the center of the picture is red; this indicates flammability. Power lines leading into the building are located directly above the area in which flammable substances are stored and there is no fire-fighting equipment visible.

Bottom. Remote collection of drums. Sites such as these can be found on isolated areas of farms and ranches and in areas behind manufacturing facilities. Drums that originally contained something else (e.g., pesticides) were often kept and used for storage of other materials or for accumulation and/or burning of wastes. Activities such as chemical storage and waste disposal might suggest the possibility of soil or groundwater contamination.

Top. Wall stains "point" directly to the ground and an area where vegetation has died.

Bottom. An old underground storage tank that has been removed. The visible evidence of corrosion and decay suggests that it had been leaking before removal.

Top. Periphery of a site with storage adjacent to fencing. In this photograph, one can see where water run-off from a storage area has created "pathways" of stained soil and dead and dying vegetation.

Bottom. Large, aboveground storage tanks. The presence of any kind of chemical manufacturing or large-scale chemical storage serves as a signal that one should check for groundwater problems.

APPENDIX G

Sources of Information

The organizations, associations, publications, and other sources of information listed here are offered solely as a guide to the array of environmental material and resources that is available to the real estate professional. Material can be procured by purchasing or subscribing to publications; contacting companies, associations, or publishers; or visiting libraries. Additional book titles and periodicals can be identified through library card files and in *Books in Print* and *Periodicals in Print* published by R. R. Bowker. This list is not intended to be all-inclusive, nor does the author or the Institute of Real Estate Management endorse any of the organizations or publications mentioned here.

GOVERNMENTAL AGENCIES

There are many governmental agencies that regulate activities related to the environment. All federal agencies mentioned here are located in Washington, D.C., unless otherwise indicated. Some are independent of the executive departments of the United States government. One such body is the Nuclear Regulatory Commission (NRC). Another is the Environmental Protection Agency (EPA), which is among the best known of the independent agencies. The EPA administers environmental policies, research, and regulations. Its branches include water; solid waste and emergency response; air and radiation; pesticides and toxic substances; and research and development. The EPA is divided into ten regions, each made up of several states. The list that follows includes the locations of the regional offices.

Region 1, Boston, Massachusetts
Connecticut
Maine
Massachusetts
New Hampshire
Rhode Island
Vermont

Region 2, New York, New York
New Jersey
New York
Puerto Rico
U.S. Virgin Islands.

Region 3, Philadelphia, Pennsylvania
Delaware
Washington, D.C.
Maryland
Pennsylvania
Virginia
West Virginia

Region 4, Atlanta, Georgia
Alabama
Florida
Georgia
Kentucky
Mississippi
North Carolina
South Carolina
Tennessee

Region 5, Chicago, Illinois
Illinois
Indiana
Michigan
Minnesota
Ohio
Wisconsin

Region 6, Dallas, Texas
Arkansas
Louisiana
New Mexico
Oklahoma
Texas

Region 7, Kansas City, Kansas
Iowa
Kansas
Missouri
Nebraska

Region 8, Denver, Colorado
Colorado
Montana
North Dakota
South Dakota
Utah
Wyoming

Region 9, San Francisco, California
Arizona
California
Hawaii
Nevada
American Samoa
Guam

Region 10, Seattle, Washington
Alaska
Idaho
Oregon
Washington

The EPA provides information on a vast number of environmental topics. Publications that are offered to the public address such issues as asbestos, radon, pesticides, and much more. Important EPA phone numbers include the following "hotlines."

- Asbestos   1-800-334-8571
- Pesticides   1-800-858-7378
- RCRA and Superfund (CERCLA)   1-800-424-9346
- TSCA   1-202-554-1404
- National response center (emergency response)   1-800-424-8802
- Whistle-blower   1-800-424-4000

Some of the executive departments of the United States government include offices or agencies that may have responsibilities related to the administration of environmental regulations and may also conduct environmental research and distribute related information.

- Department of Agriculture
  Animal and Plant Health Inspection Service
  Soil Conservation Service
  Forest Service
- Department of Commerce
  National Oceanic and Atmospheric Administration (NOAA)
- Department of Defense
  Army Corps of Engineers
- Department of Energy
  Energy Research Advisory Board
  Environment, Safety, and Health Agency
- Department of Health and Human Services
  Public Health Service
  National Institute of Health (in Bethesda, Maryland)
- Department of Housing and Urban Development
  Solar Energy and Energy Conservation Bank
- Department of Interior
  Bureau of Mines
  Minerals Management Service
  U.S. Fish and Wildlife Service
  U.S. Geological Survey
- Department of Labor
  Occupational Safety and Health Administration
- Department of Transportation
  Office of Hazardous Materials

Federal, state, and local agencies are usually listed in telephone directories.

PROFESSIONAL AND OTHER INDUSTRIAL ORGANIZATIONS

Professional organizations within the real estate industry include: the Institute of Real Estate Management (IREM) in Chicago, Illinois; National Association of Realtors (NAR) in Chicago, Illinois; Building Owners and Managers Association (BOMA) in Washington, D.C.; International Facility Management Association (IFMA) in Houston, Texas; International Association of Corporate Real Estate Executives (NACORE) in West Palm Beach, Florida; International Council of Shopping Centers (ICSC) in New York, New York; National Association of Home Builders (NAHB) in Washington, D.C.; National Association of Industrial and Office Parks (NAIOP) in Arlington, Virginia; and the Urban Land Institute (ULI) in Washington, D.C. These organizations may publish articles in their newsletters and periodicals concerning the effect of environmental issues on the industry.

Outside of the real estate industry, there are many technical, professional, and industrial organizations that can provide useful information regarding the environment and related issues.

Alliance for Responsible CFC Policy in Arlington, Virginia
Aluminum Recycling Association in Washington, D.C.
American Academy of Environmental Engineers in Washington, D.C.
American Forest Council in Washington, D.C.
American Petroleum Institute in Washington, D.C.
American Society of Heating, Refrigerating, and Air Conditioning Engineers (ASHRAE) in Atlanta, Georgia
Asbestos Information Association of North America in Arlington, Virginia
Association of Energy Engineers in Atlanta, Georgia
Association of Local Air Pollution Control Officials in Washington, D.C.
Chemical Manufacturers' Association in Washington, D.C.
Chemical Specialties Manufacturers' Association in Washington, D.C.
Hazardous Materials Advisory Council in Washington, D.C.
Hazardous Waste Treatment Council in Washington, D.C.
Institute of Scrap Recycling Industries in Washington, D.C.
Manufacturers of Emission Controls Association in Washington, D.C.
National Association of Environmental Managers in Washington, D.C.
National Association of Environmental Professionals in Washington, D.C.
National Association of Solvent Recyclers in Washington, D.C.
National Electrical Manufacturers Association in Washington, D.C.
National Fire Protection Association in Quincy, Massachusetts.
National Pest Control Association in Dunn Loring, Virginia
National Pesticide Telecommunications Network in Lubbock, Texas
National Safety Council in Chicago, Illinois
National Solid Waste Management Association in Washington, D.C.
U.S. Chamber of Commerce, Office of Energy and Natural Resources, in Washington, D.C.

OTHER ORGANIZATIONS

Other possible sources of information include organizations that have been established within the private sector to conduct research, distribute information, or to advocate or discourage particular activities relative to the environment.

Alliance of Environmental Education in Washington, D.C.
Citizens Clearinghouse for Hazardous Wastes in Arlington, Virginia
Clean Water Action Project in Washington, D.C.

Environmental Defense Fund in New York, New York
Friends of the Earth in Washington, D.C.
Greenpeace USA in Washington, D.C.
National Coalition Against the Misuse of Pesticides (NCAMP) in Washington, D.C.
National Recycling Coalition in Washington, D.C.
National Wildlife Federation in Washington, D.C.
Natural Resources Defense Council in Washington, D.C.
Rachel Carson Council in Chevy Chase, Maryland
Worldwatch Institute in Washington, D.C.

PUBLICATIONS AND OTHER SOURCES

Environmental information can also be gleaned from articles in newsletters and periodicals, brochures, books, and tapes (audio and video). Some publishers or distributors of environmental information may offer related courses and seminars. Educational offerings can be pursued through junior colleges, colleges, and universities as well as private sources (e.g., environmental consulting firms).

Published Materials

Dangerous Properties of Industrial Materials, Seventh Edition (Three volumes; Van Nostrand Reinhold, New York, N.Y.)

Energy (Windstar Foundation, Snowmass, Colo.)

Environmental Dispute Handbook: Liability and Claims (John Wiley & Sons, Inc., New York, N.Y.)

Environmental Law Handbook, Eleventh Edition (Government Institutes, Inc., Rockville, Md.)

Environmental Liability and Real Property Transactions (John Wiley & Sons, Inc., New York, N.Y.)

Environmental Regulatory Glossary, Fifth Edition (Government Institutes, Inc., Rockville, Md.)

Everyday Chemicals (Windstar Foundation, Snowmass, Colo.)

Fire Protection Guide to Hazardous Materials (National Fire Protection Association, Quincy, Mass.)

Guidance for Controlling ACM in Buildings (Environmental Protection Agency, Washington, D.C.)

Guidance for Data Usability in Risk Assessment (Environmental Protection Agency, Washington, D.C.)

Guide to Respiratory Protection for the Asbestos Abatement Industry (Environmental Protection Agency, Washington, D.C.)

Hazardous Waste Law and Practice (John Wiley & Sons, Inc., New York, N.Y.)

Managing Asbestos in Place: A Building Owner's Guide to O & M Programs for ACM (Environmental Protection Agency, Washington, D.C.)

Managing Environmental Hazards (JPM Reprint; Institute of Real Estate Management, Chicago, Ill.)

Managing Indoor Air Quality (Fairmont Press, Inc., Lilburn, Ga.)

Recycling (Windstar Foundation, Snowmass, Colo.)

Summary of Symposium on Health Aspects of Exposure to Asbestos in Buildings (Institute of Real Estate Management (IREM) Foundation, Chicago, Ill.)

Understanding the Small Quantity Generator Hazardous Waste Rules: A Handbook for Small Businesses (Environmental Protection Agency, Washington, D.C.)

Wetlands and Real Estate Development (Government Institute, Inc., Rockville, Md.)

Video Tapes

Environmental Issues for the Property Manager (E, H & S Educational Enterprises, Salt Lake City, Utah)

Environmental Issues in Business and Real Estate Transactions (E, H & S Educational Enterprises, Salt Lake City, Utah)

The Essentials of an Environmental Site Assessment (Government Institutes, Inc., Rockville, Md.)

Leaking Underground Storage Tanks (Government Institutes, Inc., Rockville, Md.)

Measuring Radon in Structures (Government Institutes, Inc., Rockville, Md.)

Medical Aspects and Controls of Sick Building Syndrome (E, H & S Educational Enterprises, Salt Lake City, Utah)

MSDS: Cornerstone of Chemical Safety (Government Institutes, Inc., Rockville, Md.)

Reducing the Risk of PCBs (Government Institutes, Inc., Rockville, Md.)

Glossary

Abatement   A reduction (partial or complete) of the intensity or concentration of something (e.g., contamination).

Absolute liability   Liability for an act that causes damage or harm to persons, property, or the environment, regardless of fault.

Adsorption   Adhesion of molecules to the surface of a solid or liquid, as when activated carbon is used to remove organic matter from air or water.

Ambient air   Air that is not confined by any structure; unconfined outside air.

Aquifer   An underground geological formation containing significant amounts of water (i.e., groundwater).

Asbestos   A fibrous mineral used to impart fireproofing characteristics to building materials, automobile brake linings, etc.; also used to provide insulation. Asbestos particles that become airborne (as friable asbestos) are a human health hazard.

Asbestos-containing material (ACM)   Any material that contains more than one percent asbestos by weight.

CERTIFIED PROPERTY MANAGER® (CPM®)   The professional designation conferred by the Institute of Real Estate Management (IREM) on those individuals who distinguish themselves in the areas of education, experience, and ethics in property management. (See also *Institute of Real Estate Management.*)

Chlorofluorocarbons (CFCs)   A group of inert halogenated organic compounds used in refrigeration, air conditioning, aerosol propellants, etc.

Claims-made insurance   A policy under which only those claims made (occurring) and reported during the current contract period would be covered. This allows the carrier to charge a lower premium because it eliminates all claims made after the policy expires (even if the damage occurred while the policy was in effect).

Clean Air Act (CAA)   Enacted in 1970 and amended in 1977 and 1990, a federal law that sets forth air quality standards and determines administration of the same.

Clean Water Act (CWA)   A federal law that establishes standards for water quality and sets forth mechanisms for the administration of those standards. Originally enacted in 1972 as the Federal Water Pollution Control Act (FWPCA), it was renamed in 1977 and amended extensively in 1987.

Comprehensive Environmental Response, Compensation, and Liability Act (CERCLA)   Enacted in 1980 and substantially revised through the Superfund Amendment and Reauthorization Act (SARA) in 1986; the collective law is often referred to as *Superfund*. Superfund provides funding and enforcement authority for cleaning up hazardous waste sites.

Comprehensive Environmental Response, Compensation, and Liability Information System (CERCLIS)   A national list of potential Superfund sites.

Comprehensive General Liability (CGL)   A single insurance policy that provides basic liability protection for premises, operations, and incidental contractual exposures.

Contaminant   Any substance that has an adverse effect on air, water, soil, or any life form.

Corrosion   The dissolving and wearing away of a material, usually by chemical reaction.

Cost recovery   The process by which money spent by the government for Superfund cleanups may be recovered from responsible parties.

Dioxin   A family of chemical compounds (known as dibenzo-*p*-dioxins) that are often found in conjunction with chlorinated hydrocarbons (e.g., pesticides). Concern about dioxins arises out of their potential toxicity to humans and animals.

Discharge   To let go or get rid of; emit. Defined differently in various environmental laws as spills, leaks, emissions, dumps, or other release of hazardous materials into the environment, excluding those discharges which are specifically permitted or excluded.

Disposal   Final placement or destruction of waste, which may be accomplished through legal or illegal means, including but not limited to such methods as incineration, utilization as landfill at designated sites, ocean dumping, etc.

Due diligence   In the environmental idiom, a general term referring to the appropriate or sufficient level of care and attention that should be given during the examination of a property.

Effluent   Wastewater that is discharged into the environment.

Electrostatic precipitator   An air pollution control device that charges particles, causing them to adhere to oppositely charged metal plates located inside the precipitator.

Emission   In environmental idiom, pollution discharged into the atmosphere.

Environmental audit   See *environmental site assessment*.

Environmental impact statement (EIS)   A document that reports the findings of a thorough analysis performed to determine the environmental impact of a proposed action. An EIS may be required for federal actions (especially when the habitat of an endangered species is involved) or by the EPA for any other proposed action, as is deemed necessary.

Environmental Protection Agency (EPA) An independent agency of the United States government, established in 1970 to bring together parts of various other governmental agencies involved with pollution abatement and control.

Environmental site assessment An environmental study from which a report is created that documents the environmental status of the investigated site (a determination of the presence or potential presence of contamination). Such assessments vary in the level of scrutiny applied to the subject property. A preliminary site assessment (PSA) is a general environmental investigation that does not involve any on-site testing of materials. A Phase I Assessment (Phase I) is a slightly more detailed examination that includes some testing. A Phase II Assessment (Phase II) examines specific problems or potential problems as identified in an earlier PSA or Phase I and, if necessary, tests specific plans for cleanup or remediation. A Phase II that includes the testing of an action plan is likely to be followed by a Phase III program of cleanup or remediation. At the end of this process, whatever assessments have been performed on the property are collectively known as the environmental audit. Environmental site assessments are performed by environmental specialists and are much more thorough than a simple environmental inspection conducted by a property owner or manager. Environmental assessments are not to be confused with the much more detailed Environmental Impact Analysis that results in an Environmental Impact Statement (EIS).

Errors and omissions (E & O) insurance A form of professional liability insurance that protects against liabilities resulting from honest mistakes and oversights (but not from gross negligence).

Estoppel certificate A written certificate in which a tenant sets forth the condition of the lease agreement at the time of certification, any modifications made to the lease, and whether any promises made by ownership have yet to be fulfilled. Required by potential buyers or mortgagees of property, as assurance that the leases held by ownership are valid and without offsets or claims pending. In the context of real estate-related environmental issues, property owners or managers may require estoppel certificates from tenants to obtain written confirmation of some aspect(s) of the environmental status of the leased property.

Federal Insecticide, Fungicide, and Rodenticide Act (FIFRA) Enacted in 1947, this law originally called for all pesticides to be registered with the United States Department of Agriculture (USDA) and established labeling requirements. FIFRA was amended by the Federal Environmental Pesticide Control Act (FEPCA) of 1972 as well as FIFRA amendments in 1975, 1978, 1980, and 1988 to further regulate the use and distribution of pesticides under the EPA.

Friable Easily crumbled or pulverized, as when rubbed between the fingers.

Generator As defined by the EPA, a person, facility, or mobile source that emits, leaches, releases, or otherwise contributes to pollution in the air or to hazardous substances in the water or soil. Under RCRA, they are designated small quantity generators

(SQGs) if they produce less than 1,000 kg (but more than 100 kg) of hazardous waste per month and large quantity generators (LQGs) if they produce more than 1,000 kg of hazardous waste per month.

Groundwater　Water located below the earth's surface in porous rock strata (accessed by drilling wells) and springs; a major source of drinking water.

Heavy metals　Metallic elements such as mercury, lead, chromium, cadmium, and arsenic that can be harmful to humans at low concentrations.

Herbicide　A chemical pesticide designed to destroy plants.

Hydrocarbons (HC)　Any of a multitude of compounds containing carbon and hydrogen molecules in combination (e.g., fossil fuels).

Incineration　In the context of waste disposal, a treatment technology involving the controlled burning of wastes at high temperatures.

Indemnification　Legal exemption from responsibility for a loss that may occur in the future or for a loss or damage already suffered.

Institute of Real Estate Management (IREM)　A professional association of men and women who meet established standards of experience, education, and ethics with the objective of continually improving their respective managerial skills by mutual education and exchange of ideas and experience. The Institute is an affiliate of the NATIONAL ASSOCIATION OF REALTORS®. (See also *CERTIFIED PROPERTY MANAGER®*.)

Insurance　A mechanism for reducing economic risk; an agreement to reimburse the insured for a loss—up to a specified dollar amount—in the event of fire, casualty, liability, or property damage, etc., in consideration of payment of a premium by the insured to the one insuring (the insurer, carrier, insurance company, etc.).

Landfill sites　Designated disposal sites where solid wastes are spread, compacted, and covered over with various materials.

Large quantity generator (LQG)　See *generator.*

Leaching　The process by which soluble components of substances are dissolved and carried away by a liquid.

Leaking underground storage tank (LUST)　See *underground storage tank.*

Lease　A (preferably written) contract for the possession of a landlord's land or property for a stipulated period of time in consideration of the payment of rent or other income by the tenant; may also be called an occupancy agreement or a rental agreement.

Lessee　See *tenant.*

Liability insurance　Coverage that protects a property owner from insurance claims arising out of incidents that occur on his or her property and result in injuries to other people or damage to other people's possessions.

Lien The legal right of a creditor to have his or her debt paid out of the property of the debtor.

Listed wastes Wastes named and listed as "hazardous" in the Resource Conservation and Recovery Act (RCRA).

Management agreement A legal contract or letter of understanding between the owner(s) of a property and the designated managing agent, describing the duties and establishing the authority of the agent and detailing the responsibilities, rights, and obligations of both agent and owner(s); also called a management contract.

Material Safety Data Sheet (MSDS) A compilation of information regarding the hazardous properties of chemicals. Usual information includes composition, physical and chemical properties, known hazards, and recommended cautions for handling, storage, and disposal.

Maximum contaminant level (MCL) The highest permissible level of a contaminant in water that is delivered to a free-flowing outlet for human consumption.

Mitigation Reduction or elimination of the impact (as of a hazard) by a specific course of action.

Monitoring wells Wells used to obtain water samples for water quality analysis (to determine the presence of contaminants) or to measure groundwater levels.

Montreal Protocol An international agreement that establishes a comprehensive schedule for the phase-out of ozone-depleting chemicals, specifically CFCs (established in 1987).

Mortgage A conditional transfer or pledge of real property as security for the payment of a specified debt; also the document used to create a mortgage loan.

Mortgagee The lender in a mortgage loan transaction.

Mortgagor The borrower in a mortgage loan transaction; the buyer of the real estate who conveys his or her interest in the property as security for the loan.

Named insured The individual(s) or organization(s) specifically identified as the insured parties in an insurance contract; one of several parties that are provided coverage, including and sometimes in addition to the individual or entity purchasing the coverage.

National Pollutant Discharge Elimination System (NPDES) A national permitting program (a provision of the Clean Water Act) that imposes and enforces pretreatment requirements for wastewater and regulates discharges of wastewater into the waters of the United States.

National Priorities List (NPL) The EPA list of the most serious uncontrolled or abandoned hazardous waste sites identified for possible long-term remedial action under Superfund.

Occupational Safety and Health Act of 1970 (OSHA)   A law requiring employers to comply with job safety and health standards issued by the U.S. Department of Labor.

Operation and maintenance (O & M) program   Action taken to monitor a situation to assure that contamination or potential contamination is properly managed to achieve prescribed levels of safety.

Operator   As defined in CERCLA, the entity or person responsible for the overall operation of a facility.

Owner   As defined in CERCLA, the entity or person owning title to land or a facility.

Ozone   Triatomic oxygen (O_3). When found in the lower atmosphere (troposphere) it is a major pollutant; in the upper atmosphere (stratosphere), ozone provides a shield from the sun's ultraviolet radiation.

Person   Under environmental law, an individual, corporation, firm, company, joint venture, partnership, sole proprietorship, association, or any other entity, state or political division, or municipality.

Pesticide   A substance used to inhibit, destroy, or repel a pest.

pH   A measurement of the acidic or basic (alkaline) nature of a material on a scale from 0 to 14, with 7 representing chemical neutrality. Values below 7 (toward 1) indicate increasing acidity; those above 7 up to 14 represent increasing alkalinity.

Phase I, II, and III site assessments   See *environmental site assessment.*

Pollution   A state of uncleanness. In environmental idiom, the presence of matter (or energy) whose nature, location, or quantity produces undesired or hazardous environmental effects.

Polychlorinated biphenyl (PCB)   A class of chemical compounds used in electrical transformers to provide insulation. Because of their toxicity, new use was banned by law in 1979.

Preliminary site assessment (PSA)   See *environmental site assessment.*

Pretreatment   Reduction or elimination of pollutants in wastewater prior to discharge, especially into a publicly owned treatment works (POTW).

Property manager   The person who administers and supervises the day-to-day management of a particular property or group of properties according to the owner's objectives.

Publicly owned treatment works (POTW)   A treatment works (i.e., any device or system used to treat municipal sewage or liquid industrial wastes) as defined in the Clean Water Act, which is owned by a state, municipality, or intermunicipal or interstate agency. Note that a privately owned treatment works is *not* a POTW.

Radon   A naturally occurring radioactive gas formed by the disintegration (radioactive decay) of radium.

Real property The rights, interests, and benefits inherent in the ownership of real estate; also used as a synonym for the terms "real estate" and "realty" (which refer to the land itself and everything attached to it).

Recycling Minimizing the generation of waste by recovering usable materials that might otherwise become waste.

Release Any spilling, leaking, pumping, dumping, pouring, emitting, emptying, discharging, injecting, escaping, leaching or otherwise disposing of a substance into the environment.

Remediation The act or process of remedying something. In the context of environmental problems, action that is taken to address the presence or threat of contamination, including but not synonymous with cleanup, which is the most extreme remediation.

Rent A fee paid for the privilege of using property.

Rental agreement See *lease.*

Resource Conservation and Recovery Act (RCRA) Enacted in 1976 and amended in 1984, the federal law that provides "cradle-to-grave" control of solid wastes.

Risk assessment Evaluation performed in an effort to define the risk posed to human health or the environment by the presence or potential presence of specific substances.

Safe Drinking Water Act (SDWA) Enacted in 1974 and amended in 1986, the law that sets federal regulations for drinking water systems and provides for their administration.

Security deposit A preset amount of money advanced by a tenant and held by an owner or manager for a specified period to cover damages and to ensure the faithful performance of lease obligations by the tenant during the lease term.

Sick building syndrome Symptoms that adversely affect building occupants while they are in a building but dissipate when they leave it.

Small quantity generator (SQG) See *generator.*

Superfund The name commonly given to the laws encompassed in CERCLA and SARA. (See also *Comprehensive Environmental Response, Compensation, and Liability Act [CERCLA].*)

Superlien Created under CERCLA, a lien that can be imposed to repay the government for cleanup or remediation of contamination. Superliens take precedence over all other liens on a property.

Tenant One who pays rent to occupy or gain possession of real estate, also known as a lessee. The estate or interest held is called a tenancy.

Toxicity The degree of danger posed by a substance to living organisms.

Toxic Substances Control Act (TSCA)   Enacted in 1976, the law that authorizes the EPA to require testing of chemical substances and to regulate hazardous substances.

Treatment   Any method, technique, or process designed to change the chemical or biological character or composition of a substance (e.g., a hazardous waste).

Underground storage tank (UST)   A large container located partially or completely underground that is designed to hold petroleum products, chemical solutions, etc. A leaking underground storage tank (LUST) can be an environmental hazard.

Virgin material   A previously unused raw material or an undeveloped natural resource that may be used as a raw material.

Volatile organic compound (VOC)   Any organic compound that can be emitted into the air as a vapor; a sometime component of air or water pollution. In environmental idiom, any organic compound that participates in atmospheric photochemical reactions.

Waste   Unwanted materials left over from manufacturing; refuse from habitation and operation.

Wastewater   Spent or used water from homes, industries, communities, etc.

Wetlands   Those areas that are sufficiently inundated or saturated by surface or groundwater to support a prevalence of vegetation typically adapted for life in saturated soil.

Acronyms

ACM	Asbestos-containing material
CAA	Clean Air Act
CERCLA	Comprehensive Environmental Response, Compensation, and Liability Act
CERCLIS	Comprehensive Environmental Response, Compensation, and Liability Information System
CFC	Chlorofluorocarbon
CGL	Comprehensive general liability
CWA	Clean Water Act
E & O	Errors and omissions
EA	Environmental assessment
EIS	Environmental impact statement
EMF	Electromagnetic field
EPA	Environmental Protection Agency
FIFRA	Federal Insecticide, Fungicide, and Rodenticide Act
HC	Hydrocarbon
IAQ	Indoor air quality
LQG	Large quantity generator
LUST	Leaking underground storage tank
MCL	Maximum contaminant level
MSDS	Material safety data sheet
NPDES	National Pollutant Discharge Elimination System
NPL	National Priority List
O & M	Operation and maintenance
OSHA	Occupational Safety and Health Act
PCB	Polychlorinated biphenyl
POTW	Publicly owned treatment works
PSA	Preliminary site assessment
RCRA	Resource Conservation and Recovery Act
SARA	Superfund Amendments and Reauthorization Act
SDWA	Safe Drinking Water Act
SQG	Small quantity generator
TSCA	Toxic Substances Control Act
UST	Underground storage tank
VOC	Volatile organic compound

Index

About the Institute of Real Estate Management

The Institute of Real Estate Management (IREM) was founded in 1933 with the goals of establishing a Code of Ethics and standards of practice in real estate management as well as fostering knowledge, integrity, and efficiency among its practitioners. The Institute confers the CERTIFIED PROPERTY MANAGER® (CPM®) designation on individuals who meet specified criteria of education and experience in real estate management and subscribe to an established Code of Ethics. Similar criteria have been established for real estate management firms that are awarded the ACCREDITED MANAGEMENT ORGANIZATION® (AMO®) designation.

In 1992, the Institute's membership included nearly 9,000 individuals as CPM® members and nearly 550 AMO® firms. Among U.S. commercial properties alone, CPM® members managed nearly 30 percent of the shopping centers and 25 percent of the office buildings under professional management. The Institute of Real Estate Management publishes books on real estate-related subjects, primarily related to property management, and offers numerous educational courses and seminars for career training in professional real estate management. This publication is part of the Institute's continuing efforts to provide quality education in the professional management of income-producing properties.